IN MY MIND'S EYE

MICHAEL REDGRAVE

IN MY MIND'S EYE

AN AUTOBIOGRAPHY

WEIDENFELD AND NICOLSON
LONDON

Extract from *The Family Reunion*, copyright 1939 by T. S. Eliot; renewed 1967
by Esme Valerie Eliot. Reprinted by permission of Harcourt Brace Jovanovich
Inc and Faber & Faber Ltd. Extract from 'The Player, Part I' by Lillian Ross
reprinted by permission; copyright 1961 The New Yorker Magazine Inc.
Extracts from a letter by Tyrone Guthrie reprinted by permission of Hughes
Massie Ltd. The lyrics of 'Could You Please Oblige Us With A Bren Gun'
copyright Noël Coward Estate, reprinted by permission of Dr Jan van Loewen
Ltd, London. Extract from a letter by J. M. Barrie reprinted by permission of the
Estate of J. M. Barrie. Extracts from letters by Dame Edith Evans by courtesy of
Bryan Forbes and the Estate of Dame Edith Evans. Poem by John Purdy
reprinted by permission of Rank Film Distributors. The early part of the list of
performances is based on that in Richard Findlater's *Michael Redgrave: Actor*
(1956). Unless otherwise credited in the list of illustrations, all photographs are
from the author's albums.

First published in Great Britain by
George Weidenfeld & Nicolson Limited
91 Clapham High Street, London SW4 7TA
1983

ISBN 0 297 78278 9

Text set in 11/12½ pt Linotron 202 Bembo, printed and bound in
Great Britain at The Pitman Press, Bath

TO
CORIN

ILLUSTRATIONS

(*Between pages 88 and 89*)
Roy Redgrave in an Australian bush drama
Daisy Scudamore as Glory Quayle in *The Christian*, c. 1909
My mother on the day of her marriage to J. P. Anderson
My mother as Lady Bracknell in *The Importance of Being Earnest*
My stepfather and some friends on a shoot
F. A. Scudamore, my mother's real father
Me at the age of four or five
As Lady Macbeth at Clifton College in 1925
As Captain Absolute in *The Rivals*, Clifton, 1926
With Arthur Marshall in *Captain Brassbound's Conversion*, 1931
With my mother, stepfather and Viscount Falkland
As Hamlet at Cranleigh School in June 1933
As King Lear at Cranleigh in June 1934
An engagement photograph of Rachel and me
Miss Linley of Bath, Liverpool Repertory Company, November 1935
With Lloyd Pearson and Jane Baxter in *A Hundred Years Old*
The Wind and the Rain, Liverpool, December 1935

(*Between pages 120 and 121*)
As Mr Horner to Edith Evans's Lady Fidget in *The Country Wife*
With Edith Evans in two scenes from *As You Like it* (above: Angus
    McBean)
Edith Evans as Rosalind
As Laertes to Olivier's Hamlet, Old Vic 1936–7 season
As Tusenbach with Peggy Ashcroft as Irina in *Three Sisters* (Houston
    Rogers)
With Margaret Lockwood in Hitchcock's film *The Lady Vanishes*, 1938
As Charleston in *Thunder Rock* in 1940
In the Royal Navy, 1941
On location for *The Way to the Stars*, August 1944

vii

The Redgrave family (Pictorial Press)
Fritz Lang welcoming me to Hollywood in 1947
A scene from *Secret Beyond the Door*

(*Between pages 184 and 185*)
As Macbeth, London and New York, 1947–8 (Angus McBean)
On holiday at Bexhill, Sussex, in 1948
With Kirk Douglas and Katina Paxinou in *Mourning Becomes Electra*
With Brian Smith in *The Browning Version*
As Antony in *Antony and Cleopatra* at Stratford-upon-Avon (Cecil Beaton/
    Sotheby's)
The family in the garden of the house in Chiswick
As Hector in *Tiger at the Gates*, 1955 (Snowdon)
A Touch of the Sun with Diana Wynyard and Vanessa (Angus McBean)
With Rachel, Corin, Lynn and Vanessa (*Daily Express*)
At Angkor Thom, a break from shooting *The Quiet American* (Raymond
    Voinquel)
As Hamlet at the Moscow Arts Theatre in 1958–9
A publicity shot for *The Master Builder* (Angus McBean)
As Samson in *Samson Agonistes* at the Yvonne Arnaud Theatre, 1965 (Zoë
    Dominic)
A Month in the Country with Ingrid Bergman and Emlyn Williams (Zoë
    Dominic)
In the title role of *Uncle Vanya* (Angus McBean)
In *Hobson's Choice* at the National Theatre, 1963–4 (Sandra Lousada)
With Vanessa in *King Lear* at the Roundhouse, London, in 1982 (Newsline)

I

It was after breakfast, and Aunt Mabel and I were alone in the dining-room of my stepfather's house off Belgrave Square. She had been telling me stories about Roy, my father, whom I did not remember, and of whom I knew next to nothing, and little good.

My stepfather had left for the City at nine-thirty, as usual. He had been a tea and rubber planter in Ceylon, and now was a director of various companies. My actress mother, when not rehearsing, usually had her breakfast in bed. Mabel, my actress aunt, with her cigarette bobbing up and down as she spoke, would now and then whisk her hand over her blouse whether ash had fallen there or not. Mother was always alarmed by Mabel's habit of smoking in bed.

Aunt Mabel – or 'Miggles' as Mother called her because her name began with an 'M' (Mabel called Mother 'Diggles' because her name was Daisy) – had just finished telling me of how my father had gone down a street at night, tearing the knockers off the front doors. It was understood, of course, that he had been drunk.

I murmured something. As Bacchus, my legendary father was nothing new to me. I had not pictured him as Hercules.

'Oh, yes,' said Mabel and giggled. 'You know,' she added, as if offering an official stamp to what she had just told me, 'I think Roy only touched Diggles once, and you, my dearest little Micky Doodlums, were the result.'

To Mabel's news I feel sure I said nothing. When deeply interested I frequently say nothing. Those who know me well say that at such moments expression drains slowly from my face and I am the picture of boredom. It was certainly quite a moment. As I recall it I can almost taste the Ceylon 'Breakfast' tea, see again the gloomy light of that dining-room, with its dark red damask curtains, its embossed wallpaper looking like crocodile skin, the Persian carpets, the electrified alabaster bowl which hung above the oddly square dining-table and cast such a waxy light on the faces of the diners, the rows of books bought by the yard, Dickens and Scott in Library Editions, *The Beaux and Belles of England* in half-leather bindings which all too neatly filled the glazed upper parts of the huge three-piece secretaire whose lower parts housed the best tea service and the cut-glass tumblers and wineglasses, the large, handsome sideboards, the heavy decanters of whisky and port, the epergne shaped like a cluster of tall tropical trees with a cut-glass fruit bowl resting in their delicate silver branches and a Singalese shepherd reclining in their shade (a gift to my stepfather from the Ceylon and Eastern Agency when he retired). All these, I feel, as I remember Aunt Mabel that day, might still be there, if only I did not know for certain that they are not. Still there, still kept in spotless order by Mary, the parlourmaid from County Wicklow, mute witnesses of dining-room conversations that were usually strained, because nothing unpleasant, no discomfortable fact, must ever be mentioned, and long silences, even at breakfast, were not allowed. It was the one room in the house which I really hated; it was so hard to escape from it.

On occasional Sunday evenings, when guests came, I remember it seemed far less gloomy and the faces beneath the light from the alabaster bowl looked less strained. 'The Captain', my stepfather – he had kept his Army rank after the war – was a kind man, a good and a just man, and a charming host. He was also a very conventional man. I feared him. Yes, a charming host. But for most of the year that dining-room in the house off Belgrave Square was a terrible room.

But that morning, Aunt Mabel's information, though somewhat stunning, elated me. My father now seemed a sort of Jove, descending lustfully on his unsuspecting love. I became a Perseus or a Minos, chance offspring of one improbable but gaudy night. This, at the time, did not seem to conflict in any way with the fact that Mother had more than once told me that my father, Roy, was a wonderful lover, or that she had attended seances to get in touch with him after his death, or that they had, after all, cohabited off and on for nearly three years. (The seances proved somewhat inconclusive. Roy, through the medium, informed Mother that he had never forgotten, simply couldn't bear, in fact, her way of sitting with her hands folded, as if silently reproaching him. It seemed very convincing, until Mother remembered that she had been sitting, just so, with her hands folded, throughout the seance.)

For her part, Mother, in her rare confidences to me on the subject, though she extolled his charm, his physical allure, and his acting talent, managed to implant in my mind at an early age the knowledge of her chief fear : that I might grow up to be like him. 'He used to point at things with his middle, instead of his index, finger, and once when you were about four you pointed at something with your middle finger and I nearly screamed.'

Not knowing a hundredth part of all I now know about my parents' marriage, and being aware that the two half-sisters were close to each other, I accepted Mabel's fantastic surmises with bewilderment but without question. Mother had already told me Roy had been married before, to an actress called Judith Kyrle, who had three children by him.

'"Judith Kyrle,"' I exclaimed, 'what a beautiful name!'

'She was a beautiful woman. *Not*,' Mother added with slight acerbity, 'a very good actress.'

There had been a divorce.

Roy had met my mother, Daisy Scudamore, in a theatrical 'stock' company at Brighton in the summer of 1907. Daisy was in her mid-twenties and Roy was thirty-six. She married him, she once told me, because she thought she could 'save' him. 'Men loved him,' she said, 'and women adored him.'

Mabel's version of the marriage was less romantic. Shortly before they met, said Mabel, Roy had had an affair with the wife of a well-to-do newspaper proprietor. The husband was to divorce his wife, citing the actor as co-respondent. Roy, according to Mabel, took what seemed the easiest way of preserving his 'quaint honour' and married the young actress in haste even if it meant repentance at leisure.

Little can be found to support this story of Mabel's. Nevertheless, there was certainly a third woman and, moreover, another child, a boy of whom Roy was passionately fond. The woman was referred to as 'Miss C.' or 'the lady'. There is no evidence that Roy wanted to marry Miss C., but his love of the child – his fourth – battled with his infatuation for Daisy.

How strange [wrote Daisy] that you should see 'the lady' in the train. Well dear, nasty or not, it doesn't matter now, it's all over and done with, and she's only herself to blame. Happiness was easily within her reach, and she's thrown herself and it away. Am glad to hear the boy is getting on so well, it will do you the world of good to see him ; you must get him to yourself as often as you can. I do hope *she* won't be anywhere near at the time. We're doing wretched business here.

The jaunty tone of this letter is misleading, I fancy.

Men and women in love, writing to each other once or even twice a day, often do not date their letters beyond writing the name of the day. But some short time after Daisy's chirpy letter there is one from Roy which must have struck fear into her heart. He says in it that Miss C.'s divorce will soon be through and that 'my first duty is to her and the boy . . . my name of course figures in the case and I shall marry her as soon as she is free.' He goes on to say that it will seem brutal to Daisy for him to write in this way, but that it is the only 'right thing' he can do. 'Heaven knows,' he exclaims, 'how this other trouble of yours hurts me and you know I shall do all I possibly can to straighten matters.'

'This other trouble' was, presumably, myself, to whom he refers later as 'the future event'. I can only conjecture Daisy's answer to this, but I am certain that few men would have wanted to be in Roy's shoes when he received it. Whatever it was, it won the day, game and set, if not, as it turned out, match. It produced a complete volte-face from, as he signed himself, 'your old worried Roy'.

He had surely much reason to be worried. His liaison with Miss C., whoever she was – and here perhaps Aunt Mabel was right, though I'm inclined to think that she, too, was an actress – was over, but from numerous references it is clear that he adored the son she had given him and that this love was returned by the child.

My dearest,
I am writing this at the theatre. Have come down early this evening. I have just wired you and shall be restless until I get your reply. I don't know why, but I've been so restless all day, and now I've finally made up my mind.

If you reply saying you will have me, then dear we will be married the next time we meet in Glasgow.

I know I love you. I believe you love me and if you will bear with me I will do my level best by you. I know I am not a saint but dear, with the right hand at the helm I can and will steer straight. I can say no more. Believe me I have not come to this conclusion in a hurry. I have thought and thought all ways. I can see *no other* way but this. I feel sure this *is* right.

I think we shall both feel happier when we have things settled. Believe me I appreciate the sacrifice you make – or would make – for me. I think you know the sacrifice I have made.

I *can't* have the boy. We must have our own.
My love dear wife
Your
Roy

4

The sacrifice he had made refers, I can only suppose, to his having, by his decision to marry Daisy, given up his rights to his son by Miss C. What Daisy's sacrifice could have been I am not so sure. Perhaps that is just conventional gallantry. 'I *can't* have the boy. We must have our own,' is a fine curtain line of the period.

The letter is written in his neatest, most well-shaped, and soberest hand. His writing varied much, as do most handwritings, I guess. Daisy's reply is written in the bold, large, generous script she maintained to the end of her life:

My Roy, my dear dear Roy,
    Your wire came just as I was going on the stage. I read it and went on in an excited dream – not conscious of one word I uttered during the prologue.
    Oh my dearest your message tonight is the most sacred of all you have ever given me – whether I am your wife in name matters not – but that you call me so in your heart – means, oh my darling, it means all the universe to me.
    I am going to bed tonight the happiest woman in the world. It seems all too good to be true that you love me so much and yet I know it is true – but I feel – oh I feel I want to shout it tonight from the housetops. I love you and you love me.
    Dearest, say it again in your letters and whisper it to me when we meet. Wife, wife, don't you know – can't you guess what it means? My darling my darling – God bless a thousand times –
        Daisy

Roy's next letter is strange, to say the least. Having dragged his feet over marrying Daisy, he now appears anxious to be married in all possible haste, in a form of marriage designed for 'mariners, travellers, etc.', which, he assures her, will be 'legal and binding the world over'. It has the great advantage that he can be simply labelled 'divorced', without having to produce any papers to show how, when, or why. Could this be, I wonder, because he never had, in fact, been divorced from his first wife, Judith Kyrle, so that his marriage to Daisy was bigamous?

2 Birnam Terrace
Craighton Road
Govan

Thursday

My dear love,
    I have just returned from Glasgow. Have had a good long talk with the registrar and now beg – fair lady – to make my report.

I have *settled* nothing! Nor can I do so until I hear from you. That's why I want you to particularly *understand* this letter and wire me by 12 tomorrow. *Because* (now the explanation) we can, if you like and are still willing, be married on Monday *next* before Sheriff MacKenzie. I have been all through it with him this morning and he says that if we can produce two witnesses to say we have both lived in Scotland for 21 days prior to the ceremony he will manage to get it through early for us on Monday, so as to enable me to catch my train for Bradford. Now I can't very well keep any of our crowd behind to act as witnesses, can *you* manage that part? It doesn't matter who they are really, so long as they don't mind signing their names 4 or 5 times to different affidavits and being – *for sure* – at the Registrar's in Minerva Street, Glasgow by 10.30 on Monday morning. The whole affair will be over by 11.30 and is as binding for all in *any* part of the world as though we gave the 21 days' notice and had the clergyman etc. I have gone well into the thing myself with him and am sure it is just as good and binding and as legal. The only thing is it is a bit more expensive. I enclose you a form which he has marked for me and which I have to fill up (I have a copy). This special marriage ceremony I may tell you is *allowed by a special revision of the marriage laws made last June* and I want you dear to decide for yourself. Personally I am quite satisfied, but if you would prefer it, make enquiries – you can do it at any Registrar's in Dundee on receipt of this. Mention the paragraph I've underlined because I believe that until this revision was made in June this particular law was only for Scotland. It has been repealed and revised for the benefit of those – such as mariners, travellers etc. – who are not 21 days in residence at one place, to hold legal and binding the world over.

This procedure of marriage has the *great* advantage that *I* am just labelled 'divorced' and need not necessarily produce papers etc., shewing when, how, date etc., which will take trouble and money and time to get. . . .

We can come into Glasgow early Monday, go to the registrar's with our witnesses at 10.30 and the whole thing will be done in an hour, in fact just in time for me to get away and our honeymoon will have to be postponed.

Thus by Monday midday you will be Mrs Redgrave and I shall be 'with you – with you'.

I want you to wire me yes or no – as near 12 tomorrow Friday as possible. I shall be at the theatre from 11.30 till 12.30 on the watch. Address Lyceum Theatre, Govan. . . .

A good idea – could you not get that friend you wrote me about to be one of the witnesses? We don't want any more 'outside members' than we can help to know the exact date of our marriage on account of the future event. I shall be all excitement till I hear from you. I've given you till 12 in case you want to go round to the Registrar's yourself.

That's all settled now, isn't it?

Now dearie, about myself. I am quite like my old self again today, quite lively and bright. So glad to hear my dearest is still keeping well. . . .

Well dearest and best of girls I must off to catch the mail. My best and fondest love to you dear love.

> Your devoted husband and lover
> Roy

These letters come from two dress-boxes marked 'Woollands, Knightsbridge', a shop where in later, palmier, if less halcyon days, my mother bought many of her clothes. The boxes were sent to me from Stanmore, where she lived in a nursing home during the last few years of her life. She sent me the boxes after she had started writing her 'notebooks', school copy-books I had sent her, suggesting that since she remembered so much about the theatre of her days it should be recorded. 'Don't write what you thought of this or that actor or actress,' I said, 'so much as what you were paid, working conditions, landladies, Sunday "train-calls" and the rest of it.'

She had been a good seamstress when young – you had to be if you were a touring leading lady on five pounds a week, finding all your own clothes – but she had lost the knack and the patience. In later days she had no use for cards, except for telling fortunes, or for crossword puzzles, or knitting. She still read avidly, mostly memoirs, but it irritated her not to be able to remember what she had just read. I hoped that the notebooks would provide some sort of occupational therapy. She completed nearly five of them.

The contents of the boxes are what must be all my father's letters to her, some telegrams, a few press-cuttings recording his death in Australia at the age of fifty, and her letters to him before and shortly after their marriage. One telegram, however, is missing, if we are to believe Aunt Mabel.

'You know,' she said on that dark morning in that dark dining-room, 'Roy only acted in the West End once. He preferred to be a big fish in a small pond. But shortly before you were born he did get a West End engagement. Daisy didn't hear a word from him when you were born, but suddenly a few days later he wired her, saying, "Come at once and bring the boy."' Aunt Mabel paused here, I think, for I remember her looking at me to see how I was taking it. She added, 'You see, his play had flopped.'

She went on to tell me other and even more scarifying things about Roy. Some of them I cannot entirely disbelieve. Although that curt telegram is not among the rest – and surely it would be if it existed, for it seems Mother kept everything – Roy's letter which greets her first letter about his new son can hardly have been the one which Daisy had hoped for. After not getting a letter at the house (lodgings in Clapham), he was, he writes, 'a little fidgety in case' she should not be well, and delighted therefore to find a letter waiting for him at the theatre where he was rehearsing.

The theatre was the Pavilion in Mile End Road, 'hitherto known as "The Drury Lane of the East"', says a newspaper cutting of 22 March 1908, whose 'traditions' would be again revived on 28 March, when, 'entirely redecorated, the theatre will be re-opened. The new management intend to spare neither money nor effort in providing the best possible entertainment that can be placed before the public of the eastern portion of the metropolis, and will produce on the opening night an adaptation by Mr Alfred Dampier of Rolf Bolder-wood's famous novel, *Robbery Under Arms*, which has not been seen in London for some fourteen years. Mr Roy Redgrave, so long the favourite of the Britannia Theatre, Hoxton, will appear as Captain Starlight.'

The cutting is dated two days after my birth in 'digs' above a paper shop on St Michael's Hill in Bristol. Mabel, it seems, was mistaken about the West End engagement – or perhaps it was I who was mistaken; perhaps she said a London engagement. Anyway, *Robbery Under Arms* was a big success in its way. Roy had indeed been a favourite at the 'Brit', as it was called. 'It was an institution,' writes W. Macqueen-Pope. It had

> its own traditions, and its history is unique in London's theatrical annals.
> No theatre had ever been so long under one management. Authors wrote
> for it exclusively, actors joined it as boys and remained until old age. Its
> main support came from people of the surrounding neighbourhood, who
> loved it and revered its manageress, Sara Lane. In its pantomimes (which
> always ran until Easter) she played the Principal Boy until she was in her
> seventies. ... The Britannia was the last London theatre to give up its
> own local and democratic drama and take in touring companies. After
> the death of Mrs Lane, mourned by the entire neighbourhood, the
> theatre passed into the hands of relatives and became a cinema.

It was a cinema when I first saw it. Quite by chance – for I had no idea that what I used to think of as 'my father's old theatre' still existed – I was strolling jubilantly down the High Street of Hoxton, returning from seeing the showing of my first screen test, at the old Gainsborough Studios in Islington, which had resulted in my being offered a film contract starting at what to me seemed the dizzy sum of one hundred and fifty pounds a week. It was a fine late afternoon in the early winter of 1938, and I was walking to look for a telephone box from which to call home to tell Rachel, my wife, that I had overcome my scruples and accepted the contract. I did not have much doubt about her reaction, but I was less sure of what my dear friend Edith Evans and my colleagues at the Queen's Theatre, John Gielgud and Peggy Ashcroft and Glen Byam Shaw, would say. Films were frowned upon by many 'serious' artists in the theatre in those days, and it should be remembered that, with a few memorable exceptions, British films before 1939 were regarded as something of a laughing-stock in England and were almost unknown abroad. Among the exceptions, of course, were the films of Asquith and Hitchcock, and it was with the promise that Hitchcock would direct my first picture – *The Lady Vanishes* – and the to me all-important clause that I should have absolute freedom to work in the theatre for six months every year, that I had agreed to the contract.

I was feeling extremely pleased with myself as I strode along Hoxton's High Street. Suddenly I saw the posters outside a cinema. It was the old Brit, my legendary father's legendary theatre. I paid and went in. It was difficult to see much of the auditorium in the dark. It seemed huge. As I came out I went into a corner pub, ordered a drink, and asked if I could use the telephone. As I drank I asked the barmaid, 'How long has the Brit been a cinema? I didn't know it still existed.'

She called towards the other bar. 'Fred! How long have they had flicks at the Brit?' While he was scratching his head she went on: 'You see, my husband and I met at the Brit. I was a dresser and he was a stage-hand. A scene-shifter, you know.'

'My father used to act there . . . Roy Redgrave.'

'You're *Roy Redgrave*'s son?'

After several drinks I left them. It was clear that they adored Roy. I could not resist telling them of the film contract. I told them I would be filming in Islington quite a lot in the years to come and would look in to see them.

I never did. I made only one film at the Islington Studios and during the making of that I was acting at the Queen's Theatre at night, and a year later the Second World War came, and during the Blitz the Brit was bombed.

I had for some time one relic of it: a rolled-gold signet ring given to my father by Sara Lane, the old actress-manageress, whose picture as a young girl in the role of Columbine can be seen in old 'tuppence-coloured' prints. But during the Blitz our house was burgled, and among the things which disappeared was Sara Lane's ring. It was worth no more than five bob or so but was, apart from a few photos, the only possession I had which was a link with Roy.

He had acted at the Brit for many seasons – everything, it would seem, that a leading man could play: Marcus Superbus in *The Sign of the Cross*, Hamlet, the lot. I don't know if he was still there when the old lady died, in 1899. He must have made his first marriage by then.

I have only two memories of my father. The first is of a tall man bending down to press the toe of my new shoe. I cannot be sure that it was Roy and not a shop assistant or some other grown-up. Yet something about this man in my mind's eye convinces me that it was he. The second is only slightly less fragmentary. I am looking through the bars of my cot. There is a fire in the grate, and standing in front of it are a man and a woman, arguing. Their voices are raised and he seems to be scolding her. Perhaps Roy and Daisy were rehearsing a scene from a play, but it seems all too probable that this was a real argument.

Both recollections must date from Australia, where Mother had taken me to join Roy. In the spring of 1909 they had been touring together, in England, in a melodrama called *The Christian*, and I was in the care of Auntie May, one of the numerous aunties who looked after me when Mother was away. After I was born, Roy, Mother told me in the notebooks, had been 'fairly well-behaved' – which, I fear, he all too rarely was after the first months of their marriage. But suddenly he had announced that he was off to Australia again: 'That's where the money is.' And off he went. (He had played there before, according to a newspaper obituary, in the company of a popular Australian actress, Minnie Titell Brune.) The tour of *The Christian* came to an end, and Mother was left penniless and alone.

It was not, it seems, Roy's intention to desert her. He wrote a letter a day from the boat on the journey out, some of them fully as passionate as the letters of his courtship. But Daisy knew all too well what would be the effect of a long separation. Both for my sake and for her own she was determined not to give him up for lost. Finding the money to follow him to Australia, however, was an almost insoluble problem. By a stroke of astonishingly good fortune she learned that a Mr Phillipson, the very manager who had hired Roy for his company in Australia, had recently come to England, so she sought him out and persuaded him to hire her as well. This must have taken some doing, as Phillipson had already engaged a leading lady and had a full complement of players for his company, but somehow she prevailed upon him to take her on as well, and even to advance her twenty pounds.

Besides these two memories of my father, I remember very little of Australia : the trams in Melbourne ; standing beneath the hosepipe in some backyard whilst the landlady hosed me down and left me to dry fully-clothed in the scorching summer's sun ; and a furious fight with a young boy named Cyril. He was a plain little boy, but with gorgeous flaxen curls which someone had been tactless enough to praise in my hearing. I was already well-accustomed to being the centre of attention. A terrific squawking was heard from the hens in the fowl run at the bottom of the yard, and terrified cries from Cyril, whose hair I was mercilessly pulling.

It can't have been a happy time. J.C. Williamson, the most successful Australian impresario, regularly imported English actors to play the leading parts, but this was the first time that the Phillipson management had done so. Roy was a big hit with Australian audiences, Daisy rather less successful. Her fellow-players she found wanting in accomplishment and apt to resent her.

Audiences in the outback and in the mining towns were rumbustious and highly vocal in their likes and dislikes. In one of the bush dramas, *The Squatter's Daughter*, Mother had to wrestle with the two villains who were trying to steal some title deeds to land with buried treasure. Accidentally she clipped one on the chin, sending him sprawling into the footlights, and the audience rose and roared their approval. Next she had to scale a mountainside and make good her escape across a log bridge spanning a ravine. The Australian productions were immensely lavish and costly, with real sheep, real horses, and, in this play, a real waterfall à la Beerbohm Tree. Missing her footing on the log bridge, she fell twenty feet into the water tank below, making a spectacular splash and miraculously avoiding the edges of the tank. This brought the house down.

But she was fighting a losing battle to keep her hold on Roy's wayward affections. He had met us off the *Orsova* at Fremantle, and for a while, she writes, 'the old joy was there'. But eventually, what with women and wine – though Roy was, I'm certain, always highly professional despite his legendary drinking habits – the battle proved too unequal. Moreover, she says, 'he did not really care for you. The only child he ever really loved was Robin,' his son by Judith Kyrle.

Perhaps so, although he also doted on the son he had had by Miss C., and I fancy that in his erratic way Roy could have been a delightful, if seldom seen, father. Looking at him now in the two photographs I have of him, I see a tall, lean, muscular man, with the wry smile of the rover he knew himself to be. In one, a studio portrait taken in the costume of one of his bush dramas, he sits on a log, his bush ranger's hat perched on the back of his head, with curly, slightly receding hair, pipe in one hand, poking the embers of the fire with his stick in the other: wry, philosophic, manly, and sentimental.

As for me, he can have seen little of me in the sixteen months between my birth in Bristol and our meeting off the boat in Fremantle. Roy, I'm sure, would have liked to make me laugh, and that must have proved inordinately difficult. I was a very serious baby, and a solemn child, easily moved to floods of tears. Mother remarks that, when someone at the quayside asked, 'Well, Michael, and were you sick on the boat?' I answered, 'No, I was sick on the pillow.'

The tears proved very successful on my debut on the Australian stage at two years of age. I was to run on at the end of a monologue by Roy and cry out, 'Daddy!' Instead, after some agonizing pushing and cajoling from Mother and the stage management, I ran on, clung to his legs, and cried piteously. Apparently this went down tremendously well with the audience, though that certainly wasn't what Roy intended. The monologue is addressed to 'Little X':

> Oh X! Little X! Is it quite understood
> When you make your appearance, you'll have to be good?
> Great parcels of love are awaitin' yer comin'
> An' leave it to Dad for to set the house hummin'.
> There is no one 'in front' but shall know that you're here
> So just you take it quietly and 'leave the stage clear'.
> An' then when your poppa's exhausted your praises,
> *Then* throw out your chest an' yell at 'em like blazes.
> But it ain't etiquette in our bus'ness, that's flat,
> For to give 'em 'sensations' right in the 'first act'.
> Just you study Brer Rabbit; pretend to lie low
> 'Cos too much at the starting'll ruin the show.
> Mind, of all the 'big parts' a 'good character's' best

So strike out for that line, boy, and leave them the rest.
The drama called 'Life' you have got to appear in
Has plenty of howlin' and lots more of cheerin'
And althou' but a 'call boy' to start with you'll need
To remember that some day you're sure to be 'lead'.
Then, when pa and ma's played out, an' you see 'em pause
And you walk to the centre and hear the applause
Don't forget lad – in front – maybe 'up in the gods',
The old folk will be watching – you jest bet the odds,
And amid the applause that your ear then devours
You will hear them both whisper, 'He's splendid! He's ours!'

Roy was the author of several melodramas containing fat parts for himself. None, so far as I know, has survived. Of his verses I have – besides the monologue to 'Little X' – only two examples. The first is a ballad called 'Ghosts'. It is signed 'R.R., Kalgoorlie, 1905', the period of his first visit to Australia, and is the only piece of paper in his handwriting which dates from before the time he met Daisy. To whom it is written is not easy to guess, except that in 1907 he was writing to Daisy that he had had six years with Miss C.

Dear, is the daylight come so soon
Is yon pale gleam the dawn?
Oh say 'tis a glimpse of the pallid moon
Thro' the curtains closely drawn.

More light, more wine: let the music chime
And the feast again begin.
With song, with kiss, keep back the time
When day and ghosts come in.

For there in the dawn stand spectres twain
That will not be charmed away;
The ghosts of two in the night-time slain
And they only walk by day.

A fair white maid and a man with her
Like a murdered king and queen:
The ghosts of the woman that once you were
And the man I might have been.

I would – if pressed – part with most of the few mementoes I possess except for this one, so redolent of Roy, and of the morals and gestures of his time.

The other poem is Roy's own epitaph. Amongst the letters preserved by Mother, I found a cutting from the Sydney *Morning Herald*, headed ROY REDGRAVE'S RETROSPECT – DEAD ACTOR'S LAST LINES.

Shortly before his death in a Sydney hospital on May 25th [1922], Roy Redgrave, the popular actor, wrote the following:

> One of the best! Held his own 'in a crowd',
> Lived like the rest (when finances allowed),
> Slapped on the back as a jolly fine sport,
> Drank any tack from bad whisky to port.
> Fool to himself – that's the worst you can say;
> Cruel to himself, for the health has to pay.
> Months back he died, and we've only just heard,
> No friends by his side just to say the kind word.
> No relatives near and no assets at all,
> Quite lonely, I fear, when he answered the call.
> One of the best. Held his own while he could.
> Died like the rest, just when life seemed so good.

II

A YEAR after our arrival in Australia, Mother and I were on the
P. & O. liner, second class, returning home. It must have
been a hard decision for Daisy to leave Australia. She had reached the
end of her contract with the Phillipson management. If she renewed
it, they would no longer be obliged to pay her passage home, and she
knew she could never save enough to pay for it herself. Roy was
hopeless with money, and Daisy was regularly having to settle his
debts. If she left, she was sure she would never see Roy again. Was it
perhaps the image of me, peering through the bars of my cot, which
tipped the scales?

Roy wrote to her only once after her return to England, the one
letter of his which she never kept.

Returning home also on the ship were a company of English
actors. They had been in a comedy which had failed. One of them,
an actor called Kenyon Musgrove, was a friend of the actor-manager
Arthur Bourchier, who owned the Strand Theatre in London.
Musgrove and his company were travelling first class, but the
Captain allowed us to join them in the first-class compartments,
except at mealtimes. Mother and Musgrove made friends, and
he promised her an introduction to Bourchier when we reached
England.

When the ship put in at Colombo, Mother made another acquaintance, which was to change both our lives. J. P. Anderson had gone
out to Ceylon as a young man of eighteen in the employ of the
Ceylon and Eastern Agency, and, now in his late forties, was
returning home. He had made his money; he was 'well off' – though
with a person so unostentatious, estimations of the actual size of his
'small fortune' varied. 'Andy', one may be sure, was commendably
reticent about Roy, and in her notebooks Daisy claims that she

'never reviled him'. Andy did, however, ask Daisy about her marriage and, one night in the Mediterranean, over a brandy, confided that he had lived with a native woman in Ceylon whom he had since provided with an income which would at least ensure that she would never want, and that she and her two daughters would live, by Singalese standards, very comfortably.

He presented Mother with a Maltese lace handkerchief, first prize for a fancy-dress competition on board in which she appeared as Trilby and I as a pierrot. By the end of the voyage he had given her the address of his London club, and said that he would like to meet her again.

They did meet, two weeks later, at the Café Royal. Mother wore a stage frock and borrowed three and sixpence for a taxi from our landlady. With mounting anxiety she watched the taxi meter as the fare clicked up; but all was well, Andy – 'good man' – paid the fare at the other end, and paid her return fare, too.

There were many of 'our calling', as Mother's friend Allan Aynesworth would say, at Mrs Gold's establishment in Faunce Street, Kennington. I remember Mother – how beautiful I thought she was, and beautifully-dressed! – standing on the pavement outside our lodging, handing out sweets to the boys from the neighbourhood. For years I used to think of that pavement as unusually broad. In fact, as a recent visit showed, it is of the usual narrow dimensions, and Mrs Gold's must have been small and cramped. But to Mother and me it was the best of all possible digs. We shared a bed in a room at the back on the first floor. Every morning Florrie, the maid, would come pounding up the stairs with our breakfast and I would pinch Mother awake, shouting, 'Here comes Florrie with the breakfast!' It seemed heaven.

Mrs Gold was a wonderful gossip, and there was plenty for Mother and her to catch up with – the tragedy of Mother's parting with Roy in Australia, her anxieties about the future, what had happened in the theatre in her absence.

We were penniless, and Mother desperately needed work. A pall seemed to hang over the house in Faunce Street. Many of Mrs Gold's other lodgers were in the same plight, and, after a day of traipsing round the offices of theatrical managements, the actor's expressive face could tell 'volumes in folio'. But at last a job lifted its head, and in five minutes all woe had been forgotten. Adderley Howard, Roy's stepfather, not a noted actor but quite a successful one, gave Mother a part in one of his sketches. That tided us over for a few weeks, and then came a tour with a melodrama, *Two Little Vagabonds*.

First date on the tour was Sunderland. It was winter and bitterly cold. I was swathed in an overcoat many sizes too large, lent me by kind Mrs Gold. There must have been another play in town, because all the usual digs were full. Eventually, after hours of tramping about fruitlessly, we came to a pub where the publican's wife took us in and gave us a huge four-poster bed with a feather mattress, which we fell into. There had been a party for a working-men's club that night, and the landlady served us a supper of fish and cockle sauce – nothing had ever tasted better than that cockle sauce. We huddled up under the eiderdown and to get me to sleep Mother recited, as she often did, sometimes Shakespeare, sometimes Tennyson. 'A fool, a fool, I met a fool in the forest' – I loved that fool – and 'You must wake and call me early, call me early, Mother dear.'

Sundays was the 'train-call', when every actress on tour would put on her glad rags, hoping that some manager would spot her whilst she was changing trains at Crewe Junction.

We moved south, to Brighton. For the first time I was allowed to see a performance. At the curtain of the second act of *Two Little Vagabonds*, Mother had to take into her arms a small boy called Dick and, sobbing, cry out, 'Dick! My son! My son!' This was too much for me. With all the wrath of a four-year-old, I rose from my seat and cried out, 'He's not your son! I'm your son!' When telling this anecdote, Mother said that the other actors on stage 'corpsed' to a man, while a kind lady in the pit tried to lure me away by shaking a bottle of sweets, rattling it like a tambourine.

Our shipboard acquaintance, Kenyon Musgrove, proved as good as his word. Mother got her introduction to Arthur Bourchier, and was engaged to understudy his wife, Violet Vanbrugh, at the Garrick Theatre in the Charing Cross Road. A better job than it might sound, for it brought her within a step or two of the West End stage, and in those days, as she complains bitterly in her notebooks, it was immensely difficult for a 'provincial' actor to gain a toehold in the West End. Fortunately, ailments were plentiful, and actors more inclined then than nowadays to take a night off if they were ill, so Mother managed to go on for Miss Vanbrugh on several occasions.

What a strange place the theatre seemed – those garishly-painted faces. I am backstage in my mother's dressing-room. So many women in varying states of dress and undress. One of them bends down to pick me up and I start to cry. Was it, as Mother said, fright at the strangeness of her make-up? Or the fear of a small boy that he might not recognize his mother in that gallery of painted faces?

Frightening, but fascinating. In those days the company manager would always give fellow-professionals free seats for the matinée if the house was not full. Tom Pitt, the company manager at the Globe and a great favourite of Mother's, gave us seats for *The Chocolate Soldier* in the stage box, and a nice programme-seller gave me an extra hassock on my chair to perch on, so I had a fine view of the stage. Half-way through the play, I could no longer resist the impulse to join in, and started to clamber over the side of the box onto the stage, only to be hauled away, protesting, by Mother and the programme-seller. Tom Pitt made amends after the show by pinching my cheek and saying, 'I can see you'll be an actor, Michael.'

We moved to a flat in Battersea, and a Miss Holland came to look after me. We were walking one afternoon in Prince of Wales Drive when an old lady stopped us, pointing with a shocked expression at my headgear. Though otherwise presentable, I had, so Mother thought, rather prominent ears, and she devised a sort of rugby player's scrum cap to flatten them.

'Did the little man hurt himself?'

I was about to reply when, without waiting for an answer, the old lady dived into her purse and produced a new penny, which she handed me. The incident must have made its impression on me. It was the first time I had been paid for dressing-up.

Mother now had a more regular income, though still very small, and for a while life was more orderly and settled. But it was a strain having to leave me in 'Mummy' Holland's care whilst she was at the theatre every night: there was the night she came home to find me delirious with fever; there were the nightmares of our house burning down. Was it for this reason that I was sent away to stay with relations? No doubt, though there was also another reason, of which I was to remain ignorant for some time.

Fortunately the Scudamores were very numerous. There was Auntie May, in Sheffield, which I remember only for the river Don and for the layer of soot which always coated the leaves. There were Uncle Norman and Auntie Bea at Wem, in Shropshire. Norman was a farmer, and the high spot of my stay with them was walking Ruth the cow to the county fair at Shrewsbury. Their daughter Joan was about my age, and we would play together, singing songs at the piano. Or, rather, I sang and played, and Joan, though I think she could play as well as I, would listen, since I insisted on an audience.

Together we would dress up, which was always my favourite game, making fantastic costumes out of crêpe paper. An old shed was our theatre. We must have been careless about tidying away our costumes, for I remember Norman in a fury at finding crêpe paper strewn all over the manger. It was the first time a grown-up had been angry with me, and it came as a shock, as Norman was usually so gentle and even-tempered.

Best of all, there was Portsmouth. Mother would tie a label, 'M. S. Redgrave, Portsmouth', on my lapel, and I would travel in the guard's van (safer and cheaper, she thought, to send me as a parcel than with a third-class ticket in a compartment). It was a grand way to travel. You could run about, dance even, or sit on the guard's stool watching the fields pelt by through his little bay window. And for additional company there were usually animals, or sometimes a pair of pigeons.

No 8 Victory Villas, Portsea, Portsmouth, Hants, was one of a row of terraced houses, back-to-back, with an outside lavatory and a tin bath in the scullery. But it seemed to offer everything a boy of six could wish for. There was Grannie Clara, and Auntie Annie, waiting on the doorstep to smother me with kisses. The Scudamores, all except for Grandpa, were great ones for kissing. And when all the hugs and kisses were done, everyone had to move to the front parlour, where the piano stood, and I was bidden on Mother's written instructions to play my parlour piece, Grieg's 'The Watchman's Song'.

Only Grandpa William, a retired shipwright, was excused this custom. It was understood that he was too old to want to negotiate the narrow passage which separated the front parlour from the kitchen, where he sat in his armchair by the window, reading that best of all monthlies, the *Strand* magazine.

Grandpa was awesomely silent. He was also awesomely deaf. A formidable character. Only once did I provoke a reaction from him. Auntie Annie had a second-hand-clothes shop on the corner of our street, and used to let me dress up in a suit, or long dresses, smelling strongly of mothballs. I put on a bonnet, cape, and skirt, found myself a stick, and hobbled back to our house, just as Grandpa was about to come out for his walk. The corridor was so dark that he didn't see at once who I was. Then, realizing it was I, he uttered a strange growl and raised his stick as if to smite me into the ground. Grandma appeared from nowhere to rescue me from Grandpa's sudden, amazing wrath. I thought she would scold him, but no – for the first and only time, she scolded me. Even Uncle Willie, whom I adored, was unusually silent that night.

Uncle Willie, a wainwright in the dockyards, was the bread-winner of the family. Two or three times a week he would give me twopence to see the pierrots on Clarence Pier. I loved the pierrots. But best of all was our trip to the music-hall on Saturday nights. Uncle Willie was a real theatre-goer. He used to hum a lot to himself, and on Saturday evenings, when he was shaving before setting off to the theatre, he became especially melodious, and his face, as we set off to see George Robey or Houdini or Little Tich, gleamed with excitement. Sitting in the gallery, I would roll up my programme and clasp it to my eye like a telescope, so that all I could see when the curtain rose was one face in the chorus. A sort of concentrated excitement gradually unfolded and flooded over me as I unfurled my programme wide enough to see the whole stage.

The War had started. Portsmouth, they said, with its naval dock-yards would be a prime target for the Germans, so I was sent to a boys' boarding school at Leigh on Sea, on the East Coast. Robert Blatchford, the socialist writer and the editor of the *Clarion*, lived next door. Mother was a socialist and admired Blatchford, so to Leigh on Sea I went, where the Headmaster gave me a sort of entrance examination.

He produced a shallow basket in which were tufts of different-coloured wool. He held up one of these and gently de-manded, 'Now, what colour is this, Michael?'

Though mystified, I gave a prompt answer. 'Red.'

'And this?'

'Blue.'

'Yes. Pretty colours, aren't they? Now what is this?' He dangled a mauve-coloured tuft before me.

I hesitated. 'It's a sort of blue.'

'*What* sort of blue?'

'Well . . . blue.'

'Dear me, the boy's colour-blind,' said the Headmaster. 'Now, I'd like him to meet my assistant, Mrs Joce. If he comes here, he'll mostly be taught by her. We'll just see . . . she may be busy. . . .'

He rose and conducted us to his study. Although it was a bright summer's afternoon, the blinds were drawn and the atmosphere was oppressively warm. Three or four boys were gathered round a lighted candle. Mrs Joce held a golf ball, which she twirled with three fingers whilst slowly revolving it around the candle.

'You see,' she said triumphantly, 'this is the way the earth moves round the sun. We call it the earth's *orbit*.' She went on describing the earth's daily journey, but one of the boys seemed to be trying to say something.

'What is it, Peter?'

'I'm sorry, Mrs Joce,' the boy called Peter mumbled, and then was neatly sick over his shoes.

Scarcely had Mother returned to London and her theatre when the Germans started shelling the East Coast, and she rushed back in a panic. She next deposited me at Cricklewood, in north-west London, where two maiden ladies, Auntie Lou and Auntie Gwen, took me in as a boarder. No 2 St Paul's Avenue was a large Victorian gabled building, housing about eight or ten young lodgers, who on the whole were a lively lot. There was Frank Bear, who was a nice boy with whom I shared a bedroom; and his sister, who was fun; and Peggy, a little girl of four who was so backward she could hardly speak, and whom we didn't include in our games because she seemed so slow on the uptake.

There remained the problem of my education. There was a convent of St Ursula in Cricklewood, with school attached. My acquaintance with it did not have much time to develop. It was the beginning of term, and newcomers to the convent school were each in turn introduced to the Mother Superior. When it came to my turn, I was determined to show myself at my best and, in a futile effort to be amiable, I put on a broad grin and uttered one word: 'Mummy.'

For three or four seconds everything went silent. Then the nun who seemed to be conducting the interview burst out (bobbing a curtsy to the Mother Superior), 'No, no, young man, that will not do! One addresses Mother Superior with respect. It is not a joke.'

I mumbled something.

'What's that you say? Speak up, young man.'

'I said, "Mummy".'

The Mother Superior's eyes closed in deep pain. With a low voice she murmured, 'Take him home. Someone must take him home.'

Some weeks elapsed before my next school was found for me. It was known as Mr Dove's and was not far from 2 St Paul's Avenue.

Auntie Lou was putting on my coat and scarf. We were getting ready for her to take me for my first morning at Mr Dove's.

'They say you're backward. But I don't believe that. It's just that they don't understand your jokes. They're Belgian, you see.' She chuckled at her own joke. 'But don't call the Headmaster "Daddy",' she cautioned.

On arrival at Mr Dove's, I found a huge classroom with some fifteen or twenty boys who did not seem to be paying much attention to the master. But Mr Micklethwaite knew what he was doing.

'I'm going to give you someone to help you. He's passed his exam, so he can teach you to read and write.'

He put me at the back of the class, where I was joined by Skipton, a jolly boy carrying an armful of books. 'Now, take your pick,' he said. 'You know your alphabet, I suppose? Here, take one of these. It's not difficult, you know. I'll soon teach you.' Skipton was as good as his word, and in a month I could read tolerably well.

I went to sleep clutching one of G. A. Henty's adventure stories, and, waking in the early morning, I was still clutching it and began to read on where I had left off. No word in my vocabulary then could describe my feelings as I absorbed Mr Henty's bluff magic. Reaching the end of the tale, I immediately turned back to the first page and imagined myself *Out in the Pampas* all over again. I remember my pleasure at my accomplishment in reading a whole book was strangely mixed with indignation that Mr Henty had somehow duped me. How dared he bring his novel to a close?

It would be fitting if I could claim that I had read all of the author's other works. After all, it was he and Skipton who had opened the gate to this new existence. But in fact I jilted him and transferred my affections to James Fenimore Cooper, and to the authors of *A Boy of the Limberlost, A Girl of the Limberlost*, and *Daddy-Long-Legs*. Frank Bear told me that stories like *Daddy-Long-Legs* were 'soppy' and meant only for soppy girls. But that did not shake my admiration one jot.

Amidst this plethora of words, two were missing: my name. And I decided to write a story myself. There was a children's paper called *Puck*, which I noticed was prepared to give two prizes for essays describing 'My Christmas Holidays'. I entered the competition and was awarded the second prize of half-a-crown. The paper's illustrator drew a picture of me, together with a picture of the girl who had won the first prize of five shillings. He did not manage to make much of a likeness. I had to be content with a back view of myself. But my main object was achieved. There ought to be a special word for people who like seeing their name in print.

My next effort was more ambitious. Mother was playing in H.B. Irving's company at the Savoy Theatre, in J.M. Barrie's *The Professor's Love Story*. When we met Barrie in the street outside the Adelphi, she introduced me to him, and asked if she could send him a story I had written. Permission was granted, and we waited to hear what the famous author thought. His reply, when it came, was a model of tact:

> My dear Michael,
>   Your wicked witch put a lot of books on top of your story so I lost sight of it, but i have found it now and i like it very much. I am sending it back to u with many thanks for letting me read it, and some day i expect u will be the author of printed books if there is nothing better for u to do.
>   your fellow scribe
>   J.M. Barrie

One Saturday afternoon near Christmas, Mother collected me as usual from Auntie Lou's and took me on the bus to the Garrick Theatre. The show we saw that afternoon was a bewildering entertainment called *The CockyOllyBird*. After the show we went backstage to the girls' dressing-room. My eyes opened wide as, for the first time in my life, I saw a host of females undressing. But one in particular caught my attention, Joan Carr, a girl of fourteen or so with a mass of golden curls, like Mary Pickford's, and an enchanting smile. She had tea with us and afterwards took the bus back with us to Cricklewood. There, at Auntie Lou's, I kissed Mother goodbye till next weekend, and was hoping that Joan would kiss me too, when, to my astonishment, Mother kissed Joan goodbye, and I realized that she was going to stay.

'Your mother says you play the piano very nicely, Michael,' said Auntie Lou that night, tucking me into bed. 'Tomorrow Joan shall play for you.'

'That'll be nice,' I thought. But I little guessed what an influence this pretty child was to have on me. Within a few days she had become a sort of fairy godmother, and everything she did or said was remarkable in my eyes.

The next day, after breakfast, Auntie Lou, as promised, asked Joan to play for me; but Joan refused, saying she wasn't ready to perform at that time of day. Towards evening she relented, however, and played Rachmaninoff's most famous prelude. In later years she was to deny ever having played that hackneyed piece, but I know she did, and I remember the three opening chords as she played them that evening, which sent shivers down my spine. When she'd finished, I didn't know what to say. I gazed at her, dumbstruck. I had never heard music of that kind played 'live', as we would say now. When the time came for Joan to go to the theatre I begged Auntie Lou to let me accompany her, but she said, 'Another day.' Another day came and went, and day after day my wonder at such a magical human being grew. I remember with particular affection the sight of Joan, one January morning, wrapped in scarf and thick overcoat, holding a little box. What was in the box, I asked. 'Feel it,' she said. I put my hand to pick it up and nearly dropped it in surprise; it was a little charcoal burner, which Joan held in her muff. She was going to the rehearsal rooms of Rosenthal in South Audley Street for her weekly lesson.

She was a wonderfully accomplished pianist, and liked acting, too. She and I improvised ballets to the music of an old gramophone which Allan Aynsworth, Mother's actor friend, had given me, and plays, too, which we would write together. No two youngsters can ever have been more stage-struck. We knew what was on and who were the stars at every London theatre, learning the list off by heart from the daily papers.

One day she was absent from breakfast. I was told she wasn't very well, and that after breakfast I might tap on her door and hope she would soon be better. I raced upstairs and tapped rather loudly.

'Come in,' said a feeble voice.

'Auntie Lou said I could give you a kiss and hope that you'll soon be better.'

She was lying stiff and straight, and to signify that permission was granted she pursed her lips and closed her eyes. I tiptoed to the side of her bed. When I reached it she flung out her arms – still keeping her eyes closed – clasped me to her, and gave me the juiciest kiss I had ever received. When I recovered from this, I asked her what was the matter with her.

'I don't think you'd understand. You have to be grown-up to understand.'

'Grown-up?'

'Yes. Listen,' she whispered. 'I know how babies come into the world.' I didn't know what to say. 'I'll tell you one day.'

I was bitterly disappointed. I couldn't have cared less how babies came into the world.

'You may kiss me again.' Perhaps she sensed my disappointment. It was the first and only time she ever implied the difference in our ages.

The time came when Joan left Cricklewood. She was training to become a professional pianist. She promised that she would come back and see me from time to time, and would take me out to tea or to a cinema. I missed her greatly. There was no one to take her place, not even Hilda Bayley, an actress in H. B. Irving's company who treated me like a grown-up. I made one attempt to get in touch with Joan. Having somehow obtained her telephone number, I rang her up and asked her if she would like to come and play in the afternoon. She answered that she would have loved to, but that she was getting married on Wednesday. Some time later I asked Mother if she knew where Joan now was. 'She married a violinist. An Australian, I think.' Later I heard it said that she had gone into the theatre and was one of the sensational totem chorus in *Rose Marie*. Then the *Daily Mail* mentioned her name and said that she was in Hollywood. At the start of the Second World War her name figured prominently in the announcement of the BBC's newly-formed repertory company. And then there was an advertisement for Pond's facial cream, which stated that she used no other – she being by now dark-haired, so the picture in the advertisement suggested, and, what was more, a well-known society beauty. 'Viscountess Moore', said the caption. Could it be the same Joan I had known at 2 St Paul's Avenue? It could. It was.

Without Joan, life at St Paul's Avenue seemed rather flat. And then one day a car pulled up, driven by 'Uncle' Andy in his uniform of Captain in the Middlesex regiment. (He was too old for active service, of course.) He and I had had only a nodding acquaintance since meeting on the ship home from Australia. There had been a dinner one evening at the Café Royal, made memorable by the creamed rice pudding with a plentiful topping of hundreds-and-thousands they gave me. And then, early one morning, when we lived at the flat in Battersea, I glimpsed him in his uniform as he was leaving. And again one afternoon when Mother and I visited the barracks of the Middlesex regiment and Andy showed us round. 'So this is the son and heir!' had said a fellow-officer to Andy as we walked through the mess. Son and heir?

And here he was again, in a big black motor car with its hood up, calling for me at St Paul's Avenue.

The motor car was the symbol of another life, something very grown-up and very sophisticated. And good heavens, look at Peggy, what was she dressed like that for? Poor dumb Peg, so backward she could still hardly speak and was never allowed to join our games, dressed heaven knows why in a party frock.

'Would you both like to go to the Trocadero tonight ... or tomorrow?' asked Andy.

'Troca-what?' I asked. Andy laughed. 'Is it Tamil? Ask me if I can speak Tamil, Uncle Andy.'

'Can you speak Tamil, Michael?' he asked, dutifully.

'*Collipa pumbli, collipa ambli, collipa ahl,*' I said triumphantly.

'Fancy your remembering that.'

I examined the car and sounded the rubber bulb of the horn several times until Auntie Lou told me to stop. It made a noise like a sick cow, reminding me of Ruth, one of Uncle Norman's cows at Wem.

The two aunts waved us goodbye.

'Where are we going?' I asked Uncle Andy.

'You'll see.'

'Where's Mother?'

'At home. Shan't be long now,' Andy replied.

I imagined he must mean Shepherd Market in Mayfair, where Mother had rooms and I would visit her at weekends. But no, we drew up outside a different house, 9 Chapel Street, with Mother waiting for us on the doorstep. I was bewildered. Mother looked worried, and so did Uncle Andy as he brought in our bits and pieces of luggage. In this he was aided by a young woman with a strange head-dress of crinkly white linen. I had never seen a domestic servant before, but Mother seemed to know her quite well, and called her 'Mary'.

'Now,' said Mother, when we were all in the house, 'would you like Mary to show you your room?'

Mary led the way up the stairs. 'This is the drawing-room,' she said, 'and here's a fine piano for you to play on. You'll like that, won't you, Master Michael?'

'It's a grand piano,' I said.

'So it is. So it is,' said Mary, who came from County Wicklow.

We went further upstairs, to a room at the back of the house, which Mary said was to be a nursery. Then she said, 'And here's your room, Master Michael.' It was a small room, with a brand-new, smart-looking bed and chest of drawers. Next to this we entered another bedroom, with two beds in it. The furniture here was altogether different, a bright white, with pretty transfers of butterflies and birds and cheerful children. 'And this is Miss Peggy's room,' said Mary.

I didn't like to ask why there was a room for Peggy. But when Mother and I were in the nursery alone, I was to discover. Mother sat in a big chair and drew me to her, brushing my forelock off my forehead. (For some years afterwards I was to bridle when she made this gesture.) She gathered me into her arms and we sat together in the big chair, and for a moment or two I thought she was about to cry.

When she spoke, her voice was soft and low. 'You see,' she said, 'Peggy is your sister. Your half-sister,' she corrected herself. 'And Uncle Andy and I, for better or worse, are married.'

I did not at once make out what this meant. She must have seen my bewilderment and, putting on a stauncher tone of voice, she extolled some of Andy's excellent virtues, his kindness, his honesty : 'He is . . . a man you can trust.'

After a long silence I hesitantly said, 'Are we going back to Australia, then?'

'No, my darling, no,' she said, and hugged me. 'Now,' she said, 'I want you to go downstairs to the morning-room, where Uncle Andy is, and sit on his knee, and give him a kiss, and call him Daddy.'

I do not remember what Andy said when I perched myself on his knee and kissed him on his tobacco-smelling moustache.

As for Peggy, my half-sister, how and when had she come on the scene ? I remembered that, some time before, when Mother and I were staying at a friend's house in Pinner one weekend, I had said, 'Race me !' and set off down the lawn. I had looked back at Mother, and noticed how heavy she had become, and out of breath, though still beautiful. But that was long before Joan Carr offered to teach me the facts of life, and I had thought nothing of it.

The other occupant of the white night-nursery, furnished by Heal's of Tottenham Court Road, turned out to be a formidable lady with leg-of-mutton sleeves, long since out of fashion, and a way of giving emphasis to platitudes which I thought plain silly. I ragged Miss Goss unmercifully. She insisted on reading to me, despite the fact, as I reminded her, that I was now quite capable of reading for myself. But nemesis was near at hand.

The Germans started to bomb London again, driving the population underground and into the Tubes. Andy decided that the whole household at Chapel Street should huddle under the kitchen stairs in the basement. I rather enjoyed this, and knitted half a balaclava helmet, while Mary the parlourmaid kept us amused with tales of County 'Wickerlow'.

Miss Goss was given her notice. Why, I don't know. She reacted waspishly. 'Your name is Scudamore . . . a foreign name, isn't it ? One has to be so careful these days, don't you think ?' (A wave of xenophobia swept London in the War, especially after the bombing.)

Mother came swiftly to the defence of the Scudamores. 'It's a French name. The French are our allies. The name means "shield of love" – *scutum amoris.*' Mother was very proud of her name. On the landing at Chapel Street hung a photograph of 'Poor Dadda', Fortunatus Augustin Scudamore, in the regalia of the Norman Conquest. Harris Scudamore, another relation, had almost bank-rupted himself trying to prove that we latter-day Scudamores were descended from the Norman invaders.

It was about this time that Mother changed her name from Daisy to Margaret, more suitable for the West End actress she wanted to become, and which, at this time, she gave every promise of becoming. When she played Lady Bracknell at the Theatre Royal, Haymarket, however, in the first revival of Wilde's masterpiece, *The Importance of Being Earnest*, she was considered too young. She never, in fact, became a leading lady.

As for Andy, he never really came to terms with the theatre. Unfortunately for his and my relationship, I cared for little else.

Best of all, I loved my visits to the Savoy Theatre, when Mother was in H. B. Irving's company. I had the unique experience of watching H. B. playing his father's most celebrated role, Mathias in *The Bells*, from the flies. I could sit up there with a couple of stage-hands, behind the great double doors of Mathias's inn. Far below was the figure of Irving, bent double, agonizing in the front of the stage. Even the big black satin head-dress which, from my vantage point, completely obscured my mother's face, became a symbol for my imagination. Was not that paper snowstorm, falling gently from the flies, part of my creation?

It was a Sunday afternoon in autumn. Andy was away in Scotland, fishing or shooting. Mother was out. Peggy was staying with friends. I was an inquisitive boy. Some impulse prompted me to satisfy my curiosity by looking in Andy's bedroom. It was dull and sombre, in its way as forbidding a place as the dining-room. I saw it each day before school, when Peggy and I had to wish Andy good morning, but at other times it was – without, of course, anyone's saying so – out of bounds.

It smelled, faintly, of Andy, of the Gold Flake cigarettes he smoked through a cherrywood holder. On the mantelpiece were twelve elephants, carved in ivory. I used to picture their originals sitting in a row in front of his bungalow in Ceylon, trumpeting for Andy. Indeed there was a touch of the elephant about Andy himself, with his long Scotts nose and heavy feet. On the chest of drawers was a medicine bottle with some colourful pills. These dated from the occasion when Andy had had hiccups for three days running, and we had to tiptoe into his bedroom to pay our last respects, and Mary and the staff crossed themselves and spoke with lowered voices, for it was understood that after the second day of hiccups a man might die.

The wardrobe contained Andy's suits, overcoats, shoes, and, on the top shelf, two or three hats. In the chest of drawers I found gloves, scarves, etc. I had never seen Andy wear spats, but there were two pairs of them. And what was this – a watch-glass? Screwed rather clumsily into my eye – an eyeglass! The monocle effected an instant change in my personality. I grabbed a grey Homburg hat, which, somehow, besides being too big for me, failed to produce the dashing effect that such a hat can bestow. But when I turned down one half of the brim and set the hat at as rakish an angle as it could bear without actually falling off, a character began to emerge. I turned my attention to the spats.

> I'm Gilbert, the Filber, the knut with a 'K',
> The pride of Piccadilly, the ladies' roué . . .

I stood back from the long mirror to see the total effect. Spiffing! I raced downstairs, nearly forgetting an essential prop – you couldn't be a knut without a cane. I selected a Malacca walking-stick from the hall hatstand and strolled up Chapel Street to Belgrave Square. There were very few people about in the Square – in fact the only time I ever saw a crowd in Mr Cubitt's masterpiece was on the day of the peace procession – so I shifted my ground to Grosvenor Gardens, and then into Hyde Park. On a Sunday morning, surely, they would be riding in Rotten Row? They were, but neither riders nor pedestrians took the slightest notice of me. It was all rather disheartening. I strode on to Piccadilly, intending to walk as far in an easterly direction as Lyons' Corner House, where I would treat myself to a Snowflake Sundae – ice cream, whipped cream, and shredded coconut, with a white grape on top. Here I got a polite nod from an old lady – I always seemed to attract old ladies – who stopped stock-still, looked at me, smiled, and shook her head. Not at all the effect I was hoping for. Crestfallen, I tried limping. But now I had become self-conscious, and cutting short my walk I scuttled back to Chapel Street. I tried to enter unnoticed by the basement door, but was met by Mary the parlourmaid. 'You've missed your tea. I'm off to confession.'

Andy had his two clubs, the Badminton and the Junior Athenaeum, and doubtless he had friends there. But in the evenings, alone with his beloved P.G.Wodehouse, that most prolific of authors whom Andy would curse for not writing enough books, he seemed to have no friends to invite to dinner. No one ever 'dropped in' to see Andy. Even on Peace Night, when every room in Chapel Street was crammed with friends, I remember only one friend of Andy's, a Major Papillon.

No, he didn't care for the theatre. Mother would book seats for the three of us, Andy, Peggy, and me, for plays such as *The Cat and the Canary*, or musicals like *Lady Be Good*, or *Hit the Deck*, and these were thought to be sensationally good. But not by Andy, who found them noisy, and who didn't much care for an American accent wherever he found it.

'Yes,' he would say, 'I liked it very much ... but you know it can't compare with the musical comedies I saw when I was a young man on leave.'

'What were they, Daddy?'

'Oh, you know ... things like *Les Cloches de Corneville* ... Ah yes, now! I'd give the whole lot of your American comedies for one night at *Les Cloches de Corneville*.'

Later, when I was an undergraduate, we had the chance to prove the worth of this exchange, for a season of old operettas was announced for the London Casino Theatre in Soho, and to open the season was dear old *Les Cloches de Corneville*. I bought two tickets and offered to take Andy as a birthday present. The curtain rose on the first act and my heart sank. The scenery was out of date and looked as though it needed more than one new coat of paint. The star of the show, Hayden Coffin, had no doubt shone in the original English production, but time had not dealt kindly with him. Nor did his name – no fault of his – do much to set the bells of Corneville ringing. The male chorus, representing the male population of Corneville, seemed embarrassed at the endless 'ding-dongs' of the show's hit number. Somehow we sat it through to the end. 'Those fisher-folk were rather fishy,' I said as we left, trying to cheer Andy up.

'Times change,' said Andy – sadly, I thought.

III

A T CHAPEL Street a new school had to be found for me. It turned out to be Gladstone's, a preparatory school for about fifty boys, conveniently nearby, in Eaton Gate. There was a mistress who taught the smaller boys; a Mr Vipan; and Mr Gladstone himself, a sweet man who seemed to find something humorous in the art of teaching boys. In winter afternoons, just before dusk, whilst we were finishing our essays, he would turn on the light on his desk and his gentle voice would strike a musical note as he said, 'Come ... with me.' A gratified murmur would run through the class. It was the signal for a story, or reading from some history book for about half an hour, and that was the end of work for the day.

We played soccer in a field somewhere near Acton. In summer we went to the Buckingham Palace Road baths (now demolished). Once or twice a term we went to the Natural History Museum, and at Christmas time, together with another school, we were treated to a performance by Maskelyne and Devant at their theatre in Langham Place. Once we went to the Chiswick Empire and saw a rough-and-ready performance by Ben Greet and his company of *Macbeth*.

The question of a public school eventually presented itself. This posed a slight difficulty. None of Mother's relations had been to a public school and Andy had spent too long away from England to feel confident of choosing a school himself. The question was referred, as often such questions were, to a friend of Mother's, Ruthie Harker, a pretty, jolly woman whose son Geoffrey was at Clifton and was said to be quite happy there. So I was put down for Clifton for the same House that Geoffrey was in.

Mr Gladstone sent a pleasant reference to my new school:

M. S. Redgrave has been a pupil of this school for the past two years and six months.

His conduct during that time has been excellent. He works well and is fairly advanced for his age.

He has great musical talent.

Nothing in that is remarkable, except perhaps the last sentence, and that needs some qualification.

At one of the concerts which my piano teacher, Miss Smith, organized for her best pupils, Mother, who was always very fair, asked why the audience hadn't applauded John Casson (the son of Sybil Thorndike and Lewis Casson) more than me. 'Surely he played better than Michael?' Mother asked.

Miss Smith agreed. 'But, you see,' she added, 'when Michael gets up to play, he starts to *act*!'

I did progress at the piano, however, and I was sent to the Royal Academy of Music in Marylebone to study with Harold Craxton. The great teacher approved of my playing but found that I had an almost insuperable problem. I was stiff at the wrists. To get expert advice on this disability I was sent to Tobias Matthay, who sat close to me on the piano stool and, when I was least expecting it, dealt a sharp blow from underneath at my forearms. Matthay showed me how they should fly up, if they were relaxed, so that only the weight of the hand went into the keyboard, allowing the wrists to rotate freely.

Richard Prescott Keigwin was the Housemaster of my House, Dakyn's, at Clifton. He combined the best mixture of scholar and athlete. He had been 'capped' at university for cricket and hockey and he was one of the few masters who had any semblance of being up with the times. His own house adjoined Dakyn's, and a small queue of new boys had formed in the passage connecting the two. A House Prefect organized the introductions.

'Ah, Redgrave,' said Keigwin, 'how is my old friend Gladstone? And that reminds me,' he went on, addressing the Prefect, 'the piano in the library badly needs tuning. I don't think our friend Redgrave would condescend to play on such an instrument.' He laughed in an easy, relaxed sort of way.

'You've been studying under Mr Craxton. Let's see ... what games do you play?'

'Soccer, of course. Oh! and cricket. I bowl a bit.'

'Good, good, splendid. It's rugger here, actually, as I expect you know. Well, you'd better run along. You'll be in the small dormitory. Our friend Bissell will keep an eye on you.'

'Thank you, sir.'

'Which study is he in, Bissell?'

'"D," sir. With Cundy, Charters, Clayton minor, and Wong.'

'Right,' said Bissell, as we left Keigwin's study, 'now for Gee-Gee.'

'Gee-Gee?'

'Mr Gee to you. Assistant Housemaster. An awful swank. But don't say I said so.' He knocked on Mr Gee's door.

'Enter!' said a sharp voice. Mr Gee was seated on a sofa with a cup and saucer in his hand. At his side was a big box of Bourbon biscuits. 'Have a biscuit,' said Gee. 'Take two.'

I did so.

Mr Gee seemed to have no wish to prolong the interview. 'That's all right,' he said, waving us away, 'show him his study.'

'This is the largest study,' explained Bissell. 'That's because it's for five people. You'll like Wong. He's the best three-quarter in the business.'

Wong was sitting on a window-seat. 'I've bagged this,' he said. 'I'd bag a chair if I were you. Have you seen our dormitory?'

Standing by a bed in the small dormitory was the Matron, who had already unpacked most of my clothes. 'Where did you get this?' she asked. Mother had packed my clothes in a theatrical skip, instead of the prescribed trunk, insisting that it would last for years. It looked like a large laundry basket, with my name, 'M. S. Redgrave', painted in big bold black letters on its lid.

'Mother thought it would be more practical,' I mumbled.

'Are you fond of animals?'

'Um . . . yes.'

'Good. I've put you on "Zoo-side".' She indicated which was to be my bed, and at that moment a piercing cry came from over the road. 'Peacock,' said Matron.

'Zoo-side' was so called because it bordered the Clifton Zoo.

'Which reminds me,' she continued, 'how old are you, Wong?'

'Thirteen,' said Wong.

'I shall leave the light on in the passage . . . just in case . . . ' said Matron as she bade us good night. 'You'll soon get used to the menagerie.'

Later, when we were all in bed, we talked in hushed voices, and Charters and Cundy answered questions from the new boys.

Soon the others fell asleep. I was kept awake by the cries of the peacocks. For some reason I was reminded of one of Mother's favourite poems, Blake's 'Tyger! Tyger! burning bright / In the forests of the night.' (She had never been able to make me understand what 'fearful symmetry' meant.) There was no mistaking the sound which came from across the road. It was a huge belch proceeding from the cavernous jaws of a big cat, as if a clap of thunder had split the little dormitory, and there was I marching into the forests of the night.

I lost no time in writing home:

Dear Mother,

I am getting on fairly well. I didn't sleep at all well last night and woke up with a ghastly headache. There are four other boys besides myself in my study called Charters, Cundy, Clayton and Wong. Charters and Cundy are old boys who have been here for some terms, but Clayton is a new boy. I evidently don't have to have an order for my clothes, but the school shop is closed this afternoon.

I have not seen Geoff anywhere today.

I am by far the youngest in my form and am finding things rather difficult. It all seems like a dream and it seems very funny to wake up in the middle of the night and wonder where I am. We have a nice little study and everything is comfy barring the beds! They are rather like the bare ground!

I was tried for the choir this morning but they didn't quite think my voice was strong enough but I think I am in the choral society. This afternoon I went to the music school and played a few things to Mr Beachcroft and I am to go on Monday to arrange about my music lessons. We had to prepare Lesson 27 in the Old Testament this evening.

Auntie Bea's cake and tart are ripping and are much appreciated.

It was freezingly cold today and we went for a long run (compulsory) this afternoon, with nothing but a thin vest and short pair of trousers. It is absolutely true that when I came in afterwards I fell on my bed and did not move for five minutes because I was so cold and tired.

I have nothing else to say (except that I shall write to Daddy tomorrow) so here I will close.

your loving son
Michael

'Ah! The very chap I was looking for! You're Redgrave, aren't you? A little bird tells me that we have here the rival of the Divine Sarah. Are you she? Myself I am but a lowly stage-manager. But where would you be without me? Up the spout! One turn of the switch and you are plunged in darkness. What do you say?'

McOstrich was the humorist of the House, the wag. He saw that I was carrying a book, which he took from me.

34

'What have we got here? Mathematics! Who wants mathematics?' He went back into his study, saying, 'Come in here. Would you like to be in the school play?'

'Is there a school play?'

'Oh yes. One a year at Commem. This year, *The Critic*, by Richard Brinsley Sheridan. Produced by A.C.K.Toms. Lighting by McO., another Irish genius. Come in here. Shut the door.'

In exchange for my maths book, he showed me a book of his own. 'Now there! A fifth Irish genius, the greatest man in the English theatre, the scourge of the critics, the one and only George Bernard Shaw!' He sat down and burst into wild applause. And then abruptly dropped the bantering tone. 'Are you thinking of going on the stage?'

'Good Lord, no!' I said. 'My stepfather would have a fit.'

'But your mother's an actress, isn't she?'

'Yes, but that's different.'

'I tell you what,' said McOstrich, 'you come and do your early prep in here, seven o'clock every morning, and I'll introduce you to Toms. He listens to my words. *De Toms en Toms*.'

Mr Toms cast me as the second niece.

'Big School', a vast, cavernous building, with its painful acoustics and difficult sightlines, was totally unsuited for the presentation of plays of any period. The ventilation was almost non-existent. That summer we performed the school play in a heat wave, with bath-tubs filled with huge blocks of ice, and electric fans playing across them, assisting the general inaudibility. But none of these defects prevented me from having, as they said, a whale of a time. My only disappointment was that Mother, who was acting in the West End, could not be there. The second niece is not a very rewarding part, but I played her 'up to the hilt, and somewhat more,' said Mr Taylor, the geography master, who had a sarcastic tongue. He added that the second niece was undoubtedly pretty, though her looks were rather those of *une fille de joie*.

The part of the second niece would not make anyone's fortune, but Mr Toms was sufficiently impressed with my acting to promote me in the commemoration festivities the following year. As Lady Mary in Barrie's *The Admirable Crichton*, I made a discovery. Lady Mary is the eldest of Lord Loam's three daughters and, when the family is shipwrecked on a Pacific island, Crichton – the butler – takes over as chieftain, and Loam and his daughters and sons-in-law find their social roles reversed. Lady Mary, with bow and arrow, becomes the huntress and falls in love with Crichton. When finally a ship is sighted off the island, Crichton makes ready to signal to it. Lady Mary in an outburst of passion begs him to let the ship go, but Crichton is firm, and the family return to England and to their former social status. Accompanying them to the ship is a rescue party of marines, who arrive just as Lady Mary has made her passionate plea – 'Let the ship go, Guv! Let the ship go!' I found on the first performance – there were only two – that I was shedding Lady Mary's tears. At the second performance, the marine nearest me on-stage saw that I was crying and whispered from the corner of his mouth, 'Blubbing again!' I discovered that I could turn on the water taps at will. Laurence Olivier calls it 'the gift of tears'. A very doubtful gift: unless the text specifically calls for tears, they are better left unshed.

The day before the end of my second term, McOstrich told me there was going to be a grand party in the senior dormitory that night. He had thought of inviting me, he said, but had decided against it because if I were to be asked the others in the junior dormitory might feel left out. There was to be wine, and candlelight, and formal invitations, and it was thought that Barlow had shown a pretty wit in his acceptance: 'Yours, to the last cork.'

It was impossible to go to sleep that night with so much conspiracy seething up in the darkness. A sentinel had been posted to tiptoe up and down the staircase which led to Keigwin's part of the house.

McOstrich put his head round the door of my dormitory and beckoned. 'Come and look,' he said. The senior dormitory by candlelight looked like a scene from *Peter Pan*, with some of the revellers in masks, and I was disinclined to go back to the small dormitory. But McOstrich said no, I was not to be involved in any way and, rather to my surprise, kissed me on the forehead, something he had never done before. Then, with a gentle pat, he ushered me back to my own bed. He seemed perfectly sober then. This could hardly be said of him later.

I do not know how long I slept, but I was woken by someone sitting on my bed. 'Hello, McOstrich,' I whispered.

'It's not McOstrich, you silly little fool.' It was Simpson, the butt of the House. He leant over me and said, 'Bloody good party.' His breath smelt absolutely foul.

'Yes,' I said, feebly, 'was it?'

His voice went on mumbling. 'Look here, I'm getting cold. Let me get into bed.'

I managed to slip out the other side of the bed and start for the 'rears'. I shut the door, bolted myself in, and waited for Simpson to go away. But he only became more insistent.

'Don't be afraid. I wasn't going to do anything.' He kept this up for about five minutes in loud whispers. 'Come on out. Come on, don't be silly.'

Suddenly there was another voice. 'Bugger off, Simpson.' It was McOstrich, sounding so drunk that I still didn't dare to unbolt the door. I could hear the sound of a scuffle. It became more vigorous and sounded as if at any moment it might develop into a brawl. There was the sound of a body falling on the floor and a groan from McOstrich, and the outer door of the 'rears' slammed. I swiftly unbolted the door of my cubicle and knelt down beside McOstrich, shaking him by his shoulders. I could smell the wine on his breath and, prig that I was, became angry with him. I slapped his face two or three times. To my surprise it seemed to rally him a little.

'Don't do that,' he said, 'stop it.'

'You're drunk,' I said.

'Of course I am. Bloody good party.'

'Come along, Mac, get up.' With difficulty I hoisted him to his feet.

McOstrich suddenly laughed.

'What are you laughing at?'

'You. Helping me. You don't know how funny that is.'

Mother was able to see me in only one of the three remaining plays during my time at Clifton (as Lady Macbeth, Mrs Hardcastle in *She Stoops to Conquer*, and Captain Absolute in *The Rivals*), and it may be that my performance as Lady Macbeth made her think twice about my becoming a professional actor. In her notebook she recalls a piece of business from the sleep-walking scene: 'you not only really seemed to be asleep, you bowed your head just before the end of the scene and your head seemed to drop as though you were tired to death. ... It was a lovely bit of business.' Yet she had always been firmly against my becoming an actor. I was 'too tall', the stage was 'no life for a man'. This last, of course, referred to Roy. The shadow of my father haunted her until she was an old woman. I have already mentioned her fear that I might become like him. And to this was added her concern for what might displease my stepfather: 'the master who produced the plays was terribly keen on your being an actor and begged me to send you to Oxford or Cambridge and then let you go on the stage. Good advice, I am sure, but I knew Andy would be against it, so I did not encourage the idea.'

IV

I F I SET aside my early trip to Australia and back, I suppose my first foreign holiday occurred when I was about sixteen, when Mother, Andy, Peggy, and I went to Normandy, to the small, delightfully-named watering-place Veules-les-Roses, where we stayed at the important-sounding Hôtel des Bains et de la Plage, a small, second-rate hotel near the sea. The bathing was poor, off a shingle beach, backed by chalk cliffs. The hotel food was sometimes suspected of being of equine origin, dressed up with watercress.

But it was 'abroad'. There were charming, poppy-sprinkled walks through the fields at the top of the cliffs. There was a 'casino': a rather shabby affair where one could dance to a trio, and an inner room where the grown-ups could gamble for small stakes. 'Yes, We Have No Bananas' was the rage of Veules that year and I danced to it evening after evening with a beautiful, tall, dark American girl with the Shakespearian name of Mary Arden Stead. I imagined myself to be in love with her, and I do not think she was averse to me. She was, perhaps, three or four years older than I, and several years more worldly-wise. On an excursion to Rouen I bought her a bracelet of olivewood, marked 'Jerusalem'. Her embarrassment at being presented with this dismal object must have been keen, but she concealed it well enough and certainly wore it that evening. A very sweet young woman.

However, she was not to be the visiting star of that holiday. When we had been at Veules-les-Roses for about a week, Andy broke the news that the son of the British Prime Minister, Stanley Baldwin, was expected.

Oliver Baldwin was a socialist and had been canvassing as a Labour candidate for Dudley, a constituency close to his father's. That he was known to be Labour was sufficient to damn him in my stepfather's opinion; that he should attempt to win a seat on the

39

opposite side of the House to his father, the Prime Minister, placed him, as Andy put it, 'beyond the pale'. This was enough to make me prepared to like him.

In a day or two he arrived. Tall, with straight, reddish-gold, silky hair, a trim officer's moustache, and pale but piercing blue eyes, he had an air of distinction and, indeed, beauty which would not have disgraced a pre-Raphaelite hero. He was accompanied by two other young men. The elder of these was a florid, merry-looking fellow of about Oliver Baldwin's age. The younger looked very singular. It appeared as if his head had been shaved or closely cropped. He looked what later would have been called 'butch', but 'butch' with a difference. That long scarf, flung round his neck, those birdlike, roving eyes, the drop of his hand over the back of the dining-room chair . . . he seemed a singular travelling companion for the two stalwart men.

One afternoon I was strumming away on the piano in one of the lounges of the hotel, sight-reading some simple music which I had found in the piano stool. When I stopped for a moment, a light voice from behind me said, 'You play very well. Do go on.' I turned and found 'Master Silk Scarf' (as Andy had dubbed him) sitting in an armchair with his feet curled up under him.

I thanked him and added that I could play only with the printed music in front of me. Not from memory or by ear. He disregarded this and, rising from the chair, threw his scarf over his other shoulder. 'Play me some Chopin,' he said.

'No, really, I can't. Not without music.'

'Do you know any of the *Valses*?'

'Yes, but I'm afraid I can't play any without –'

He cut me short by leaning forward and spreading his hands on the keys. I slid off the piano stool to make room for him. He sat and started to play.

He played very well in what, to my thinking, was rather a florid manner. His head and shoulders swayed and, for several seconds at a time, he would close his eyes during a few bars of rubato. I was rather given to rubato myself in my own playing and was inclined to over-indulge myself with the soft pedal. I thought he went altogether too far. I had yet to discover how far he was prepared to go.

He finished playing the Chopin waltz and paused for a moment or two. I hardly had time to say something in the way of praise before he started playing again, this time Rachmaninoff's showy and pianistic 'Polichinelle'.

'Oh, I play that,' I interjected.

He stopped immediately. 'Then *you* play it.' He rose abruptly from the piano.

'It's no good,' I said, 'I can't – '

' – without music, I know. But I don't know that I believe you. You're too timid, that's what's the matter with you, my friend.' In almost the same breath he said, 'Come on. Let's go for a walk.' He redraped his scarf.

The word 'timid' had done the trick. No boy likes to be called timid. I did not particularly want to go for a walk with this rather extravagant-looking young man. Suppose I were to meet one of the family? How could I introduce him, not knowing his name or anything about him except his piano-playing?

We walked up the chine of Veules-les-Roses on to a road hedged with poplars running between fields of corn and poppies. He asked me my name, where I lived, where I went to school, who my family were: He told me he lived at Sidmouth with his mother. I asked him how he came to know the Prime Minister's son.

'Oh, don't!' he said, rather petulantly. Then, suddenly, 'Oh, God, I am *so tired*. Let's sit down somewhere.'

There was no comfortable place to sit down except against a haystack. I thought for a moment, Aha! Here we are, back at school again. But the word 'timid' still had a slight sting. We sat down and leant our backs against the haystack.

'Why are you so tired?' I asked, politely.

'They talk all night and I can hear them through the wall.'

'Who talks all night?'

'*They* do. My two gaolers.'

'Do you mean – '

'Yes. Johnnie and Oliver. They're supposed to be looking after me. But they talk all night and then wake me up at seven to order breakfast for them. You see, neither of them can speak French, even though they were at Eton together. They had all my hair cut off – I don't know what my mother would say if she knew. Shaven and shorn I was, like a lamb.'

'How awful. Why don't you tell her? Then you could go back home.'

'Mother paid for their so-called holiday – fares, hotel bills, everything. They were supposed to be looking after me, but they treat me like a skivvy. Oh, it's too tedious. I can't *tell* you.'

Looking back, I cannot imagine how I believed all this. The words 'pathological' and 'paranoiac' were unknown to me and, I fancy, to all but a minority in those days. Pansies were for thoughts.

I felt myself moved and indignant on Sidney's behalf. That was his name: Sidney from Sidmouth. It was not long before I was disillusioned.

Coming downstairs before dinner that evening, I heard footsteps behind me. They were accompanied by a grave, gentle, but authoritative voice.

'Redgrave. I wouldn't believe everything that young man tells you. Not if I were you.'

I stopped and turned and found myself facing the dastardly Baldwin.

'Well, I think it's rotten, *rotten*, the way you've treated him.' There was a tremor in my voice, and he smiled.

He did not speak for several seconds but seemed to be weighing the situation up. My outburst had left me slightly shaky with emotion.

'Would you like an orangeade before dinner?' he asked at last. The wind was immediately and completely taken out of my sails.

'All right. Thank you.'

We sat in the gravelled courtyard and he ordered two orangeades. Waiting for these to be served, he asked me what school I went to, how long I and my family were staying in France, and other politenesses. I told him that my father had been an actor. I said I thought Roy was dead. And then he explained about Sidney.

Sidney's mother, a widow and an invalid, seemingly doted on her only child. She wanted him to travel but could not accompany him. Baldwin had been a friend of her family for some years. She was also a friend of Rudyard Kipling, who was Oliver's godfather. (This impressed me vastly.) Hearing that Baldwin was going to France, she besought him to take Sidney along. This, said Baldwin, was easier said than done. The youth was not only a congenital liar, but his appearance, even on his home ground, was considerably daunting. On a tour of Normandy and Brittany there was only one word for it: impossible. The mother's request was acceded to, but on conditions. Sidney could not be given a complete *laisser-aller*: he must first of all cut very short his artificially-bright golden hair and promise not to make up his face. Not even in the evenings.

'You see,' said Baldwin, 'he was known as the "Painted Lady of Sidmouth".'

I was so taken up with this glimpse of a mode of life so different from that of my stepfather's house and the purlieus of Belgrave Square that I was late for dinner.

I was not questioned about either of my acquaintances, which was a relief, but an ominous silence prevailed until Mother, who was always the first to try to break the dreaded pauses, asked me what I had been doing all day. As it happened, the great *Lieder* singer Sir George Henschel was staying at the hotel with his wife and daughter, and I had met Georgina, the girl, that morning when we had discussed the idea of getting up some charades in the lounge one evening. It was my idea. Inflamed by my success as Lady Macbeth in the school play, not to mention an hysterical Clarence in the murder scene from *Richard III* in the Christmas-term House Play, and a French maid in one of my Housemaster's one-act French plays, entitled *Par un Jour de Pluie*, I was always thinking in terms of 'theatricals', as Andy called them.

I revealed my and Georgina's general plan.

'You'd like that, wouldn't you, Peg?' said Mother.

I had not even thought of including my half-sister in the project. Peg was shy, but game.

'*Rather!*' was all she replied, without great conviction.

'When are you going to play this game?' asked Andy.

'Oh, it isn't a game exactly. More like a performance. We shall rehearse it all first.'

'A performance! Who's going to watch?'

'The residents.'

'You mean French people?'

'If they want to. There are heaps of English in the hotel. Of course, they'll have to pay. Same as the English.'

'Pay!' Consternation mounted. 'You won't get many if you make them pay.'

'On the contrary. Lots more.'

Mother reverted for a moment to being a 'pro'. 'There's something in what he says, Andy.'

There was a pause. Then Andy said, 'What will you do with the money?'

I hadn't thought of that. 'We haven't decided. We shall only charge a few centimes, anyway.'

For the rest of the meal I talked about Georgina's father, Sir George, who, it was reputed, at the age of seventy and even though he smoked cigars, could still sing 'Erlkönig'. When I told Georgina that my Housemaster had a record of him singing 'Erlkönig', she persuaded him to sit at the piano and sing it for me. His cigar lay in an ashtray and was still alight when he finished. His voice sounded much the same as on the old record, the cries of the dying child as passionate. 'When you have learned to sing a song properly, you can always sing it,' the old man said. 'It's like riding a bicycle. A bit rusty, perhaps, but it still goes.'

Georgina and I invented and rehearsed the charades. I had put up a notice in the lobby and we had a full house. (No cinema and, of course, no television. Nothing much else for the guests of an evening.) After the performance, when the audience was dispersing, Baldwin invited the cast to orangeade and ices in the courtyard. He asked us if any of us liked ghost-stories. 'Oh, yes!' some of us said.

We were all elated by the success of our charades, and the beach-huts were only a few yards down the road. About eight of us packed into one of them. It was completely dark, and there were squeals of pretended fear and some giggles. Baldwin waited until we were all seated on the floor.

'No whispering,' he commanded. The whispers died and he held a long pause.

The stories he told us were simple and in themselves not very alarming, but his voice had mesmeric overtones and he cleverly underplayed his narrative and would make a slight hesitation before each climax. When he thought we had had enough he was begged for more, but he said it was time some of us were in bed. He would tell us another story the next evening.

As we sauntered back to the hotel, I plucked up the nerve to say to him, 'You ought to have been an actor, Oliver, don't you think so?'

'As a matter of fact, yes, I do. If I could be smuggled into England as, shall we say, a well-known Polish actor, I'd show them how to play Richard the Second, or Hamlet.'

'Yes! Wouldn't that be marvellous?'

'I'm not serious, Michael. It would be impossible, anyway. For better or worse I'm too well-known. Anyway, I have other things that have to be done.'

I sensed that this meant politics and thought it better to keep my mouth shut about these.

'I suppose you're a Tory, like your stepfather?' he asked.

'Well . . . I don't think about it very much.'

'We can talk about it some time, if you'd like to. Shall we go for a walk tomorrow, after lunch?'

During this conversation the others had called good night or simply disappeared. Johnnie Boyle came up to us as we reached the hotel.

'Michael thinks I should play Richard II,' said Oliver.

'He'd be not bad, you know. Marvellous, in fact. He's read me a lot of it, especially the prison scene. But then he knows all about prisons. Or should do, by now.'

'We won't go into that,' said Oliver. 'But there's one thing I'm sure of.'

'What's that?'

'Michael should be an actor.'

The next day, the three of us set out for a walk. I did not ask where Sidney was, but Johnnie implied that he had gone or been sent home. We walked along the top of the cliffs in the direction of Saint-Valéry. We talked of this and that. But suddenly, Oliver, who was marching along strongly, almost like the Guards' officer he had been, sat down on a milestone and said, 'Don't wait for me. I'll sit down for a minute. I'll catch you up.'

I was for stopping and waiting for him, but Johnnie tugged at my sleeve and said, 'Come on.'

As we passed out of earshot he said it was nothing to worry about, but that 'Noll' was not as robust as he looked. Not surprisingly, he said, after what 'Noll' had been through. I enquired, tentatively, what that might be.

After the Great War, when he had served in the Brigade of Guards, he had become deeply and actively involved in the fate of what Johnnie called 'poor, bloody Armenia'. He had risen to the rank of Lieutenant-Colonel in the Armenian Army and had been captured by both the Turks and the Bolsheviks, and incarcerated in six different prisons. From one prison he had been marched out to be shot and then, for lack of ammunition, marched in again. As a result of these experiences, Johnnie concluded, Oliver had a serious set-back in health. He would wake up in a nightmare every night, or groan and call out in his sleep. They had chosen to holiday at Veules-les-Roses as the best place for his recuperation because of its quiet.

I was knocked sideways by this brief résumé of Oliver's heroism and sufferings. I looked back to where he had sat down. He was already on his feet and walking towards us. We waited for him to catch us up.

When he came abreast with us he said, with a smile, 'No gossip, I hope, Johnnie.'

'I was telling him about your book.'

'Oh, that.'

45

I thought it was about time I said something. 'What's it called, your book?' I asked.

There was a pause. Johnnie answered: 'This one's called *Six Prisons and Two Revolutions.*'

I forget what Oliver said but he abruptly and firmly changed the subject.

Later, back at the Bains et Plage, an awkward little incident blew up which was embarrassing to all concerned and agonizing for me until it blew over.

It seemed that my stepfather had struck up a bar-room acquaintance with a friend of Oliver's. Andy's strong Tory prejudices still resented the mere presence of the young Baldwin in the same hotel, and I dare say something had reached him about the beach-hut entertainments. That the 'Bolshie' should be placed 'beyond the pale' was no longer strong enough. He should be 'horse-whipped'. The other man expostulated, presumably, and Andy calmed down sufficiently to say he would like to talk to the feller and would the friend convey an invitation from Andy asking the deluded young man to have a drink with him, even if this amounted to asking Oliver to step inside the 'pale' for a few minutes.

'Your stepfather has invited me to have a drink with him.'

'Oh, dear!'

'Don't worry. I shan't go, of course.'

My anxiety was by no means relieved at this. Oliver's non-appearance might be taken as a 'cut' and lead to anything.

He then related what was supposed to have taken place.

I was panic-stricken. 'Are you going to tell him why you can't go?'

He explained that, since the invitation had not been issued in person and had threats attached, he thought it better to ignore it. What he had seen of war and revolution had made him a pacifist.

'When the next war comes, as it will, I shall be proud to lead a regiment of young men sharing my convictions into prison.'

Good Lord, I thought, it's just as well if he *doesn't* meet Andy.

But when we met for dinner that evening, the dreaded subject of Oliver was never mentioned. I can only suppose that the friendly go-between had told Andy about his war service when under age, and his career as a Lieutenant-Colonel in the Armenian Army in the war, which had dragged on and which few spoke about because comparatively few had ever heard about it.

Then, one day, all too suddenly, Oliver and Johnnie left Veules-

46

les-Roses. Life became very dull. Mary Arden Stead had found a new cavalier. The Henschels had gone.

But what I chiefly suffered from was not loneliness but impatience. For before they left, Johnnie had asked me to stay with them for a week during the remainder of the 'hols'. To apprise Andy of this, as things were, I should have had to pluck up more courage than I think I possessed. But Johnnie took the matter in hand. He was, if anything, more socialite than socialist and he had a very jolly way with him. He explained that their little house was in Oxfordshire, at Shirburn, quite close to his sister's place, Shirburn Castle – on the same land, in fact. Did Andy know the Macclesfields?

I do not mean that it was only this mention of his aristocratic relations that did the trick. Not entirely. For John Boyle, when he set out to charm, seldom had a failure. He remembered that I had said Andy usually went shooting or fishing at the suitable times. 'Where are you shooting this year?' he asked. That was what did it, though I think the Earl and Countess helped.

My stepfather simply said, 'Have you told your mother?' I said I hadn't, yet.

But Johnnie had another card up his sleeve. 'We must take him over to Chequers some evening.'

Chequers, I fancy, was brought in not only for Andy's but for Oliver's sake. Many people must have assumed that the Baldwins *père et fils* could not be on speaking terms, which was scarcely the case (as Keith Middlemas and John Barnes testify in *Baldwin: A Biography*, published in 1969).

Anyway, we did go to Chequers, as one of my childishly-written diaries records: 'This morning Oliver and I had a long talk about many things. In the evening we went to Checquers [*sic*] to dine.'

What we talked about that morning was Socialism and Sex. We were sitting in a little hut at the end of the garden, a place Oliver used for his painting and in summer for writing. A peacock and peahen were on the lawn.

'I have a question for you,' said Oliver, 'but I'm not sure you'll like it. Shall we toss a coin for it? If you win, you don't have to answer.'

For a moment I thought he was joking, but he looked deadly serious. 'All right,' I said, thinking it would be unsporting not to agree; besides, I was curious.

'Shall I ask you the question first or shall we toss first? I think toss first, don't you?'

This, I was too slow to perceive, was cunning of him, because if I won the toss I should be agog to know the undivulged question. So, like a fool, I said, 'Yes, let's toss first.'

I won the toss.

Oliver smiled. He knew he only had to wait. 'Well, then, I'll ask you another question: Do you believe in socialism?'

I hesitated and then said, 'I suppose so.'

'It's not a question of supposing, it's a question of belief. It's a positive question.'

'I don't know.'

'You haven't really thought about it, have you? You would believe whatever the last person told you, wouldn't you?'

'Oh, I don't know about that. ...'

'Well, I do. But I could make you believe in socialism without much talk or argument. I could *show* you and you'd have to believe your eyes.'

'How?'

'Come with me for a day, or even a few hours, to Dudley. I'd show you the living conditions. I'd show you the difference between the privileged and the people.'

I couldn't help looking at the peacocks.

'Before Mother married Andy I used to see lots of poor people. In Portsmouth and ...

'It isn't poverty I'm talking about. I'm talking about misery. Britain is Two Nations: the Rich and the Poor.'

I expect Oliver may have used Disraeli's famous tag on countless platforms. He can seldom have found a more receptive listener than myself, ignoramus that I was. But from that day I could not politically call myself anything but a socialist.

When I returned home I was already a different fellow to what I was before I visited Shirburn. Of course, I played Shirburn Castle and Chequers for all they were worth and skirted round Andy's awkward and dreaded question 'Was the PM there for dinner?' with a line I had thought up on the train back to London: 'Oh, I would think he has far too much on his plate at the moment. Wouldn't you?'

Betting on the chance that Andy had no more idea of what the Prime Minister had on his plate than I had, I thought discussion of Chequers was closed. There was a pause in the conversation. 'What's he got on his plate?' asked Andy suddenly.

'Oh, you know,' I replied limply.

When I was reading in bed later that evening, I was surprised that Mother came into my room. She sat on the bed and her hand patted mine.

'Don't let him think you've become a socialist,' she said, with an anxious smile, 'it only makes things more difficult.'

'Yes, I know.'

'Well, don't, then. There's a dear. It upsets him terribly. He doesn't understand that one has these convictions when one is young. I used to be a socialist. Do you remember how I introduced you to Robert Blatchford when you were a little boy? He was a fine man.'

'Yes, I remember, vaguely.'

'You were only six.' She kissed me and I hugged her.

On the mantelpiece stood a framed photo of herself. Carelessly I had used it to prop up a photo of Oliver in front of it. As she rose to leave, it caught her eye. She looked at it and picked it up. I thought she was going to say something, but she didn't. She just laid it flat on the mantelpiece and said good night. I had not leant Oliver's photo there with any purpose of defacing hers. But there it was and there was nothing I could say without making matters worse.

Oliver was my first hero, and for a time he could in my eyes do no wrong.

My later memories of him are scattered, but somehow he always remained 'in character'. One characteristic was his desire to shock. Of this I became aware when gnawing curiosity made me ask him to put the question to me which I had escaped by the turn of the coin. I had thought he might be going to ask me something portentous.

And he did.

'Have you ever been to bed with a woman?'

I shook my head slowly.

'I think, if I were you, I would.'

V

I N THE 1920s it was commercial death for any manager to mount a
production of Shakespeare in London, and no West End actor
would want to be called 'Shakespearian'. Nor would Mother, I
think, have cared for the label. Yet it was she who was largely
responsible for the 'Fellowship of Players', an admirable enterprise
which set out to perform, in London, the entire Shakespearian
canon. The plays were cast from out-of-work actors, and sometimes
leading actors if they could spare the rehearsal time. There were two
performances: one on Sunday evening, and a matinée on Monday.

I was at a loose end. I had left Clifton in the summer of 1926 with
no job to go to, and no particular prospects. When Mother suggested
I might 'walk on' in *The Taming of the Shrew* as one of Petruchio's
servants, I was over the moon, especially when I heard that Robert
Loraine was to play Petruchio. Though not such a beautiful man as
Henry Ainley, whom I revered and, alas, never met, Loraine was a
wonderfully magnetic actor and a great favourite. The production,
if you could call it that, was by Ben Greet, the staunch and
much-loved Shakespearian.

I was told that I was to play the cook. Not much of a part, really,
but Greet had inherited a surefire piece of business where the cook,
on his name being called, was sent twirling from one servant to
another until, at the end of the line, he almost fell into the arms of the
dread Petruchio.

This I performed at the dress rehearsal to Loraine's satisfaction, I
suppose. But at the first performance I was inspired to try something
a little more vivid. Instead of being caught by Petruchio, I eluded his
grasp, fell flat on my face, and lay winded and panting at his feet.
This produced a big laugh. Loraine, I thought, mistook it for a
genuinely accidental fall, though I was told by his dresser that he

could see I was an actor's son by the way I held the fall and got a much bigger laugh. At the second performance I was all set to elaborate my pratfall, but Loraine was too quick for me: as I reached him he started to speak the next line and walked away a pace or two with a broad smile, taking the audience's interest with him.

Many years later I undertook Strindberg's *The Father*, which had not been seen in the West End since Loraine had made a tremendous success in it. My notices were good; some very good. Some, though good, said that my performance had not erased the memory of Loraine's. I myself could still picture Loraine vividly in the part. I was puzzled, however, by a mental image of him seated in a wheelchair. This I placed as coming from a curtain-raiser – Barrie's *Barbara's Wedding*. But why had he thought a curtain-raiser necessary? *Barbara's Wedding* played for at least half an hour, and *The Father* was long enough in itself.

I was haunted by Loraine. After the last matinée performance at the Duchess Theatre, I was visited by Loraine's widow. I asked her why Robert had needed a curtain-raiser. 'He didn't. But he thought he did.' He couldn't, she said, bear to be thought of as a weak man, even on the stage. So he cut every line of the Captain's which showed his weakness, thus turning the play upside down.

'But the critics . . . ?' I exclaimed.

'Ah, yes, the critics. Most of them, you see, had never read the play.'

And now, I thought, their knowledge of the play, for the most part, was the imagined remembrance of Robert's rugged, forceful, and highly-effective performance, which many of them had not even seen.

The results of my School Certificate examination arrived. I had failed. Andy, who had borne the expense of my five years' public schooling – and all for nothing, it seemed – never once reproached me for this dismal failure. In fact, he scarcely ever reprimanded me. He was never angry, and he tried hard not to be impatient; but one by one, every little thing that went wrong, or wouldn't work, came to seem – even if obliquely – my fault.

Two newspapers were delivered at number 9: *The Times* and the *Daily Mail*. The *Mail* was for the whole household; *The Times*, it was understood, was exclusively Andy's. One morning he was a little late taking his bath and I dared to take *The Times* into the lavatory with me. Something must have caught my eye, for I sat there quite a while, reading. As I emerged from the cubiculo I collided with Andy, who had been searching for his newspaper beneath the breakfast table.

'Oh, sorry, Dad,' I said, handing him the paper. Suppressed anger made his hand shake as he seized it from me. 'Sorry, Dad,' I said again.

'I suppose you know,' he said at last, 'that you would be turfed out of any London club for that?'

Mother produced a sort of careers brochure for school-leavers, and she, Andy, and I worked our way through its suggestions. Accountancy, architecture, bee-keeping (bee-keeping?) . . . catering management, draughtsmanship, engineering . . . The trouble was that to embark on any one of them I should need some qualifications, and I had none. As I leafed through the catalogue, the realization dawned on me that really I should like nothing so much as to do nothing at all.

Andy gave a sigh. 'Of course, there's always that.' He pointed towards the mantelpiece, to a watercolour of a Ceylonese scene. I looked at Mother in some astonishment. Andy caught my look. 'Of course, you're too young. But I dare say the Agency might stretch a point.'

There were a few seconds of silence. Andy went on: 'We could wangle it somehow, I'm sure. It's a fine life. You'd have your own bungalow, and servants. And the climate, well . . . it's not like India. A beautiful place, really.'

'Sounds idyllic,' I said. So it did.

'Of course,' Andy went on, 'you'd have to ride twenty miles for your game of bridge.'

There was a long silence.

'Never mind,' said Andy, 'just a suggestion. Not the life for Michael, really.'

'Don't worry,' I said. 'I'll find something.'

I had, in point of fact, found something; or, at least, there was something there for the taking. It was Margot Dempster, back from Hollywood, full of vitality and 'oomph'. Margot was a friend of Mother's; in her late thirties, an independent woman whose job, I knew, had something to do with films. We had met the year before, on holiday at Pornic in France. She invited me to her flat and I arrived with a pot of chrysanthemums.

'You've grown,' she said.

'Everyone says that.'

Her manner had much changed. At Pornic, she had seemed always to be holding back. Here, in London, and with the aura of glamorous Hollywood still about her, she startled me at first. Before, she had kissed me on the cheek. Now she kissed me full on the lips, and went straight into a monologue about Gary Cooper, Norma Shearer, Clara Bow, Chaplin, and other personalities. She spoke with a hint of an American accent, an assumption which I found immensely pleasing.

'And what about you, Mike,' she asked, 'what are you doing?'

'Nothing very much.'

'British studios! You know they really take the cake! They keep you hanging about for hours. They've no idea of the value of publicity.'

'No . . . I dare say,' I said.

'I'm seeing this man at Teddington on Wednesday. Now, if this were Hollywood, they'd have some creature to follow me around, carry my camera, run errands, look up telephone numbers. Chaplin always sent a car for me . . .' Suddenly it seemed as if some important thought had crossed her mind. 'What are you doing Wednesday? Or Tuesday, for that matter?'

'Nothing,' I said.

'Well, would you do that for me? You know, run errands, look after me? How are you off for money? What does Andy give you?'

'Oh, well . . . you know. . . . '

'Strictly professional,' she said, slipping a five-pound note into my breast pocket.

A few days later she gave a cocktail party – 'Just a few chums. You must come, Mike.'

It was all so unlike Chapel Street, where a cocktail meant a rather weak Martini. At Margot's, cocktails were cocktails: Tom Collinses or Clover Clubs, served with Hollywood showmanship, the rim of the cocktail glass neatly coated with sugar. I downed three or four in rather quick succession. Suddenly Chapel Street seemed very far away, and very hard to get to.

'I'd sit down for a moment if I were you, Mike.'

'I think I'd better.' The other guests had all departed.

'I could put you up for the night.'

She wore black silk stockings, which were new to me; flesh-coloured stockings were the fashion then. I asked her why. 'I've a friend who likes me in them,' she said.

What followed, on the carpet in front of the fire, was new to me also, and would never have occurred to me without her guidance. Many years later, on a trip to Pompeii, I was reminded of it – at the *gabinetto*

53

pornografico, where our guide tactfully dismissed the children. He pointed at one of the frescoes. 'You see?' he said. '*La donna è sopra.*'

It was Mother who procured half a dozen letters of introduction for me to take round Fleet Street, in hopes that one at least might provide the entrée to a career in letters. I gave *Punch* the privilege of first choice, and I felt quite cheerful as I entered a handsomely-furnished room – could it have been the boardroom? – where a smartly-dressed, youngish man shook my hand warmly and invited me to sit down. It was all very gentlemanly, and we spent a few minutes talking about the world in general; and when we had done with the world, he focussed my attention upon me. By degrees his suave manner changed, and he became rather brisk. He asked me what I thought *Punch* could do for me. I chuckled to show that I was quite up to the sub-compliment. A pause followed.

'Have you brought anything which I might read?'

I thought of poor feeble Mr Bate of Billingsgate, with his twenty-five rhymes on the syllable 'hate', and rejected him hastily.

'No, I'm sorry ... I wasn't expecting ... '

His manner became even more brisk. 'I'll tell you what,' he said, 'you send me a few things of yours, and I'll drop you a line when I've read them. Then, perhaps, we could meet again.' He rose and opened the door for me and shook my hand.

A telephone call put me in touch with Sir Ernest Benn, a big noise in Fleet Street, who, like the young man from *Punch*, was most cordial. After a little chit-chat he said, 'Now, let's talk about you. You have, of course, your School Certificate?'

'Er ... no, I'm afraid not.'

'Oh dear! It's rather a yardstick, you know, the School Certificate. Never mind, we'll soon find out. ... Tell you what, I'll give you a job on the *Western Farmer's Journal*. You won't like it, but it'll give you a toehold in Fleet Street, and that's the main thing. ... '

Next on my list was the publisher Mr Ivor Nicholson of *Nash's* Magazine, who was about to launch the firm of Nicholson and Watson. He was just leaving his office when I asked to speak to him, but he made time to see me the next day. I told him what Sir Ernest had said, and asked his advice about the *Western Farmer's Journal*.

'He's quite right, of course,' Nicholson said, 'you'd hate it there, I fancy. What are your languages up to?'

'To be honest, not much.'

'The trouble is,' he said, 'you have nothing to offer. Who sent you to Clifton?'

'My stepfather.'

'Couldn't he send you to France and Germany for a few months?'

'I don't like to ask him,' I said. 'He suggested I be a tea and rubber planter, though I don't think he's too keen on that, either. I really don't think I can ask him to send me abroad.'

'Has he money?' asked Nicholson.

'Yes, he's well off.'

'Well, then, *I'll* ask him.'

To my surprise, Andy received Nicholson's suggestion with something like enthusiasm. Later it occurred to me that he didn't in the least mind parting with some cash – not such a lot by today's standards, anyway – if it meant getting me out of the way. The Orbachs were called in. George Orbach and his wife lived just round the corner from us, in Chesham Street. With immense zest, George, being German, went into the salient characteristics of Munich, Berlin, Leipzig, Mannheim, Hamburg. 'But of course,' he concluded, 'Michael would not be happy in any of these places. Let us think of the smaller, artistic milieu, such as he would find – say – in the Black Forest . . . or Heidelberg. Aha!' he said, as he slapped his plump thighs. 'Yes, Heidelberg! That is the place for Michael!'

If Ivor Nicholson's kindly interference had filled me with happy expectation, George's enthusiasm for Heidelberg was like strong drink. I couldn't contain myself; I danced round the supper table.

'You seem damned anxious to get away from us,' said Andy.

'Oh, no!' I said, suddenly realizing how much the whole project depended on Andy's generosity. And it was hard to tell from his look whether he was not suffering from some distemper, whereas George – who, come to think of it, always took my side – was wreathed in eupeptic smiles. He started to sing, '*Alt Heidelberg du feine, du Stadt an Ehren reich . . .* '

It was all so sudden. Had anyone ever sung before at that forbidding table?

Mother came up to kiss me good night.

'Won't it be wonderful?' I said.

'It hasn't happened yet,' she said, 'but yes, it will be good for you . . . for both of you.'

It came with something of a jolt to realize that she meant it would be a relief for Andy, as well as for me. For a very brief moment I had a glimpse of my own selfishness. The idea of Ernest Benn's offer, though I felt I had to be polite about it, had filled me with distaste; worse, with rank boredom. And then I must have fallen asleep.

'Today, my friend Chichele Waterston and I went skiing in the Black Forest,' I wrote to Mother. We had set off in a train starting at about four in the morning, with a party of students from Heidelberg. Now, we were back in the acetylene-lighted hut which served as an hotel, waiting to pile into the truck which was to return us to the station.

The students started to sing, '*Ich weiss nicht was soll es bedeuten, dass ich so traurig bin.*' I felt rather *traurig* myself. What a waste the day had been. Another wasted day! For the hundred and first time, I resolved to work harder. Not for me, I thought, this suicidal sport. Better use could be made of my money by going to the theatre, or even the cinema. Better by far to steep myself in Goethe's mighty lines.

And who better to speak them than Maria Andor, grave of face and sweet of tongue, the leading actress at the Stadttheater? I wished a thousand times for the nerve to present myself at her stage door. I tried hanging about near the theatre, but never succeeded in exchanging a single word with her.

Later, when I left Heidelberg, I did catch a glimpse of her on the next platform, waiting for a train going in the opposite direction. I was on my way to Mainz, at the order of Andy. I was to bring my half-sister, Peg, back from Germany to England, with all possible speed. Peg, I should explain, had asked to be sent to Germany in my wake. Why she wanted to go I cannot now remember, nor why she had chosen Mainz. But now it appeared that she had fallen in love with a German doctor and was talking about marriage. She had written to Andy about this, and Andy had gone up in smoke. Peggy must return at once. It was arranged that he and I together should fetch her.

She met us at the station at Mainz, accompanied by an agreeable-looking fair-haired individual of very German countenance. Peggy immediately let forth a torrent of German, smiling and laughing till I thought Andy would burst. It came as something of a shock to realize that she spoke German far more fluently and idiomatically than I. Peg was staying at a small but rather elegant pension, while Andy and I were to share a room at the Vier Jahreszeiten Hotel. The four of us met for dinner, where again Peg kept up a stream of fluent German, Andy demanding of me all the while, 'What's she saying? What was that?' The trouble was I couldn't always follow what they were saying, and when this occurred, I was obliged to improvise.

Andy announced that they would return home in three days' time. I was ordered to organize the return journey through an itinerary which included Paris. This was intended to sweeten the prospect of Peg's enforced departure.

I was fond of my half-sister in a 'dear old Peg' sort of way, and was quite unprepared for the sight of the truly tragic young woman who presented herself on the station platform on the morning of departure. She had not shown, or I had not noticed, any great grief the previous three days, but now her tears and strange, choking, wailing sounds made me think that surely Andy would relent, or at least permit some stay of execution.

Feverishly she looked about for her doctor, and at last he appeared, running down the platform. As he approached, the train started slowly to move. It was all too much for Andy, who uttered the unfortunate expletive 'Good grief!' The train quickened its pace. Peg's doctor was left standing. He called out, in perfect English, 'Don't forget! Write to me!'

I returned to Heidelberg. But life at Fräulein Rauch's Pension Sylvaner now seemed humdrum. My fellow-lodger Chichele Waterston had gone for two months' skiing. I missed him. He continually used words which were unfamiliar to me ('occlusion', 'increment') and had a way, which I was to copy when I came to Cambridge, of always carrying a book under his arm.

Christmas came and my German lessons were suspended. What command of the language I had acquired with the help of Professor Wildhagen, my tutor – a dear old creature of incredibly dirty appearance, whose passion was translating Turgenev – began to ebb away.

New Year came, and with it David Loveday, who had been the Assistant Chaplain at Clifton.

Before he left he had put forward a bold scheme. Someone should persuade Andy to send me to Cambridge. I had been a late developer, he said, but now I was at the stage where university might set me on my feet intellectually. Would Andy agree to this prospect? I said I strongly doubted it. David announced his intention of talking it over with him. I was to return home in a few weeks, and it was arranged that David would visit us at Chapel Street.

He was a nervous man but not a timid one. He pressed his case very clearly and sympathetically. And Andy, though far from timid himself, was perhaps a little awed by the Cloth and the 'Reverend'. After about half an hour it was settled. What clinched the matter was David's offer to coach me himself for the entrance exam. I would spend six weeks at Bristol. He would coach me in Latin, and a mathematician from Bristol University would be persuaded to 'cram' me with maths. This would be followed by three months in France to improve my French, the idea being that I should read Modern Languages. The thought of my being coached in this way at no extra cost so appealed to Andy that he even swallowed France without blinking.

Monsieur Sémézies, who was entrusted with the task of burnishing my French, was styled *ancien professeur de l'École Berlitz*. I took this to mean that he was ancient, or ageing, half-expecting a Gallic version of my Professor Wildhagen, and was surprised to find a young man, with a very attractive young wife. They lived at the Château l'Estiou on the Loire, near Beaugency. There were three other pensionnaires – two German boys and Luis, a Spaniard, who spoke very fast and incomprehensibly.

Word came from David, who had friends at Magdalene, that I had passed the entrance exam in Latin and English, and that the College would take me provided I had achieved a pass mark in Maths.

In the afternoons I would walk across the fields to the river. The German boys would appear in their boat, constructed by a former pensionnaire, a wonderful punt with a carpet for a sail. The Loire was very shallow at this point, and the current strong. Upstream, with a breeze behind us, our little craft would manage about four hundred yards an hour. Downstream, it covered the same distance in about ten minutes. I would hang on to the boat, and they would pull me up very slowly to the top of the beach. Two of us would bathe, while the third held the boat. Then we would skim back downstream, moor her in a backwater, and walk back across the fields.

After dinner we would play the gramophone. Or sometimes I would play the piano, or accompany M. Fritz, one of the German boys, on his cello; and then go to bed.

We were playing croquet on the gravel in the back garden one afternoon when the postman appeared with a telegram for me. *Accepté par la Madeleine*, it said. Years of public school French and a month with M. Sémézies and his wife had not prepared me for instant translation. La Madeleine? That big church in Paris? Or the little cake which, according to Chichele Waterston, Proust dipped in his tea? It took me a minute or two, sitting in the garden of the Château l'Estiou, to realize that here was the key to the next three – or, as it turned out, four – years at Cambridge.

VI

M Y FIRST year in Magdalene, in 1928, I had rooms in Bridge Street, only a few yards from the entrance to the College, over the bridge. In the rooms above me was Robin Fedden, a fellow-Cliftonian. It was thought for that reason that we should like to be boarded together. In fact, we scarcely knew each other, since at School we had been in different houses.

Robin's sitting-room or study was graced with watercolours by his artist father, Romilly Fedden; mine with coloured reproductions of ballet designs by Bakst, taken from *L'Illustration* and framed in passe-partout.

I hired an upright piano and bought gramophone records of Beethoven's last quartets. There was often a vase of flowers on a table by the window.

At midday the bus to Newnham would stop opposite my window, and the Newnham girls on the top deck would be able to look straight into my sitting-room on the first floor, where they could see me, playing the piano or seated at the table piled high with dictionaries and colourful books, casually looking up to see if any one of them was interested. None of them ever looked back. I could not think why. Too well brought up, I supposed.

During the first week or so, several characters called on me. During my last summer term at Clifton I had taken up rowing. I did not care for rowing. I had taken it up chiefly because of a romantic affection for a small boy who was a cox, and a marked loathing for the game of cricket. I told my first visitor that I had a dicky heart. A totally unnecessary lie. But how was I to declare what was indeed the truth: that I had already taken up, perhaps unwittingly, the role of a University aesthete?

My next visitor brought with him the proposal of athletics. In spite

of my 'dicky heart', I received him with a show of warmth. I really
enjoyed running, especially cross-country. I told the second caller that
I might be of some slight use as a long-distance runner. My distances
at Fenners, the University playing fields, were the mile and three
miles. Both were run in the same afternoon, and I managed to scrape
into third place twice, for which, to my surprise, I won two bronze
medals. These were delivered to me when a voice from a window
the other side of Magdalene Bridge called out my name. I looked up
to see Richard Bonham-Carter, who called down, 'Half a minute.
You'd better have these,' and chucked the medals into the street.

My third visitor was from the Amateur Dramatic Club; he
had heard, from some old Cliftonians, of my renditions of Lady
Macbeth, Mrs Hardcastle, Captain Absolute, etc., in the school plays.
Rather to my surprise I heard myself saying that, until I had
completed the first part of my Modern Language tripos, I could not
think about theatricals. But of course I was grateful for being asked.

I cannot say that I worked hard my first year. But I did work. I
biked to tutorials and attended most of the lectures on French or
German literature. I gained an Upper Second (2.1) in the first part of
the Modern Languages tripos, which was not discreditable, and the
College gave me a bursary of twenty (or was it ten?) pounds. Next
year, I thought, I'd really get down to it. Meanwhile, I had two
weeks before the start of the long vacation to do as I pleased.

Early on the first morning of this fortnight I received a visit from
Frank Birch, a professional actor and producer. He was directing a
production of the Goldoni comedy *The Servant of Two Masters* for
the Amateur Dramatic Club, and the part of the romantic lover,
Florindo, had fallen vacant due to a sudden illness. Would I take
over, with one week's rehearsal? I said I must ask my tutor at
Magdalene for permission. This was easily granted. And so began a
delightful and hectic six days of rehearsals, followed by a week of
performances in May Week.

Until this ADC production I had resisted the lure of the footlights
at Cambridge. But I had undertaken a number of activities which in
no way assisted me in the Modern Language tripos.

I do not remember how I got myself on the staff of the University
magazine *Granta*, but I did and was appointed chief film critic. There
were five cinemas in Cambridge at that time. The 'talkies' had not
yet reached the Fen country. A small orchestra, a piano or His Master's
Voice accompanied the films with what was frequently wildly
inappropriate music, often rendered inaudible by the comments and

derisory noises of the undergraduates. At the cinema in Market Square the audience achieved a ceaseless running commentary of laughter, cheers, ribald remarks, and rude noises. The favourite stars of the moment – Clara Bow and Laura La Plante – came in for much adoring dirt. It was not easy to review the films in which these two delectable stars appeared.

One day, towards the end of our first year, Robin Fedden and I went for a walk to Grantchester. It may have been the evocative place-name and the legend of Rupert Brooke that set us talking of poets and poetry, of which, certainly at that time, we both knew not very much. What Cambridge needed, we had decided, was a literary magazine.

So shallow was our editorial experience that it came quickly to the boil: as we returned, a rough plan was made, and before we were back in College even the name of the magazine had been chosen: *The Venture*. Not a very bold title, perhaps, but not too pretentious. It hardly occurred to us that the project might not be financially viable. After all, *Granta* and *The Cambridge Review* appeared weekly and had successfully done so for many years. Was there not room for another periodical?

My first approach was to the printers R.I. Severs. This proved to be a very fortunate choice. Severs was not only enthusiastic but patient. Four years later I was still paying off my debt to them, my co-editors having from the start perforce waived all financial responsibility.

It had never occurred to us that there might not be enough poets and writers blushing unseen but bursting to appear in print. I began the search for potential contributors by writing round to the editors of the college magazines and of *The Cambridge Review*. The response was not very promising. I also wrote to Oliver Baldwin. I remembered that, framed above the piano in Oliver's cottage in Oxfordshire, was a sonnet by John Drinkwater, which I asked his permission to print. Then Mother, off her own bat, persuaded Clemence Dane to contribute a short story, 'The Youth Who Longed to Shudder'. From Oliver, again, came an introduction to J.R. Ackerley, who sent us a short poem. Why my fellow-editors did not stamp on these three contributions whilst the first number was going into print, I don't know. They were enough to sink any literary magazine. Perhaps, like me, they were too polite to reject them.

It was Robin who suggested we should have a third editor. He put forward the name of a young post-graduate student at Trinity, Anthony Blunt. I never got to know Anthony well, and he did not, as I recall, take a very active part in editorship, but his contributions to *The Venture* – 'Self-consciousness in Modern Art', 'John Michael Fischer and the Bavarian Rococo' – lent a real and much-needed note of distinction.

The day of publication was at hand. Excitement ran moderately high. Never had my desire to see my name in print come so near to satisfaction. There it was, beneath the title, as Editor, and amongst the list of contributors as author of 'The Widows', a short prose fragment. (I was much given to fragments in those days.) I hired a barrow with a large poster to be parked in various strategic spots, and a dozen sandwichmen were paid to walk up and down King's Parade.

The Venture sold fairly well at its first appearance. But what nearly eclipsed that first edition was the arrival, at much the same time, of another literary magazine, edited by Jacob Bronowski and William Empson. I thought poorly of some of the poems which our competitors had printed: Empson's 'She cleaned her teeth into the lake', for instance, seemed too self-consciously anti-poetic. But *Experiment*, as the rival magazine was called, *was* genuinely experimental. In its light *The Venture* was shown clearly to be what it was – a farrago of juvenile trifles.

Nevertheless, we persevered and improved, publishing six issues, one a term, for two years, and in the course of these we published several writers who subsequently made their mark: Malcolm Lowry, John Lehmann, Julian Bell, and John Davenport.

The rivalry that was supposed to exist between *The Venture* and *Experiment* was more the invention of *The Cambridge Review* than of our making. In fact, I had come to admire Empson tremendously. When he was sent down, or 'rusticated,' on account – it was said – of contraceptives being found in his rooms, all literary Cambridge exploded. John Davenport, Hugh Sykes Davies, and I hired the Masonic Hall. Dressed *à la Bohème*, with a jug of beer on a candle-lit table, three mugs, and a pile of manuscripts, we read or declaimed Empson's poems for the best part of an afternoon before an enthusiastically partisan audience.

'He's really rather a nice old chap. But he will not go to bed. You must sit up with him until the early hours of the morning or he becomes a bit tetchy. But the food and wine are first-rate, and he has some nice pictures. I think you could do worse than to spend ten days or so with him.' It was my friend Francis Cook telling me about an elderly man, an invalid, who lived on Lake Garda. It was the long vacation in 1928, and as I would be returning from Sicily through Italy, it seemed a simple matter to break the Journey at Verona and catch the train on to Lake Garda, and it was duly arranged that I should be a guest with Fothergill Robinson.

He was standing on the steps of the villa, waiting to greet me. He was dressed in a sort of pyjama suit. Both his hands were heavily bandaged. He was rather charmingly effusive. He wanted to hear all about Sicily, which he said he had not visited for years.

'Would you like to bathe?' he asked.

'Just what I was hoping you would say.'

'We shall get on famously, I can see that,' said he.

Tea was served by a man in a white jacket.

'I must introduce you to Marco. He is my butler, my valet, my amanuensis. He also plays the piano, not very well, but quite pleasingly. Don't you, Marco?'

'My name's not Marco,' said the latter. 'Never was. He likes to pretend I'm Italian. I ask you, do I look Italian?'

'You do, a bit,' I said, smiling.

'Ah, there! You see?' said Fothergill Robinson. 'He's on my side!'

During the following ten days I found myself frequently on Marco's side. But I seldom liked to contradict F.R., as he preferred to be called. Marco's real name was Sam, and he had been a chorister at a church in Leamington when F.R., as a young clergyman, had been incumbent there. The two of them pursued a seemingly endless bickering. Yet, from time to time, a great affection could be seen.

'Thank God you're here, sir,' said Marco after dinner that first evening. 'There are times when I think I'm going potty. You will sit up with him, won't you, and listen to his talk? When he was young he knew everybody, and it irritates him when I don't know half the people he's talking about. Oh, and don't forget, if you should find yourself dropping off, try not to let him see it. He can be very funny that way.'

Fothergill Robinson had been in holy orders as a young cleric in a fashionable church. He had had, as a boy, a pleasing treble voice, which had ripened into a very fine tenor. He had been a very handsome man, and some of the ladies of Leamington had 'shot many an amorous dart in my direction', as he put it. The time came when, bolder than the rest, a beautiful Leamingtonian young lady, who happened to have a comfortable income, proposed to him and was joyously accepted. It was a Society wedding, and among F.R.'s friends, believe it or not, was the painter Romilly Fedden (father to my friend and co-editor, Robin). There were some very handsome presents, among them a portrait by Fedden of the bride.

It was now two o'clock in the morning. We were sitting on the porch. He had been talking for almost three hours. At the mention of the portrait, the old man's voice shrank almost to a whisper. There was a long pause while he lit a Turkish cigarette. The pause grew so long that I thought I should say something.

'Was it a good portrait?' I asked.

'Technically, yes. A good likeness. The painting of the dress of broderie anglaise brilliantly executed. But there was something about the picture which I did not like and which she – my wife – found most displeasing.'

There was another pause.

'What was it?' I asked.

The pause this time was so long that I feared he had gone to sleep. So I asked again, 'What was it in the portrait you didn't like?'

'Epilepsy. I charged Fedden with this, and he said that it wrung his heart, but that if he were to paint the same sitter for a hundred years, he would see it the same.'

'What did you do about it?' I asked.

'Poor Hilda. Her health deteriorated rapidly and she had to be sent to a nursing home. In those days divorce was not granted on the basis of physical ailments.'

There was another pause.

'What time is it?' he asked.

'Nearly three.'

'Is that all?' he said, to my dismay. 'Well, it's your first night here. I never tire, but I suppose you do. Better go to bed.'

Life at the Villa Rampolla was smooth enough. *Modo sic, modo sic. Ita vita truditur*, F.R. would say. He had a fondness for Petronius and a wealth of Latin tags. The days passed slowly, and the nights were interminable. In the mornings I would write poems, much under the influence of Arthur Waley and his translations from the Chinese. At midday I would go for a swim, sleep in the afternoons, and in the evenings listen to F.R.

Lake Garda is a long stretch of water, and one day, towards the end of my stay, I took one of the steamers and sailed round the lake, stopping at the various landing-stages. When the steamer reached the last but one port of call, there was some merriment going on. A wedding was in progress, and the happy couple and their retinue were dancing to the tune of an accordion. It was all very jolly. And then I began to realize that I might be late for dinner.

As I came in through the front door, an unmistakable voice said, 'Is that you? Where have you been?'

'Shan't be long,' I called out. I hurried upstairs to change for dinner.

Sam was hovering nervously on the landing. 'I think you'd better go down and break the ice, sir. He's in one of his moods.'

'You must find it rather dull here,' said F.R.

'Oh, not a bit!' I said. 'I'm terribly sorry, I . . .'

'No, don't apologize. It is dull, isn't it, Marco?'

'It comes and goes,' agreed the latter.

'It wasn't so always. A lot of people used to come here. All sorts of people, every summer. But they're mostly dead now. I've enjoyed your stay very much.'

'So have I,' I said emphatically. I felt very guilty. That night F.R. suddenly terminated our conversation after brandy and insisted that we go to bed. It was not even midnight.

And then something happened. Next morning, I was in the bathroom, shaving; F.R. was in bed, writing letters. I was singing – bits of Schumann and Schubert, echoes of Heidelberg, among them Schumann's superb setting of Heine's 'The Two Grenadiers', a song which asks as much from the actor as from the singer. I was just leaving the house for my morning bathe when he appeared in the doorway of his room.

'Sing that again,' he said.

I put down my towel and bathing costume.

'Have you had any training?'

'A little,' I said, 'nothing much.'

'Who taught you?'

'No one, really. I've always loved singing.'

He walked about the room impatiently.

'Has anyone ever told you that you have the makings of a fine voice?'

'No.'

'A very fine voice. I don't mean an operatic tenor, but a fine tenor-baritone. Like Steuart Wilson, or . . . sing the Schumann again. You know, I know what I'm talking about. I was a member of The English Singers for years. Agnes Nicholls, Dora Labette . . . I'll tell you what I want you to do. I will send you to Munich so that Beibig may hear you. And what would please me most would be that you should work under him. Don't worry about the money. I have plenty.'

'But,' I said, 'I don't think I love music enough to want to devote myself to it entirely.'

'My dear fellow, you surely don't suppose that singers have to think, do you? Or even love music? What are you hoping to be if not a singer?'

'Well, I really want to be a poet.'

'A *what*?'

'A poet.'

'What have you written? Go on, fetch something.'

I went to my room and found a poem which I had finished that morning.

'Read it to me,' he said.

I read:

> Like an actor in an antique tragedy
> The young cat creeps out onto the porch steps,
> And then returns into the dark house
> To look for the birthplace of her children.
> The ugly cat stalks out of the ferns,
> Pauses on the steps, turns at some sound,
> Showing the dull red wound in his neck,
> And walks on into the flowers, which hide him,
> Hateful, and humiliated, and alone.
> The grey one is just seen in the dark doorway,
> Easing herself of her burden on the ground.
> These actors speak a foreign tongue,
> Only the gist of the play is understood;
> Stripped of softening, explanatory speeches
> And accompanied by the thin squeak of bats,
> Their mime touches me more than a play.

'Rubbish,' he said. 'Oh . . . I know how it is when one is young. They think they can do anything, and they go frittering their time and their talent away, and it's only when it's too late that they sit down and think. I would not be telling you the truth if I encouraged you to be a poet. We'll talk about it after dinner tonight.'

We talked until about three o'clock in the morning. The old man's tenacity was most disturbing. Again and again he would almost convince me that I had to be something bigger than my present existence allowed for, and that such stature could come only through music. Finally the situation became impossible even for him, and he told me – or, rather, commanded me – to go to bed.

I was very tired and I slept poorly. Next morning I had an urge to sing. I wanted to sing very much, but I checked myself to a pianissimo in case the sound of my voice should prompt him to start all over again. I left the house early for a swim. As I walked through the garden, across the road, and down the pebbly beach to the water's edge, I could hear the sound of F.R.'s gramophone, *La Marechiare . . . la Marechiare . . .*

I paused and listened to the end of the song.

The water was cool and clear. I thought of Heidelberg . . . of Munich *. . . I don't mean an operatic tenor, but a fine tenor-baritone. Like Steuart Wilson, or . . .*

As I walked back through the garden, F.R. stumbled out of the house.

'That song you were playing,' I said, 'it's lovely! *La Marechiare . . .* who was it singing?'

'Tito Schipa,' he said. 'Have you packed? Your train leaves at eight.'

As I sat in the train I thought, 'Poor old man. Kind old chap. A sick man wanting to be in the swim again. Sitting up in bed at the Villa, sending cheques to me, or to Beibig. . . . '

And yet . . . and yet . . . could it be arranged, I wondered, that I should meet Beibig? All those framed photographs in the morning-room of the Villa Rampolla . . . Caruso . . . McCormack . . . I had given them only a casual glance. I had the same urge as in the morning: I wanted to sing. The train carriage was full. I stepped into the corridor and sang, quietly at first, 'The Lass with the Delicate Air'. I looked around to see if I was being overheard. They were all reading, or admiring the sunset. I tried a bar or so of *La Donna è mobile*, and decided that I was aiming too high. Then, no doubt to the astonishment of my fellow-travellers, I launched into my version of 'Every valley shall be exalted'. The noise of the train prevented me from sounding at my best. But I was not displeased with myself. When I dried up, having gone as far into the valley as I could remember, I came out with a medley of songs from *The Beggar's Opera*. I was more satisfied. 'Let us take the road' . . . good! 'Fill every glass' . . . Aha!

Nevertheless, as our train rolled on through Italy and into France, I was brought back, by degrees, to my first conclusion: that there was a world of difference between the professional and the amateur.

Chantmesle, my next port of call, twenty miles or so from Paris, had once belonged to Charles Conder, the English impressionist painter.

My first visit there, to stay with Robin Fedden and his parents, had not been an unqualified success. I had chattered on interminably about the Château l'Estiou, intoxicated with the sound of my own conversation. The bedroom walls upstairs were thin, and, going to bed that night, I overheard Mrs Fedden saying, 'Does that young man never stop talking?' I was horribly crestfallen, and the following day, on a trip to Chartres, I tried to make amends, asking, as I hoped, all the right questions and confining my remarks to expressions of polite interest such as a model guest might make. I succeeded in being more dull than the night before.

So when Robin asked me to stay again, after the Villa Rampolla, I murmured something about things being very busy, and privately decided not to go. Impressions were very important to me, and I feared I had made a very poor impression on that first visit. I wrote from the Villa Rampolla to say that, no, I should not be able to make it to Chantmesle that summer.

But Robin was not to be put off. He wrote back to say that he hoped I would change my mind, especially since Margaret Coss and her sister Mary would be staying, and Mary was dying to meet me again. 'Mary', said Robin, 'says she has fallen in love with you.' This put a very different complexion on the invitation. I wrote back at once to say that, after all, I would be delighted to come, if only for a day or two.

Margaret and Mary Coss were Americans who had been sent by their parents to Europe that summer in search of culture. Margaret, though attractive, was a rather over-earnest intellectual, at least in her appearance. Robin, I thought, was keen on her. Mary was strikingly beautiful. So much I knew from having met her at tea one afternoon in Robin's rooms at Cambridge. She had said nothing, but had looked at me once, very thoughtfully. She had wide-open, very dark brown eyes.

We were sitting on a low stone wall, backed with vines, on the road to La Rocheguyon. All evening I had tried to summon the courage to ask her to come for a walk. Robin had tactfully disappeared to put the car away. The other guests had gone out to welcome a late-comer, whose arrival had caused a minor commotion, but I was seized with panic and remained tongue-tied.

Then, when everyone had come back, and I realized I had lost my chance, I blurted out: 'I think it's very hot in here. Who says a walk? Mary, will you come for a walk?'

'I'd love to,' she said.

Now in the moonlight we were talking of Cambridge. She told me that Bill Empson had reported me as 'one of the nicest people there'. This surprised and delighted me more than I could say. It emboldened me to talk about the first time I had seen her, at the tea-party in Robin's rooms.

'You were beautifully dressed in brown, with a golden chain round your neck. You sat down in an armchair opposite me.'

'I know,' she said. She spoke in a low, deep voice. 'I came to see you.'

'You'd never seen me before, had you?'

'Yes, I had. Margaret and I were walking in Magdalene Fellows' Garden, with a dreadful man – I forget his name – oh, an awful man. Suddenly you came across the lawn. You had a book in your hand. I said, "Who's that?" and Margaret said it was you. I thought any man who could look so beautiful in glasses was the one for me. I decided that I must meet you. So it was arranged, and I came to call for Margaret at Robin's rooms fifteen minutes too soon. Then Robin said that he would ask you here. Then came a long letter of his to Margaret. On the last page he said, "Michael cannot come." I was so miserable I didn't know what to do. Then we found he had written a P.S. saying, "Michael *is* coming."'

There was a pause and I took her hand.

She leant towards me. I kissed her. A sweetness, a tenderness I had never felt before. We walked along the road, stopping every other moment to embrace. The moon had gone down. I carried her for twenty yards. A dog barked at us, a little terrier, filling the whole country with its noise. Eventually we reached Chantmesle. It was half-past three in the morning, and as we stood outside the gate, a bird was singing. It was already dawn.

At breakfast she appeared wearing a lovely brown dress with a deep collar and a long scarf trailing from her shoulder. After breakfast I suggested a walk. She told me she was coming back to Europe the next year to learn French. Good, somehow I would get to France then, to see her. And after that – she would spend three years at university in America. Three years! I protested: Too long! I could get a Commonwealth scholarship, she suggested. Yes, but that would hardly bring us closer together. America seemed so vast. I hinted that I would always wait for her and tried to show her how I saw my life for years to come. How difficult but how necessary it would be to break from my family if I were to dedicate my life to poetry. How – and here the picture I painted was heavily fringed with melodrama – my home life had been overshadowed by a stepfather who misunderstood me. Such envy, hatred, malice, uncharitableness – I laid it on thick.

She looked at me, her eyes full of compassion and understanding.

'And you, Michael,' she asked, without the slightest trace of irony, as if I really might be perfect, 'have you no faults?'

'But of course I have,' I said, magnanimously.

'Tell them me.'

'I am selfish. Proud. Weak in needing encouragement. Living too much in the present ... sensual ... and vain,' I added.

She smiled, and nodded, and with all the wisdom in the world, I thought, said nothing.

After lunch we took a boat up the Seine to bathe, I rowing as impressively as I was able.

'And you?' I asked her, 'What will you do?'

'I shall read, and I shall work, and work, and work. And then one day I shall come back to England and we shall go to a tea-party together, and I shall astound you with my knowledge.'

I felt a little frightened by this. I must have overawed her, I realized, with my description of my life to come. Now she would spend the next three years trying to catch up with me. This would never do.

'Oh, don't worry, Michael,' she teased, 'I shall never be more brilliant than you. And don't,' she added, 'worry so much about how you talk. You talk quite brilliantly enough.'

We were silent all the way back to the house. I tried to hum 'Fain would I change that note', but the effort was beyond me.

Tea was a dismal affair. The girls went upstairs to get ready, and came down in their travelling clothes.

'Goodbye, Mrs Fedden,' Mary said, 'and thank you so very much.'

At the station, sister Margaret, with her lorgnettes, bought the tickets. Robin and I carried their bags to the platform. Mary was silent and miserable. The train arrived and we found them two corner seats. I shook hands with the sister first – 'Goodbye, Margaret' – then, 'Goodbye, Mary.' Her look was haunting. We got out on to the platform and watched them through the window, smiling a little.

Robin and I drank in a café in silence. On the drive back, over the hill, stopping on the way to send telegrams, I was unable to control my tears. Robin said nothing, but took my arm, and we walked the last part of the journey arm in arm back to Chantmesle.

71

Mary returned to Cambridge the following year. In America, Margaret told me, she had cut her hair very short and unbecomingly, so as not to attract any of the sophomores. Though not a Cambridge undergraduate, she attended almost all the lectures. She accompanied me every opening night to the Festival Theatre when I went as drama critic for *The Cambridge Review*. Without anything being said, or written, the two of us found ourselves out of love and not in the least missing it.

She returned to Philadelphia, where Francis Cook, on a Commonwealth Fellowship, met her. 'She's very beautiful,' I had told him, 'and I charge you not to fall in love with her.' A year or so later came a letter from Francis saying that, despite my half-earnest injunction, he and Mary had married. And then, I cannot remember how, I learned that she had joined the Communist Party and was selling their paper on street corners, and she and Francis had parted.

After the Goldoni comedy my taste for acting and all things theatrical was given a broad scope. Dennis Arundell, who was a great figure in University theatre, asked me to play the Soldier in the first performance in England in 1928 of Stravinsky's *The Tale of a Soldier*, to be staged at the ADC Theatre. Maynard Keynes, the economist, was married to the Russian ballerina Lydia Lopokova, and he and balletomane Arnold Haskell backed the venture, which, even in those days and especially in that tiny theatre, must have been an expensive trifle. Lydia played – or, rather, danced – the part of the Princess; Hedley Briggs, a talented young actor-dancer who had distinguished himself in Norman Marshall's season at the Cambridge Festival Theatre, played the showy part of the Devil. Arundell directed and spoke the words of the Narrator, and Boris Ord, the organist at King's College chapel, conducted the orchestra of eight picked professionals. Costumes were designed by Duncan Grant and the sets by Humphrey Jennings, to whose pioneering documentaries the British cinema owes so much. (One of them, *Diary for Timothy*, was to be the occasion for my renewing acquaintance with Jennings towards the end of the War. He asked me to record the commentary for it written by E. M. Forster.)

After the prestige of *The Tale of a Soldier* there was no stopping me. George ('Dadie') Rylands, a young don at King's, put on a reading of scenes from *Comus* in his rooms, himself playing the name part, with Robert Eddison and myself playing the brothers, and Lydia as the Lady. Eddison, a fine actor and a brilliant cabaret performer, excelled in our university productions in what were known as 'breeches' parts, in which the woman plays the man, with the double irony in Robert's case of the man, and an elegant, six-foot man at that, playing the woman playing the man. In the audience for *Comus* were Virginia and Leonard Woolf. I was much in awe of the beautiful Virginia, who asked me if I was nervous when acting. I replied, 'Yes, hideously.' I do not know why, for as an amateur I was seldom, if ever, nervous on the stage.

There was another performance of this programme at the Keyneses' house in Gordon Square before a scintillating audience of, largely, Bloomsbury artists and writers, including Walter Sickert, who for some unknown reason addressed Robert and myself in French: '*Messieurs, vous étiez délicieux!*'

Lopokova's broken English was adorable, but it was an acquired taste. Especially in Milton. Nevertheless, Maynard must have believed in her powers as an actress, for he took the Arts Theatre in London for a programme consisting of *A Lover's Complaint*, the scenes from *Comus*, excerpts from *Paradise Lost*, and, to end the evening, a *divertissement* of ballet. In the last item, to the music of William Boyce arranged and conducted by Constant Lambert, she was supported by Frederick Ashton and Harold Turner. The critic of the *New Statesman*, Raymond Mortimer, dubbed this 'a blue-blooded evening'.

To be acting in a real theatre, even if was only a club theatre, filled me with a comfortable conceit and, to cap it all, there was Maynard Keynes handing each member of the company a crisp five-pound note.

Among the starry audience at Gordon Square was a woman who introduced herself to me as Hilda Matheson of the BBC. She asked me if I would like to do a test for reading on the radio. Term had not then begun, and it was arranged that I should do the test one morning at Savoy Hill, where the BBC first set up shop. I was received by a tall, smiling man who looked as if he would burst into giggles at any moment. His name was Lionel Fielden.

He listened to whatever it was I had prepared and, still smiling, drawled, 'Yes, that will do *very* nicely.' I thought he was sending me up. However, within a few days, a contract from the BBC arrived by post and, by hand, an edition of Lord Chesterfield's *Letters*. I was to read from the *Letters* for three Saturday evenings, each time, I think, for about twenty minutes. It seems unlikely, now, that the BBC would put out such material even for one Saturday evening.

More improbable still that I should be allowed to make my own choice of the excerpts. But so it was, and I was paid two guineas a time. Later I was asked to read poetry, amongst other things T. S. Eliot's *The Waste Land*. This poem I did not well understand, and I wrote to Eliot asking if he could tell me the kind of delivery he thought most suitable. I received a letter from his secretary saying that Mr Eliot suggested I use as *little expression* as possible. This I did to the best of my ability, only to receive a letter from a clergyman criticizing me for my unpoetic, flat delivery. He said he had switched off after five minutes.

I did many readings for Fielden during my time at Cambridge. His sardonic humour, his air of treating the work as if it were a great lark, must have concealed a deep concern for the future of broadcasting. His entry in *Who's Who* gave as his recreation 'trying to avoid being organized'. Nevertheless, he was made Controller of Broadcasting in India, a post he held for five years. We met by chance in Italy some time later, and I lunched with him at the farm to which he had retired, not without some disgust, it seemed. He made languid scorn of everything: Right, Left, and Centre. I remembered that his Brasenose smile had always been worse than his bite.

High on the list of activities during my four years at Magdalene were the reading parties organized by a don, Francis Turner, each Easter, when some six or eight of us would meet for about a fortnight and study. We lodged in the Castle Rock Hotel, Mortehoe, in North Devon. Perched on a cliff, half-way up the hill to the village, the old Victorian building looks out to distant Lundy Island, and on one side of the hotel a cliff path leads to Morte Point, providing an excellent track for a run, up and down, down and up, round the Point and back. On the other side, after one crosses the long beach, Woolacombe Sands, is another headland, Baggy Point, which offers as pleasant a walk as one may ask.

Mornings for work, evenings for chess or card games, afternoons for walks or rustic hockey or 'waterworks' on the sands, to the pub sometimes ... plenty of exercise, plain food, no talk of war ... *Love's Labour's Lost*, Act One, Scene One.

It was Francis Turner who steered me in the direction of what, for a brief moment, might have been an academic life. After a year of Modern Languages I had embarked on the English tripos. I had achieved a satisfactory Upper Second degree in my finals, but still I had no more idea of what to do with my life than when I first went up to Magdalene. Francis suggested I should stay on for a fourth year and read for the Le Bas prize. The winning text was always published by the Cambridge University Press, and the prize carried some kudos. Francis himself had won it, and the £100 that went with it, with a treatise on *Irony*. Clearly he thought an academic career was indicated for me, and I was by no means averse to the idea.

The day came when, without trumpets, the examiners announced the set subject for the Le Bas, and my spirits took a definite and deep drop. I could hardly believe that some obscure don had wasted his midnight oil thinking up such a musty subject: 'The Idea of a Victorian University.'

As I look back on it, the subject was perhaps an interesting one, but it called for an orderly mind and I had no idea where to begin. I browsed in the library, hoping that inspiration might come. I dipped into Cardinal Newman, but it seemed that this eminent Victorian had said all that could be said on the matter.

I called on my tutor, 'Dadie' Rylands, to ask his advice, and it was agreed that I should abandon the Le Bas and read instead for the second part of the English tripos. Such merciful release went to my head. Two whole terms now stretched before me, offering renewed scope for all my extracurricular activities, and I availed myself of it greedily.

I brought the life of *The Venture* to a not discreditable end and took up editorship of *The Cambridge Review*. Boldly I broke with tradition by not printing the University Sermon, replacing it with articles such as Basil Wright's on the new movement in the German cinema. No one rebuked me. None of my friends noticed the loss. Not until the end of my stint as editor did someone think to tell me that subscriptions to *The Cambridge Review*, under my aegis, had shown a somewhat drastic decline. Parsons up and down the country, I was informed, relied upon cribbing from the University Sermon for their weekly pulpit orations.

I developed a warm friendship with John Davenport, and together we edited for the Hogarth Press two volumes of Cambridge poetry.

Davenport had the enviable gift of a photographic memory, and I was what is known as a 'quick study'. Hearing that two members of the cast in Peter Hannen's production of *The Voysey Inheritance* would have to miss one performance in order to register their votes in a Union debate, for a lark John and I learned their parts and took their place for that one performance. Somehow I also found time to write and direct a two-act operetta called *The Battle of the Book*, in which I appeared as Samuel Pepys. All this stretched the patience of our tutors a little too far. I was sent for by Dadie, and was told to stop fooling around and get down to work. Too late. I had almost forgotten what work meant.

For my last appearance in May Week at the ADC, I took the name part in Shaw's *Captain Brassbound's Conversion*, with sets designed by Guy Burgess. Very good sets, too. Burgess was one of the bright stars of the University scene, with a reputation for being able to turn his hand to anything. Alistair Cooke reviewed our production, none too favourably. He was appearing in something put on by another Cambridge dramatic society, The Mummers, and I sharpened my pen and took my revenge. 'Mr Cooke,' I wrote, 'knows all the tricks but, unfortunately, can do none of them.' I had forgotten this squib until, many years later, Cooke quoted it when introducing me on a television programme in New York.

It was the first and, as it turned out, the last time I ever acted in Shaw in the theatre. Shaw claimed, correctly, that his characters are 'actor-proof'. I think that is why I have always resisted playing them. (Gabriel Pascal came near to persuading me to play Dubedat in a film of *The Doctor's Dilemma* and, later, Apollodorus in *Caesar and Cleopatra*, but I was playing in *Uncle Harry* in the West End at the time and after seven months in a heavy dramatic part I thought that the strain of filming in the day would have been too great, so I backed out.) Shaw had the last word. He sent one of his famous postcards to Mother: 'What!!! So Michael is your son? I must re-write *Coriolanus* for the two of you.'

VII

THE YEAR I left Cambridge – 1931 – was hardly the most propitious time to find a job: the year of the run on the pound; the fall of the Ramsay MacDonald Labour government; the election of the National government, which cut the dole and established the means test for the two and a half million unemployed. But I had my Bachelor of Arts degree. Failing all else, I thought, I could teach. I went, like many another penniless graduate, to the Gabbitas Thring Agency and presented myself and my B.A. Hons (Cantab.). I had pictured an offer to teach French, German, and English in a beautiful old school somewhere on the South Downs. What I was offered was the tutelage of a small Brazilian boy, aged twelve, called Miguel. His guardian put at our disposal a room in the Piccadilly Hotel.

Miguel was a charming boy, and spoke almost perfect English. After a fortnight, our hotel room and the same walk each day around St James's Park became rather constricting, and Miguel suggested we might try the cinema. This wrecked the whole thing. One morning Miguel's guardian apprehended me in the hotel lobby and addressed me with thinly-disguised annoyance.

'Miguel tells me you amuse yourself with visits to the cinema. I have nothing against the cinema, please understand, but it is not my idea of how English should be learnt.'

He paid me my fee, and that was that. It was back to Gabbitas Thring.

As it happened, they had something more substantial to offer me. Highgate Grammar School wanted an assistant master to teach Modern Languages, French and German, able to help out with hockey, and ready to start within a week. 'They'll want a reference, of course.' I thought at once of David Loveday, whose helping hand had got me to Cambridge. David, I knew, had left his old post at Clifton as assistant chaplain and taken up the Headmastership at Cranleigh School, in Surrey.

'I don't really intend to teach,' I told Loveday, 'not for long, anyway. I don't really know what I want to do.'

'Why don't you come and give this place a try? I've a post here for a Modern Languages master. Stay a couple of terms. It won't make your fortune, but what will, nowadays?'

And so began another beginning. The salary was not, indeed, princely: £225 a year. But with bed and board for eight months of the year, it could hardly be sneezed at. The school, Victorian Gothic, built for the education of the younger sons of well-to-do clergymen, was – another point in its favour – conveniently close to London.

It is customary, in tales of schoolmasters and their lives, that one should be a young Olympian, another a crabbed and dangerous character – *Mr Perrin and Mr Traill*, *The Browning Version*, etc. Perhaps I was fortunate. My contemporaries in the Common Room seemed as pleasant a bunch of men as one could hope to find in such surroundings. Only one, Frank Devonshire, who had been at Cambridge with me, seemed out of his depth. Frank, an Etonian and a brilliant scholar, had a fatal lack of confidence, which instantly conveyed itself to the boys he was attempting to teach. After a day or two, murmuring and muffled laughter could be heard beyond the thin partition which separated his form room from mine, giving way to howls of incredulity, shouts, guffaws, and a hammering of desk tops. My class looked at me to see if my nerve would crack.

My disability was of a different kind, though no less fatal to serious teaching in the long run. I could not resist playing for a laugh. The room was a little overheated, and I took hold of the cord of one of the transom windows. There was nothing to attach it to. I stood there, cord in hand, and asked, with my most dead-pan expression, 'What do I do with this? Stand here all morning?' The form laughed. Redgrave, it seemed, was all right.

One of the set books for the Higher Certificate was Milton's *Samson Agonistes*. My sixth-form class, usually a very lively lot, were making heavy weather of it. Not even Robert Bridge's excellent guide, *Milton's Prosody*, could loosen its adamantine chains. We came to the messenger's speech. I remembered that in Greek drama the messenger speech is often the most vivid moment of the play, and so it is in *Samson*. Suddenly I threw my textbook into the air and said, 'Let's learn it.' There were a few subdued groans.

'We'll learn it,' I said, 'and act it. Here in the school library. We'll do it Sunday fortnight.'

I rigged up some costumes of buckram tabards, a beard for Manoa, a spear for the giant. Mr Bowyer, the Classics master, a dear man and a very accomplished composer, wrote some excellent music. I elected to play Samson and treated myself to a wig from Fox's Costumiers; the hair was not quite as long as Samson's should have been, but time was short. When the day came for our first performance, my class was quite cheerful, I even more so. What did it matter if Milton had ordained that his poem should not be performed? I believed that I had tumbled on an unacknowledged theatrical treasure:

> O dark, dark, dark, amid the blaze of noon,
> Irrecoverably dark, total eclipse
> Without all hope of day!

The awesome weight of Milton had been lifted.

Cranleigh, before my arrival, had the reputation of being a 'tough' school with no theatrical tradition. Perhaps it was a chance over-heard remark of some German visitors who had strayed into a rehearsal of *Hamlet* and left muttering, '*Nur Kultur und Liebe*', which riled me and helped to nurture a secret ambition that Cranleigh might have its own tradition that would bring scholars and amateurs of the theatre, in the way that the Greek play performed at Bradfield attracted classical scholars to that school.

It remained – fortunately, perhaps – a secret ambition. Another, more peremptory ambition was forming itself during my three years as a schoolmaster. In all I did six productions at Cranleigh: *HMS Pinafore*, *As You Like It*, *Hamlet*, *The Tempest*, *Samson Agonistes*, and *King Lear*, and played the leading part in five of them. Besides, only a few miles away, there was the semi-professional Guildford Repertory Company, where somehow or other I managed to squeeze in Menelaus in *The Trojan Women*, Young Marlow in *She Stoops to Conquer*, Ernest in *The Importance of Being Earnest*, Robert Browning in *The Barretts of Wimpole Street*, and Clive Champion-Cheney in Maugham's *The Circle*.

Loveday had given me every encouragement, turning a blind eye when needed to the amount of time spent on our 'theatricals', as the Bursar called them. But the inspiration which decided me came from another quarter. During the spring term, in my second year at Cranleigh, I had taken my French class to London to see La Compagnie des Quinze. The Quinze had grown out of Jacques Copeau's troupe, Les Copiaus, a young company which he had formed and trained in a village in Burgundy after his retirement from the Théâtre du Vieux Colombier. But after five years, expecting an invitation to the Comédie Française, Copeau, who, despite his dedication to the idea of a theatre without stars, had more than a touch of the *grand seigneur* about him, disbanded Les Copiaus, who thereupon regrouped themselves as La Compagnie des Quinze. They had an author, André Obey, to write for them plays such as *Noah* and *The Rape of Lucrece*; they had a collapsible rostrum with surrounding tent for a stage; they were jugglers, mimes, acrobats; their productions, wrote Tyrone Guthrie, 'were like a ballet, only they had fifty times more content than any ballet ever had'; above all they had – or, rather, they found – an audience, for Copeau in the last years at Pernand-Vergelesses had starved his company of performance. Bronson Albery had brought them to London for a short season at the Arts Theatre the previous year, and such was their success that he was able to transfer their productions to the Ambassadors and the New, and then bring them back to Wyndham's Theatre the following two years, 1932 and 1933.

What my French class made of our excursions I am not sure, though no doubt they flattered me into thinking that six seats in the gallery at Wyndham's had not harmed their chances in the School Certificate. For me, the Quinze were a revelation. There were fine actors in the company, and Pierre Fresnay gave a glittering performance in *Don Juan*. But the French actors showed us an ensemble with a style and a dedication for which there was no English equivalent. In their bright light, all obstacles – my stepfather's disapproval, the warnings that I was 'too tall', the insecurity which I would be exchanging for a safe job and a permanent salary – melted away. I gave in my notice to leave at the end of the summer term of 1934.

Andy's reaction, when I broke the news to him, was contrary to all expectation. He raised no objection at all. Perhaps he was relieved. For so many years he had paid for my education, an investment which, to his prudent way of thinking, must have seemed to yield a lamentably small return. And to make matters worse, though he never complained about it, he had had to pick up the debts I ran up at Cambridge and at Cranleigh. Perhaps, as

Mother conjectured, 'he had been salmon fishing all that month in Scotland and had had much luck, and due to that he did not seem to mind very much that you had decided to become an actor.'

Mother, at any rate, was delighted and rushed up from Windsor, where she was playing in repertory, to see Lilian Baylis at the Old Vic Theatre. Baylis, the founder and manageress of the Vic, had asked Mother to be on the committee of the sister theatre, Sadler's Wells, and would have liked her to come to the Vic, 'but I knew', Mother wrote, 'that that would mean *living* at the Vic.'

I was granted an audition, and summoned to present myself at the stage door in Waterloo Road at 10.40 a.m. The time being so specified rather daunted me, implying the presence of many other hopefuls besides myself. Listening to them, as I waited my turn to be called, I thought they were rather good. The season we were auditioning for was to be directed by Henry Cass, built around the personality of Maurice Evans, who had made a notable success at the Vic.

I had chosen one of the lesser-known soliloquies from the canon, Rumour's prologue to *Henry IV, Part II*, which I had played for the Cambridge Marlowe Society, doubling it with Prince Hal, in a very stylized performance, with much waving of arms. I thought it unlikely any of the other contestants would choose it. I was quite right. Most of them had chosen one or other of Hamlet's soliloquies. I had completed only about half a dozen lines when a voice from the stalls called out, loud and clear, 'yes, thank you. *Thank* you.' I was badly rattled. The others had been allowed to go on for about five minutes.

'I can't see anything but hands,' said the voice from the stalls. It was Lilian Baylis. 'Do something else. Can't you do anything *not* Shakespeare?'

'A little onward lend thy guiding hand / To these dark steps, a little further on ... ' I launched myself into Samson's lines, shuffling forward, arms outstretched, not pausing to reflect that Samson, as I had played him, was even more balletic of gesture than Rumour. I had spoken hardly three lines when she interrupted me again. 'You'll have to learn to use your hands, y'know,' she said, adding, 'I couldn't pay you anything. I have to pay the actors who carry the show.'

'She's trying to get you to come for nothing,' whispered Cass. 'Don't!'

I'd accept an offer of three shillings a week, I thought – anything to be able to say, 'I'm an actor at the Old Vic.'

I said, 'Yes, I will come if you'll give me something to do. I'm too old to carry a spear or wave a flag.'

'My dear boy,' said Cass, 'if you can play Romeo, you shall play Romeo. But I can't promise anything.'

As I left the stage door, Murray Macdonald, who was to be the season's stage director, walked with me a few steps and said, 'I expect you'll be with us. I hope you'll be with us.'

In spite of Murray's kindly words I heard nothing from the Vic. I went back to Cranleigh for my final term, disappointed but not downcast, thinking that I must spread my net wider, and wondering whom I should invite to come down and see what I could make of *Lear*. The Whitsun holiday arrived. Still no word from the Vic. I had written a note to William Armstrong at the Liverpool Playhouse, saying that I would be coming up to see the Saturday matinée, and would he please give me an interview. Before catching the train to Liverpool I called at Chapel Street to collect some photographs. There was no one at home, but I found two letters for me, and one of them was from the Old Vic, offering me a contract for the next season for three pounds a week.

Armstrong was polite, but seemed rather abstracted, more or less pushing my photos aside.

'I know your mother, of course, a delightful actress, but, you see, my company is nearly filled. I have some very good young men – oh, and an excellent new young assistant director – you have some experience of directing, didn't you say? – but I'll let you know.'

'When could you let me know, Mr Armstrong?' – and here I made as if to reach into my breast pocket. 'When could you let me know? Because, you see, I have a contract for the Old Vic.' I paused.

Willie looked at me with something like alarm. 'A contract for the Vic?' he said. 'How much for?'

'Three pounds a week,' I said.

'I'll give you four,' said Willie. And four it was. For an instant I regretted my honesty, as I told Willie later, having the impression that if I'd said seven, he would have capped it with eight.

The Liverpool Playhouse theatre had just been redecorated. It was, and is, one of the most attractive old theatres in England. I saw the matinée, of a play by John Van Druten, and enjoyed it. The company seemed to play to a high standard. But my mind kept wandering to the photographs in front of the theatre. How, I wondered, would mine look amongst them?

I bought myself another ticket for the evening performance, and that, too, proved a great stroke of luck, for in the audience was a very popular actor, Lyn Harding. We were introduced, and Willie mentioned that I would be joining the Playhouse for the next season. As we parted at the end of the second interval, Harding said suddenly, 'By the way, Redgrave, never let them tell you you're too tall. I was told that many times.' (Triumphantly my mind flashed to my mother's warnings, and I longed to tell her what Harding had just said. And I remembered an evening at the Savoy, where Lionel Fielden had taken me after a broadcast. Tyrone Guthrie was there. He was planning a new season. 'You should have Michael,' Fielden said. 'Michael should be an actor.' 'Far too tall,' said Guthrie.)

'How tall are you?' Harding went on.

'Six foot three.'

'Same height as Lucien Guitry. A wonderfully graceful actor. You never noticed his height when he was on stage.'

VIII

O UR FIRST production was *Counsellor-at-Law* by Elmer Rice, an excellent choice of play for a repertory company. It had first been done in 1931 in New York by the Group Theatre. The Group had Clifford Odets and Elmer Rice to write for them, and such as John Garfield, Margaret Sullavan and Luther Adler in their company. But there were no 'stars' in the Group. *Counsellor-at-Law* had, as they say, something for everyone.

In our Liverpool production James Stephenson played the Counsellor. Rather an English counsellor he seemed to me, but then we had not long had the talkies to teach us what we should sound like, and none of us except Deirdre Doyle – who could switch accents at the drop of a hat – had spent any time in America. Ena Burrill was our leading lady, but wasn't to join us until the next play, so the part of the secretary went to another actress, Lindisfarne Hamilton. Netta Westcott, who had played the part in London, was the counsellor's wife, whom I, as a 'lounge lizard', had to seduce. Netta was somewhat older, and complained that she felt a little less seduceable each day, till at the dress rehearsal I, like so many another young actor in his first part in repertory, assumed another twenty years by larding my hair with 'Number 20'.

William Armstrong, one of the most beloved figures in the English theatre, had made a reputation for the Liverpool Playhouse which, together with the Birmingham Repertory Theatre, was at that time outstanding. He was mocked, imitated, and adored. At the end of a scene in rehearsal, his voice could be heard from the back of the stalls saying, 'Oh! It's so beautiful! So moving!'

Just before he died, in 1952, he broadcast his memoirs for the BBC. He had been a leading man with Mrs Patrick Campbell, and one of his favourite stories, based on Mrs Pat, can still be heard in truncated form in King's Road, Chelsea, or anywhere that so-and-so has set up his camp. The original, according to William, concerned two young actors who appeared to be more wrapped up in each other than was strictly necessary. On hearing of them Mrs Pat remarked: 'I don't care what they do, so long as they don't do it in the street and frighten the horses.' Today the catch-phrase survives, rather as Edith Evans's inflection of 'a handbag!' is echoed by those far too young to have seen or heard the original.

I began to take stock of the company. Of all the young men, Geoffrey Edwards and Robert Flemyng seemed likely to be my chief rivals. Bobby was an expert light comedian who could shoulder broad comedy parts as well, but he was no one's idea – least of all his own – of a classical actor. Geoffrey, however, was to play Hamlet, and I confess I was not altogether pleased to learn that I should play his Horatio. I don't know if there was not a little spite one evening when, as I cradled the dying Hamlet in my arms, I contrived to weep and a large splash of warm mascara fell on Hamlet's chin. But on the whole it was a happy company. Once Deirdre Doyle tried to kill a laugh by upstaging me, but for that I had learned from Mother a surefire remedy. You simply walked upstage with the culprit until you reached the backcloth. 'They'll never do it again,' Mother had said, 'at least, not to you.' She was right.

There was James Stephenson, who had been with the company for two years, with no previous experience of acting. A dark horse if ever there was one. To most of us he seemed an honest, earnest nonentity. Towards the end of the year he was cast as the lead opposite Ena Burrill in S.N. Behrman's *Biography*. 'What's he like to act with?' I asked Ena. 'Well,' she said, 'he's *clean*, and do you notice he always wears patent-leather shoes? That's so as the audience will think he's polished them well, I suppose. Oh, James is all right ... the girls find him attractive.'

But the camera could discern something in James which none of us at Liverpool, except perhaps Willie, had noticed. James left to try his luck in London. He photographed very well, and almost immediately landed a part in a picture at Teddington studios, and had hardly finished that when he was offered a contract in Hollywood, and off he shipped himself with his young wife, to play a long string of parts, including a notable performance, opposite Bette Davis, as the defending counsel in *The Letter*.

There was Ena Burrill, our leading lady. Ena was something of a riddle. Very tall, weighty without being fat, and with a dazzling smile, she would scarcely bother to characterize a part, was almost lazy at times, and yet could walk on to a stage and command an audience's attention by the sheer force of her personality.

There was Deirdre Doyle, who was a mistress of make-up and could look at will remarkably like Marie Tempest, or Sara Allgood, or anyone she chose. Most of what I learned about make-up was from Deirdre. One trick in particular, very useful for middle-aged or elderly parts : you etched in the lines round the eye with the milled edge of a silver coin, after powdering the foundation. It produced a delicate, soft, feathery wrinkle.

There were the Sangsters, Alfred and Pauline, who were the parent figures of our company. Alfred had written several plays, one of which, *The Brontës*, had some success. He lived in hopes that Willie would stage it, and I, who had a strange ambition to play the Reverend Nicholls in it – very strange, now I come to think of it, because there is scarcely anything for the reverend gentleman to do – pleaded its case with Willie, too. But Willie resisted, probably because it needed three girls of really star quality, and Willie, expert in diplomacy, could foresee the ructions that might cause in his company. To each of his actresses he conveyed the impression that, all things being equal, and were it only a matter of his choice, she would be leading lady next season.

There was Hannah Daniel, who was determined to be a great actress, and if determination were sufficient, she would have been. There was something very touching about Hannah. She lived, breathed, and, indeed, entirely existed for the boards. A while after I had left Liverpool I bumped into her at a theatre and tentatively asked her what she was doing. She burst into tears on the spot. 'Oh, Michael, I'm married, I'm going to have a baby!'

I remembered walking her back to her digs one night after a performance, in which she had, in fact, been very effective, of Pirandello's *The Man with a Flower in His Mouth*. She kept stopping and breathing deeply, as if not wanting that precious moment to be lost. Suddenly she burst out, 'It's all so precarious! A lot of people get on just by having a pretty face. I'm not pretty, but I *know* I can act if I'm given a chance. It's so unfair.'

'Yes, isn't it?' I said.

'Oh *you*.' She sounded almost exasperated. 'You've got nothing to worry about.'

'I don't know,' I said, 'sometimes I get very worried.'

'What on earth about?'

'Well . . . I've had three successes in a row now, and I wonder if I can keep it up.'

I blush to recall my conceit.

There was little Larry Shipston, who, apart from his lack of inches, was truly unprepossessing in appearance. I shall never forget the zeal with which he pounded the Green Room table one morning, insisting that any actor ought to be able to play any part no matter what he looked like.

And there was I, who almost by luck had fallen into a job in the Playhouse, and was loving every minute of it. After three or four plays I was given my first really good part, Melchior Feydak, a Hungarian composer of musicals, in *Biography*. Speaking S. N. Behrman's excellent dialogue and accompanying myself on the piano, I felt like Noël Coward and Ivor Novello rolled into one. On a sudden impulse I bearded Willie in his office as he was writing a letter. 'Willie,' I said, 'I'm worth more than four pounds a week.'

'I know you are,' he replied, without looking up. 'I'll give you six.'

A painted sign above a rather dingy-looking staircase said: GYM. NEL TARLETON. I walked up to the top floor. Liverpool was a city of sharp contrasts. My rooms in Falkner Street were almost next door to the cathedral. Chinatown was five minutes' walk away. Bold Street was the Bond Street of Liverpool, yet it housed this dirty-looking entrance to the workshop of the Featherweight Champion of England.

Tarleton himself appeared, and I explained that I wanted to enrol myself at his gym. He seemed pleased. 'When would you like to start?' 'Now!' I answered and ran back to my rooms to get the right clothes. My eagerness seemed to amuse him. He put me through a brief work-out of exercises, skipping and punching, and afterwards filled a bath for me and washed my back. I told him how I had seen his title fight at Bellevue, Manchester, the year before. I vowed to myself I would train each day.

There was still the problem of height. So many years of being told I was too tall for an actor had had its effect on me.

We were to do John Van Druten's play *Flowers of the Forest* in March 1935. Ena and Bobby Flemyng were leaving the company to go to London in a new play, so the coast was clear for me and – and who? I was courting a young actress, Ruth Lodge, and was keen to get her into the company. I invited her up to Liverpool, where we waylaid Willie Armstrong.

'Oh!' he said. 'Oh, dear! I've already cast the part. Rachel Kempson.'

'But she's much too short,' I said.

On a visit to Stratford the year before, I had been very taken with the actress playing Hero in *Much Ado About Nothing*, Phoebe in *As You Like It*, and Ariel in *The Tempest*. Perhaps it had something to do with the Spanish costumes in *Much Ado*, with the Velásquez wigs and pannier skirts, but somehow I had got the impression she was rather short.

'I should have to go down on my knees to kiss her,' I protested.

The first night was proceeding quite smoothly, until we came to the love scene in Act Two. There was some business with a standard lamp, which I had to switch off in the middle of the scene. One thing which every aspiring actor learns in repertory is how to turn off a standard lamp: you remember to keep your finger on the switch until the light is turned off by the electrician at the switchboard. I went to the lamp and mimed switching it off, but it refused to go out. Another thing you learn is you cannot play a love scene with one hand on a standard lamp. So I left the wretched light and continued the scene as best I could and, at the very moment when I took Rachel in my arms, the lamp went out. Big laugh. I dare say we played the scene adequately. The audience were polite and laughed only once or twice. The curtain fell and we fell into each other's arms.

'Oh!' said Willie. 'Oh, dear!' We had waited until we were sure he would engage us both for the following season before breaking the news that we were to marry. 'You see,' he sighed, 'all the girls in the audience want to sleep with Michael, and all the men want to take Rachel out to supper. ... However, if you're *quite* determined ... ' He kissed us both, and a tear ran down his cheek.

Breaking the news to Willie was a sight easier than facing our respective parents. Of one thing we could be certain, we said: we did not want a church wedding with all that fuss and expense. We were soon to learn, however, how many things and people change their specific gravity when it's a question of a wedding. For instance, in the question of whom to invite, and whom not, the protagonists are shown in very different lights. And one may be sure that among them is one who will think the whole idea misplaced. How were we going to live – what would we live on? Was J.P. Anderson solvent, and if so, for how long? In short, every delaying tactic short of Tybalt's death was to hand. Tears were not uncommon. Even threats, of a kind. I was told there was a certain window in the Royal

My father, Roy Redgrave, in an Australian bush drama.

My mother, Daisy Scudamore, as Glory Quayle in the popular melodrama *The Christian* (about 1909).

Daisy (now Mrs. J. P. Anderson) on her wedding day (1922).

Margaret Scudamore (no longer Daisy) as Lady Bracknell in the first revival of *The Importance of Being Earnest* after Oscar Wilde's imprisonment and death.

My stepfather Andy (*centre*) and some friends at a shoot.

F. A. Scudamore (Daisy's real father) in the 1880s.

In my sailor hat, in either 1911 or 1912.

(*Left*) As Lady Macbeth, at Clifton. 'A little bird tells me that we have here the rival of the Divine Sarah. Are you thinking of going on the stage?' 'Good Lord, no!' I said (1925). (*Right*) As Captain Absolute in *The Rivals*, at Clifton (1926).

With Arthur Marshall as the female lead in *Captain Brassbound's Conversion*, at the Amateur Dramatic Club in Cambridge. The first and, as it turned out, the last time I ever acted in Shaw in the theatre. He claimed, correctly, that his characters are 'actor-proof' (1931).

With Mother, Andy, and Viscount Falkland on Degree Day at Cambridge (1931).

As Hamlet, at Cranleigh. This first attempt owed so much to Gielgud's performance in 1930 that I must have seemed like his understudy (1933).

As King Lear, at Cranleigh (1934).

With Rachel at Liverpool – an engagement photograph (1935).

With Alfred Sangster, Rachel, Deirdre Doyle and Eileen Douglas in *Miss Linley of Bath* (1935).

With Lloyd Pearson and Jane Baxter in *A Hundred Years Old* (1935).

With Denis Webb, Rachel, Deirdre Doyle and Cyril Lister in *The Wind and the Rain* (1935).

Naval College at Dartmouth – Rachel's father was Headmaster – where certain cadets were keeping up a constant menacing watch for Redgrave coming up the drive. Privately, I doubted this. After all, Redgrave would have been no more recognizable to any of them than the Barber of Seville.

Years afterwards Rachel and I simultaneously confessed that there had been a weakening of resolve on both sides. Eric, Rachel's father, most sympathetically, had gone so far as to say that it could still be called off. And there were moments when I would have been only too glad to hear that it had been. But I funked the role of the jilter.

According to custom, the wedding gifts were put on view in the drawing-room. Needless to say, there were more presents from the bride's friends than from the groom's. So far, so good. But my best man, Dick Green, my closest friend at Cambridge, had asked me what I wanted, and I had chosen a print by Maillol, one of a series of nudes. I was not present at the moment when Rachel's mother, Beatrice, saw the print, but Rachel told me there followed a short, serious discussion as to whose feelings would be more offended: the guests', if the nude were to remain on display, or the best man's and the groom's, if it were not (it being impossible, of course, to please both parties at once). The nude was turned to the wall.

After this, the wedding ceremony itself was plain sailing. I had not spent all those years as a chorister at Clifton for nothing, and sang lustily. Cyril Maude, an expert light-comedy actor, was the guest of honour, and made the speech. The Dartmouth cadets crossed swords and were given a half-holiday.

The time came for Rachel to put on travelling clothes, amidst renewed signs of tearfulness from mothers and aunts. We had been lent a comfortable old Morris by Rachel's father and, during the last two weeks of the Playhouse season, I had attempted to pass the driving test. My examiner professed to be an ardent fan of everyone at the Playhouse and knew that I was going to be married, and somehow I thought this might prejudice him in my favour. No such luck. With a broad grin he said, 'Sorry, old man, I'd sooner see you both come back in one piece. Failed.'

So it was arranged that a hired Daimler with chauffeur would drive us from the College to Totnes, where the old Morris would be waiting for us with 'learner plates' attached. I drove fairly competently, buoyed up with champagne, until we got to Exeter. Then Rachel, who was an expert driver, drove us through the town.

The most lavish of all our gifts was the cottage we were lent on the river Hamble, together with an excellent cook. But it was thought we would not reach the cottage in one swoop, so a double room had been booked at a hotel in Lyme Regis.

Rachel seemed rather nervous, I thought, so I volunteered to go down to the bar and have a drink while she changed upstairs. The wedding champagne was having a soporific effect on me, and two dry sherries in the bar somehow failed to produce the amorous, seductive character I was hoping to become. I thought of Margot, but that didn't help much, either. We were both eager to get into bed, yet I knew for a certainty that when we did, I, for one, would fall asleep. And so it happened. But it was a very happy awakening for both of us.

A delightful actress joined the company for the second season: a rather surprising engagement, since Jane Baxter was already a star performer. She had played leading parts in London and had made two films in Hollywood. She was every undergraduate's ideal of an English rose. I viewed her arrival with some alarm, wondering how it might affect the parts Rachel would play. But there was no need. The opportunities William gave his Company were well judged, as I might have known they would be.

There was to be a double bill: *The Copy*, by the Scandinavian playwright Helge Krog, and *A Hundred Years Old*, by the Quintero brothers. To my delight I was given the leading part in both plays. In the Krog piece I played a Schnitzlerian, worldly cynic (with a beard, to show I was cynical). The Liverpool evening paper, which always published a photo of the play after the first night, pleased my vanity by printing my picture above the caption 'Redgrave – with a beard.' To be referred to, not as 'Mr Redgrave', not as 'Michael Redgrave', but as 'Redgrave' *tout court*!

A few nights later, after the curtain call, on our way back to our dressing-rooms, Jane called to me, 'Michael, have you got a second?' She introduced me to a tall, sauve, very English Englishman, Bill Linnit. He was her agent, and had invited himself up to Liverpool to see how she was getting on. He asked me if I were going to be in any of the shows to come. I mentioned, among others, *Richard of Bordeaux*. I said I wasn't sure that I would get the part, but that it was whispered that I would.

'Ah,' said Mr Linnit, 'if you're not sure, then there is some hope for my project.'

He went on to say that watching the performance that night he had had it in mind to offer me one of the leads in Henry Bernstein's *L'Espoir* in London, 'unless, of course, you want to stay here to play Richard. I think you'd be wise to do so.' He asked me if I had an agent, and said that if he could help me in that respect, he'd be very happy to do so.

I thanked him profusely. I longed to stay and question Jane, but instinct said it was better to make a quick exit. A day later he repeated his offer by letter. But again he stressed that if I were offered Richard I should be wise to stay on at Liverpool. He would come up and see me in it. There would be many other offers.

That night Rachel and I sat up till two in the morning, by which time I had played the lead in *Richard of Bordeaux*, acquired the lease to His Majesty's, commissioned T.S. Eliot to write a play for both of us ... and what was *L'Espoir* anyway?

Linnit was as good as his word. A few weeks later he sent me a note saying that he was coming to Liverpool to see *Richard of Bordeaux*, bringing Hugh Beaumont with him. The name meant nothing to me.

Bill's face as he entered my dressing-room after the performance looked tired and sad, and for an awful moment I thought he had been disappointed. But no, his car had broken down outside Chester, and he had seen only the last two scenes of the play. In came a young man: 'Bill has told you? I *am* sorry. I *am* sorry. *What* a shame.' Almost at once he asked where the telephone was, and then began a series of telephone calls to London, and from these I gathered that this Mr Beaumont had something to do with the theatre. I looked around for Willie Armstrong, but he had fled the building. Two such stars could not keep their orbits in one sphere.

Rachel and I had decided that, rather than take them to supper at the Adelphi Hotel, it would be more chic for us to give them white wine and smoked salmon at our rooms in Falkner Street. Mr Beaumont, we learned, was a new but powerful producer, whose other name seemed to be 'Binkie'. Did I know *The Ante-Room* by the Irish writer Kate O'Brien, he asked. No, I didn't. 'Pity,' said Binkie, 'I was thinking of asking you if you would care to play the leading male part in a dramatization of it.' Diana Wynyard was to play the lead. Diana was a very big star at that moment, having done some Hollywood pictures. She was also well-remembered in Liverpool, where she had played for a season at the Playhouse. The play would be directed by Guthrie McClintic, Katharine Cornell's husband.

At nine the next morning Rachel and I were up and out, searching every bookshop in Liverpool for Kate O'Brien's novel.

My part, if the novel was to be trusted, was a good one, and the prospect of landing such a leading role in the West End was immensely pleasing. Meanwhile, arrangements would be made, said Binkie, and a script would be sent as soon as it was ready.

But, before I received it, another important person arrived unexpectedly in Liverpool whose visit was to change the course of my young career and put in the shade such ambition as I had of landing feet first in the West End – Tyrone Guthrie.

IX

I FIRST met Tyrone Guthrie in Cambridge days. I doubt whether he noticed my presence much, though his presence was unmistakable. He was a giant of a man, even taller than I, with a short military moustache and a funny, light head-voice – nowadays it would be called 'camp', though he was far from 'camp' – with which to deliver devastating one-line judgements. At the Festival Theatre just outside Cambridge, he staged witty, inventive, very theatrical productions. When you saw them you realized that times had changed.

I wrote to him several times during my interlude as a schoolmaster at Cranleigh, inviting him to come down and see my productions. He would reply expressing regret – genuine, I felt – that he was unable to come. For my final production, *King Lear*, I wrote again, and received the usual kind reply, thanking me for the notices I had sent in the hope that they might tempt him. Yes, he had heard the production was 'brilliant'; he wished me luck in my forthcoming job at the Liverpool Playhouse; but no, regretfully, he couldn't come. I made one last desperate attempt and rang him. Telephoning from school was no easy matter. There was chapel at nine, followed by lessons throughout the morning, and the only available phone was in the music master's rooms. Guthrie at eight-thirty in the morning was a little less urbane than usual. Wasn't I 'a bit of a mug' to be giving up my safe job as a schoolmaster? He wished me luck but, again, was sorry that he wasn't able to come.

It was two years before I heard from Guthrie again. We were nearing the end of our second season at Liverpool, and Rachel and I were playing the young leads in a James Bridie play, *Storm in a Teacup*. It was 1 May 1936, the sort of morning which makes Liverpool – to us who loved Liverpool – look its sootiest and most appealing. We walked, as usual, to the theatre for rehearsals for

93

Twelfth Night, the last play of the season, in which Rachel was to play Viola and I, Malvolio. The letter at the stage door had been delivered by hand that morning, from the Adelphi Hotel.

> I saw your show last night [wrote Guthrie], and enjoyed it very much. We are en route for Ireland for a short holiday. I saw William Armstrong and he tells me you have several alluring offers in view, so I don't suppose there is much likelihood of my being able to persuade you and your wife to come to the Old Vic with me next autumn. The money we can offer you will *not* compare favourably with a West End salary. But the work would, I think, be more interesting, and possibly, at a long view, more profitable even in a worldly sense. I know in Rep. one has neither time nor energy for writing, so enclose an addressed postcard which may save bother.

Malvolio that morning smiled and smiled, and Viola positively danced through rehearsal.

I did, it was true, have one other offer in view: *The Ante-Room*. This had no doubt been elaborated and added to by Willie Armstrong so as to paint a picture for Guthrie of West End managers queueing for our services. When we had told him that we wanted to leave at the end of the season, he had done his utmost to dissuade us. But now, having reconciled himself to our leaving, he was not going to allow Guthrie to think he was discovering any ordinary actors.

The postcard enclosed with Guthrie's letter read:

> We are / are not interested in the idea of an Old Vic season. We are / are not available. If your salesman calls (in plain van) around May 25 we can / cannot discuss the matter fully.

We lunched at the Bon Marché, wondering what parts Guthrie might offer us. It seemed too lucky to be true, that we should have the chance to go on working together. Supposing Binkie had brought a script of *The Ante-Room* with him, and I had already signed a contract? Supposing Guthrie had seen us in less good parts in another play? We wrote to him that afternoon.

He replied by return of post. He couldn't yet promise an exact list of parts, he said. He was in negotiation with Edith Evans, and after Christmas, Laurence Olivier would probably join the company, so the final list of plays and parts would have to wait on their acceptances.

> Olivier and you might a little tend to want the same parts, but I'm inclined to think that even with Olivier there would be enough for you to do in order to show yourself to the public and the critics in the best way e.g.

Horatio, *not* Hamlet, in the noted tragedy of that name. I think that from your point of view it would be wiser to make a very favourable impression in a few leading roles (not the big classic parts) and in good second parts, rather than take the risk of appearing straight off in the big parts in which you eventually want to make your name. I think the honest summary of the position is that I would like to use you two as the *juvenile leads* not as the *stars* of the season; though we should 'star' you in the billing. I can't say exactly about the money but it wouldn't be much – top salary is £20 per week. I expect you'd get that or somewhere near it. The following list of plays and parts is strictly provisional, but I think I can say that it represents the sort of stuff you would be asked to do. If there were any part or parts you particularly wanted I would gladly make an effort to arrange things to make it possible.

The Merchant of Venice	Portia
	Bassanio
Antony and Cleopatra	Charmian
	Caesar
Ghosts	Regina
	Oswald
Hamlet	Ophelia
	Horatio
Love's Labour's Lost	King
	Princess
Witch of Edmonton	
Within the Gates	leading juvenile parts

(produced by Michel Saint-Denis)

He ended by suggesting, 'If you want to play it we might try to do *Richard II*,' and promising, 'I anticipate getting money to spend on the productions, so the scenery and costumes will not, I hope, be tatty.'

(Lilian Baylis was notoriously tight-fisted: £25 was the budget for scenery and costumes for each production until Guthrie arrived, though, of course, it should be remembered that the theatre then had no subsidy and each play had to pay its way for its four or five weeks' run. Guthrie as director and his leading actors were engaged for the season, the supporting players from play to play, and all were on rock-bottom salaries. Baylis herself, of course, never directed, but hers was the dominant presence at the Vic throughout her life. She could hardly be said to have had a 'policy', still less a 'house style'. But more important than policy or style are vision and purpose. Baylis's vision of a popular theatre presenting its classics to a local audience was heroic. The Vic in her day never talked down to its audience, never imposed on them, and never tried to overawe them. As a result, it won their respect and their fierce loyalty to a degree unsurpassed by any other theatre.)

My reply to Guthrie was a mixture of shrewdness and sheer cheek:

The prospect of Oswald is tremendously attractive to me, especially playing with Miss Evans. [So it was: I always wanted to play Oswald, and never did.] But I imagine this would almost certainly be one of the plays which would drop out if Miss Evans did not come. [My instinct was right: Edith did come, but didn't want to play Mrs. Alving, and *Ghosts* was dropped.] I feel that supposing I played just those parts you mention, but not Oswald, I should be like a card player who has a fair hand, one to play an intelligent-enough game, but with which he could not possibly win. This is due, of course, to the fact that juveniles are, often as not, rather unexciting parts, and the exciting ones, except Oswald, would all be played by Olivier. And I wondered whether you had not perhaps noticed something of the sort when you suggest I should play *Richard II*? Your list of parts, given the plays, and Olivier, are certainly varied, but with the exception of Oswald I could play them on my head, as the saying goes. If you can find some way to give me one or two parts I could really get my teeth into, I should be very happy. I expect you want someone for Claudius with more weight than I could be supposed to assume – but I should very much like to play Laertes rather than Horatio. It seems to me that Laertes should be a young soldier, very forceful and physically bigger than Hamlet, bursting with health and proper pride, and so untouched by sorrow that his reactions to Ophelia's madness become, as they easily might, selfish, conventional, and a little unreal. I imagine that is how Matheson Lang must have played him when he was young. Then, if you would consider me as Macduff rather than Malcolm [Guthrie had said that Olivier, if he came, was keen to play Macbeth], and Archer, rather than the attendant without in *The Beaux' Stratagem* [another possibility, if Edith Evans were to come], I should feel I was really getting somewhere.

The cocksure tone of this letter, from a young actor who had yet to prove himself outside provincial repertory, is outrageous, though Guthrie, to his credit, took it in his stride. ('Laertes by all means if you prefer, though *I'd* call Horatio the better part.') I had no conception then that I could possibly fail in a part. I set no bounds on what I could do. I scarcely knew what it was like to feel nervous on-stage.

Love's Labour's Lost opened in September 1936 at the Old Vic to good notices, though rather poor houses. The stars, Evans and Olivier, had yet to join the company, and we were a very young group, with Guthrie putting us through our paces. Alec Guinness was Boyet; Alec Clunes, Berowne; Rachel was the Princess of France and I was the King of Navarre. Guthrie, introducing us in the Vic-Wells magazine, sounded rather like the *maître d'école* assessing his newest intake:

> Incidentally, the small permanent company includes two young men for whose future we have the highest hopes. Alec Clunes is not unknown to Old Vic audiences. He is still very young, but the promise of great gifts is apparent: and when time has a little mellowed and ripened them there is the possibility of great things.
>
> Michael Redgrave is a few years older. He comes with the reputation of two very fine seasons of work at Liverpool Repertory, the nursery of so many excellent actors. We believe he has the equipment of a potential star. He has refused more lucrative offers, both on stage and screen, because he preferred to work at the Vic in plays of quality. It is our hope that this season will establish him as a new leading man.

Clunes had the most beautiful voice I had heard in a young actor and was an excellent Berowne. Nevertheless, I couldn't help thinking that he and I might be rivals, and wondering why Guthrie had passed me over for Berowne. Ferdinand, as I had told him, was one of those parts I thought I could play on my head. Guinness, as Boyet, had a rather tiresome part, and succeeded against the odds in bringing it to life. He had, and still has, that most valuable asset for comedy: the appearance of possessing an impenetrable secret.

And the promise of money to spend on the productions had not materialized, at least not yet. There was a real fountain centre stage, as there had been in Guthrie's last production of the play. But at the Vic the set had a distinctly utilitarian appearance. The skycloth had seen far better days, and a gauze had to be hung in front of it to hide its wrinkles and gashes, giving the whole play an autumnal, hazy look quite at odds with its springtime theme. And I hated my costume. It was absurdly frilly and over-pretty, marabout edged in lace, like an illustration to a child's history book. Here, perhaps, was the chink in my seeming armour of self-confidence. I had a slight secret fear that I might look effeminate, that out there in the audience someone would say, 'He's a bit of a "nancy".' I would counter this by charging myself up in the wings to strike what Macready calls 'the firm manly tone'.

Besides this half-acknowledged fear, I had an inhibition, quite evident in my photographs of this period, about smiling. 'You should use your smile more, dear,' my mother would say, 'you have such a charming smile.' But I couldn't. I was embarrassed about showing my teeth. I went to the dentist to have them filed down, but it was little help. Later, in my first film part, they plugged a gap between my teeth with gutta-percha, which was constantly falling out but seemed to overcome the problem.

But these were small clouds, easily overlooked. Rachel and I had taken a small furnished flat in Greycoat Mansions, off Victoria Street. Soon we should need a larger flat because Rachel was pregnant. That much we knew, but in all other respects we were thoroughly ignorant. So when someone recommended a doctor who advised a vegetarian diet for Rachel, we accepted this as if it were the latest medical wisdom and became regular customers at the Vega Restaurant near Leicester Square, never questioning the fact that Rachel became more and more hungry and weak throughout her pregnancy.

'Have you read *The Country Wife*?' asked Guthrie, one of our first visitors at Greycoat Mansions. 'Read it, and see what you think of Horner.' He explained it would be done in co-production with an American management, and would transfer to Broadway after a six-week run at the Vic. 'I think it would be rather chic for a young actor in his first season in London to go straight to New York, don't you?'

On the first day of rehearsal of *The Country Wife* – the 'read-through' – the entire company was assembled, and there was a kind of quiver in the air; for an actor no other occasion can match this, except perhaps the first night. One or two nonsenses were spoken in asides to each other by the cast. One of the student actors whispers, 'I've got two lines – "Yes, Madam" and "No, Madam" – I'm simply terrified.' 'No need,' says another, knowledgeably. 'You'll see. Guthrie always invents the best business for his extras. He's wizard.' After the introductions were over, all eyes turned to the American actress Ruth Gordon – the unknown quantity. Miss Gordon seemed supremely confident. Well she might be; her knowledge of the play exceeded all of ours, including the director's. She had played it with resounding success in summer theatre, and she clearly knew more than her lines.

The whole production was to be far more costly than had ever before been mounted at the Old Vic. Never had the old boards creaked under the tread of such expensive shoes. The leading actors may have agreed to play for a low salary, but Oliver Messel, the designer, had it in his contract that if anything in the set or costumes did not meet with his approval, it should be changed. With no argument.

Gilbert Miller, the American impresario, and Helen Hayes, a close friend of Ruth's, had raised the money to mount the production first in England, before transferring it to New York. It had, I suspect, always been an ambition of Ruth's to be acknowledged as a classical actress, and though it might be stretching a point to claim that Wycherley's *The Country Wife* is the pure serene of the classical temple, it was nevertheless a minor classic and would serve as a 'classic' vehicle for Miss Gordon. She took it greedily and joyously with both hands. Not for her to revert to giving a mere reading. Her bright, bird-like eyes twinkled. She put down her script, having no need to consult it, and launched into a full-scale performance. Did I say I was never nervous? I was that morning.

I was conscious during the reading that those bird-like eyes were fixed to some extent on me. And every now and then she would shoot a glance at me which did not bode too well. What was to be decided was whether I was mature enough to play the lead in such a company. I felt miserable and uncomfortable. But apart from me, the cast read with great spirit. Edith Evans, as Lady Fidget, was in her element. Altogether it seemed certain that, when Guthrie had got to work on the play, all would be well.

My difficulty was that, when giving me the play to read, Guthrie had given me no indication of how he wanted me to play Horner, who, it will be remembered, feigns impotence in order to deceive the husbands and seduce the wives. Once rehearsals proper had begun, I thought I had found a clue to his character, but at each attempt of mine to fix the salaciousness of the part, Guthrie would shake his head. I did not know then, nor did I learn until the play was already in performance, that I was being directed to soften the ugly contours of the play, to placate the Old Vic's Board of Governors. Guthrie had told Lilian Baylis that such was my youthful charm that not one of them would see a jot of harm in the antics of this pleasant young scoundrel. This ploy succeeded admirably so far as the Governors were concerned. As Lord Lytton, the Chairman, wrote in a letter to the *Daily Telegraph*: 'The coarseness of the play can only be redeemed by the rendering of the part of Horner. The fact that he is performed at the Old Vic by an artist whose inherent niceness is so transparent, makes the whole thing a clean and not a dirty entertainment.' Right you are if you think you are. But it left me hopelessly at sea as rehearsals progressed.

When, three weeks later, it came to the dress rehearsal, all attack had left me. My voice sounded soft, my motions apologetic. Jed Harris, Ruth's common-law second husband, who had come over to vet the production, drew me aside and said, 'You know, Mike, if I were playing your part, I'd start with Horner in bed, and during his first scene with the doctor I'd start to dress and try and make myself more alluring. I'd maybe put him in corsets, and apply a patch to each cheek. . . .'

I listened, but couldn't think what to say. I was sure that Charles Laughton, who had come over with Jed, was working on Lilian Baylis. 'Let me play the part,' I could almost hear him saying, adding, no doubt, 'At the same salary. Just to show you how it should be done.'

To cap it all, Tony Guthrie gave me at the final dress rehearsal an almost impossible piece of business to cover a scene change. Rather than lower an act drop, he wanted me to walk across the stage laughing throughout the length of time it took to change the set. It was like corporal punishment. I was already sufficiently despairing about my capacity as a laughter-raiser, let alone a life-giver. But Tony, as always once he had set his mind on something, refused to acknowledge any difficulty. 'Go on, Mike, laugh!'

Leaving my dressing-room that night, I found my mother, tearful. 'Murray Macdonald [the stage director] says you don't appear to be even trying. What's the matter?'

'I don't know what Tony wants me to do.'

'And you should smile more, dear.'

Just then we met Edith Evans coming from her dressing-room. Mother didn't greatly admire Edith. She called her 'a spurious actress', a 'clever woman' who had somehow fooled the critics. But at this moment Edith said something which, for the moment, pushed away my fears. I had sprained my ankle at the last but one performance of *Love's Labour's Lost* and was still limping.

'Here's the hero of the evening,' said Edith, 'still soldiering on.'

'Well, dear,' said Mother, cutting Edith short, 'remember what I said. It'll be fine. It'll be fine.'

Edith's words gave me a much-needed lift. When we assembled for notes the following morning, she gave me a radiant smile, and presently she said something more, which took my breath away. In her most honeyed tones, almost a whisper, as if she and I were old friends of long standing, she said, 'You don't want to go to New York to play Horner on Broadway' – she made it sound as if only a great booby could possibly want such a thing – 'you want to stay here and play Orlando with me.' All that day I was buoyed up with the excitement her words had given me. But then, just before the curtain went up, I overheard two stage-hands talking: 'I hear Charlie Laughton's in front.' I felt as though all the wind had been taken from my sails. I could see Laughton out there saying, 'That boy's no good.' Even the elementary sense not to break an audience's laugh, which I must certainly have acquired after two years at Liverpool, clean deserted me. Guthrie had devised some simple business where I had to push Edith, as Lady Fidget, down on to a settee and she, thoroughly predatory, had to pull me on top of her. It got a huge laugh from the first-night audience. Almost oblivious of this, I was rising to continue the scene when I felt Edith's hands grip me at the waist with what seemed enormous strength, holding me there on top of her until the laughter had subsided. Somehow I braced myself to bluff my way through the remainder of the evening, and I fancy that in some measure my performance strengthened.

Certainly it strengthened sufficiently during the three weeks playing for the Gilbert Miller management to change their minds about me. I knew they had had their eye on another actor, Roger Livesey, for the Broadway production. But now they thought that perhaps they should give me a second chance. I was sent for to Miller's offices in the St James's Theatre to discuss a contract, and he came out with the suggestion that I should play the part in New York for the same salary as I was getting at the Vic, £20 a week. I pointed out that Edith and Ruth could probably afford to play for such a small sum, but that I could not, and I said this in sufficiently positive and final a manner for Miller to be taken aback. He dithered for a few moments. 'Well,' he said, eventually, 'time is short, but all you have to do is to make up your mind.' I made up my mind there and then. I would stay and play Orlando with Edith.

Ever since, I have marvelled at my good luck. Had I gone to New York at that stage, and been exposed to New York critics and audiences, heaven knows how long it might have taken me to recover. Not that I was afraid of such exposure. After a few weeks' playing I had more or less recovered my nerve, and a portion of my conceit. The London critics had been kind enough, and perhaps ignorant of the play's real intentions, to praise me quite warmly. Only James Agate in the *Sunday Times* seemed to have detected what was wrong: 'Mr Redgrave was neither old enough, nor experienced enough, nor sardonic enough, and was altogether much too nice a youth to hit upon this play's ugly and middle-aged invention.'

The rehearsal room at the Vic – too hot in summer and too cold in winter – has witnessed some remarkable scenes. Unlike so many rehearsal rooms, it seems to take on the character of the actors who are at work in it.

During the rehearsals of *As You Like It*, its walls resounded to the cascade of merriment which was Edith Evans's voice. Her voice was very particular to her. She had studied with Elsie Fogerty, the great teacher-healer. (Much could be written of Fogerty's ability to divine the source of an actor's problems. Once, when in trouble with a part, Edith went to Fogerty, who said, 'Well, of course you can't act it in those shoes.' 'So,' said Edith, 'I took them off and that was all there was to it. I had no more trouble after that.')

Each day she had lunch in her dressing-room. She was dieting to reduce her weight. She was a sturdily-built woman, and now she needed to do what she had done so successfully as Millamant in *The Way of the World*, when she is reputed to have said to some admirer, 'I just say to myself, "You are the most beautiful woman in London"' – and so, for the nonce, she was. Unkind critics, not the professional ones, would remark that the three best actresses in London were 'Bosseye', 'Popeye', and 'Dropeye'. 'Dropeye', of course, referred to Edith, whose drooping eyelid can be seen in Sickert's portrait of her. She didn't follow fashion. The works of Schiaparelli and company had no allure for her. At first glance, indeed, one could describe her manner of dressing truthfully, if not charitably, as dowdy. And now that she was forty-eight, even her most devoted admirers feared that she had left it too late to play Rosalind again.

The Country Wife had been as big a success as it promised to be, and was still playing to packed houses. The advance bookings for *As You Like It* seemed, by comparison, thin. Even some of Edith's closest friends had not booked seats for the first night.

None of these perilous thoughts seemed to touch her. Only in the first scenes were her fears evident. As Rosalind the girl, she was less than persuasive. But when she changed into a boy her whole being seemed transformed. It was not that she looked in the least like a boy. The Watteau style which the designer had imposed upon the play was most unbecoming to her. But nothing mattered except her spell – even when, once, she 'dried'. She simply laughed, in the most assured way, and one could have sworn that the word that eluded her mattered far less than the music of her laughter. She waltzed across to the prompt corner, took her prompt, and waltzed back, laughing.

I had fallen under this spell when we were half-way through rehearsals. We had worked together all morning. When we came to the exit in Act Three – 'Will you go?' says Rosalind. 'With all my heart, good youth,' says Orlando. 'Nay, you must call me Rosalind' – at this point, when we were sitting close to each other on the ground, I leant forwards and, taking her in my arms, kissed her.

For several days Edith made no reference to the incident in the rehearsal room. Then, one morning, during a break, she asked me to have dinner with her at the Café Royal, a place which still offered an atmosphere of bohemianism.

'Tell me,' she said that night, 'why did you kiss me?'

I tried to shrug it off with a laugh. 'Because I wanted to. Did you mind?'

'That makes me feel quite sick.'

I felt like a man who goes out to paddle at the water's edge, and finds himself up to his neck in deep waters. We were silent for several moments. 'Is that a new hat?'

'Yes.' She smiled. 'Do you like it?'

I realized that I was completely out of my depth. Still I floundered on. 'You have a farm? Where is it?'

She told me about the farm. Thirteenth century. Moated. Guy's pride and joy. 'You must come down and see it one weekend. What about next weekend?'

'I'd love to.'

She had surprised me again by referring to her husband. I had no idea she had been married. Very few people knew of her marriage to George (Guy) Booth, a childhood friend, who had died tragically the year before.

The following day at rehearsal I asked her, 'Would you care to try the Café Royal again?'

'I was hoping you'd say that. Why not come to my flat? What do you like to eat?'

'Scrambled eggs would be very nice.'

That night after the show we went to her flat in West Halkin Street. 'There's something I wanted to show you.'

On the mantelpiece was a photograph of Guy pruning an apple tree.

'You see, I was in New York when he died. Playing the nurse in *Romeo* with Kit Cornell. I knew nothing of his illness until after his death. But it's there, do you see? There's death in that face.'

She asked me about my family – Mother, Andy, Peggy. She was particularly interested in my Portsmouth relations. I asked her about her Welsh origins.

'I'm not really,' she said. 'Not *really* Welsh. I just let them think that because of the name.'

'I do hope that you have no notion whatever of living your life without me,' she wrote. 'You simply couldn't do it. We have such beautiful things in common. Oh – so very common. Rice pudding on the hearth rug and coats over the back of the chair. Darling, please don't alter. I love you shamelessly.'

What with rehearsals of *As You Like It* by day and performances of *The Country Wife* at night, we hoped to conceal major indiscretions with a host of minor fibs and prevarications. When, in response to her invitation that night at the Café Royal, I went to stay for the weekend at her farm in Biddenden, Alec Guinness accompanied us. A photo, taken by her chauffeur, shows Guinness, a very young man, with a few sparse curls still lingering on his crown, arm in arm with Edith on her left hand; I, windblown, laughing, a head taller than my companions, arm in arm on Edith's right; and Edith, between us, her slacks tucked into woollen socks, like a land-girl, is smiling triumphantly as if saying, 'Aha! Look what I've got!'

That evening, after our walk on the Romney Marshes, Edith asked us both, 'What is your idea of a theatre?' Alec, answering first, talked gently but cogently about a company, like the Moscow Arts Theatre, working together, developing its own repertoire and style. And I answered in similar terms. Both of us had been inspired by the theatre of Jacques Copeau and La Compagnie des Quinze. A theatre without stars. 'But what,' asked Edith, 'would there be for me in such a theatre?'

I fell head over heels in love with Edith, and she with me. She had chosen me, a young actor floundering helplessly in his first leading role, to play Orlando to her Rosalind.

Esmé Church, our producer, was of the 'Yes, dear, that'll be lovely, let's do it again' school. I cannot for the life of me recall a single note she gave me during our four weeks' rehearsal, or whether she gave me a note at all. Nor do I think it mattered. I can think of one prescription only for any young actor who is to play Orlando: fall in love with your Rosalind. And if that should fail? Try again.

After six weeks at the Old Vic, and another four weeks when Edith played the Witch in Dekker's *The Witch of Edmonton* with me in the part of Warbeck, *As You Like It* transferred to the New Theatre, where it ran for a further three months, a very respectable run for Shakespeare then. I think Bronson Albery, the New's manager, must have known about our affair. He was casting for *The Taming of the Shrew* with Edith as Kate and Leslie Banks as Petruchio, and offered me the part of Biondello, probably thinking that we wanted to continue playing together. But I, thinking that Biondello was a very insignificant part after Orlando, turned it down with some amazement that it had even been suggested. I went into *The Bat*, a once highly successful thriller, with Eva Moore, which came and went with scarcely a flutter, to be followed by two more West End plays, which disappeared with equal dispatch. And then I joined John Gielgud's company at the Queen's Theatre to play Bolingbroke in *Richard II*.

'More and more I want us to be together in the theatre,' wrote Edith, on tour with Mother in St John Ervine's play *Robert's Wife* in the autumn of 1937 whilst I was rehearsing at the Queen's. 'Murray was full of praise for your Bolingbroke and, oh, how my heart jumps with pride when people speak well of you. The situation here is so odd, and would be unbearable over a length of time. Your mother and about six of us meet every night at supper, and I feel that the home possessive atmosphere of you, not wrongfully, is very strong, and there I am sitting in the midst, my heart singing for joy because of my share in your life, and nobody knows.'

I confided in my friend from Cambridge days, Paddy Railton. Under the pen name of 'Patrick Carleton' he had published several novels, including a fine historical novel, *Under the Hog*, which gave me the idea he might write something for Edith and myself. 'I told Paddy,' I wrote to Edith, 'and boy! was he excited! He looked like Armado in *Love's Labour's* – "I'm for whole volumes in folios." You'll find yourself with a Plantagenet trilogy on your hands if you're not careful!' But Paddy was by now suffering chronically from tuberculosis and wasn't able to complete the play.

'Isn't love extraordinary,' she wrote, 'the way it releases energy?' It was so, for her. She took up riding and then, having been chauffeured for years, learned to drive and passed her test. And her dress, very ordinary and everyday before, became distinctly smart and fashionable.

Though I never learned to ride nor to drive – I had given over driving to Rachel ever since our honeymoon – I nevertheless felt immeasurably strengthened by Edith's love. She had accepted me at a very early, critical stage in my career. One day, at the start of rehearsals for *As You Like It*, she had asked me, 'What do you want in the theatre? Everyone knows what Larry stands for, and what Peggy and John and I stand for. But what sort of an actor do you want to be?' Suddenly I realized that she was suggesting that I might, if I chose, and applied myself, and put thought and passion into it, find my place in such company. It took my breath away.

Her remarks about my acting, and acting in general, were brief, but illuminating: 'I am told you are going to be most excellent as Sir Andrew.' (It was the summer of 1938 and I was rehearsing in Michel Saint-Denis's production of *Twelfth Night* at the Phoenix.) 'It doesn't surprise me. I saw all the seeds of your acting when we were so much together. A look here, a look there, told me all I wanted. I just knew that you required stability of character to hold your talents in place.' Written in pencil, these last words are scored in so heavily as almost to break the pencil lead. 'If you want things enough, you can't compromise. To like them enough you must have passion. If you want to be first-class you must grow in loving and passion.'

Years later, in America, I gave an interview to Lillian Ross of *The New Yorker*, in which I spoke about Edith. It conveys, I think, the essence of our relationship:

For me, Edith Evans has the authentic magic. Claptrap word though 'magic' may be, it's the only word for the stage. When she comes onstage, the stage lights up. She's a very strict person about her own profession and is without any of the nonsense. She's a real and dedicated artist. Her art is her life. Everything she does on the stage is interpreted through her own morality. It's the way Picasso paints. It's the way Beethoven composed. It's the thing the great artist has that makes him different from other people. I don't mean morality in a pettifogging way. I mean moral values, without which nothing is achieved, and nothing created. Part of it is caring enough about what you do to achieve something beyond the mundane.

Acting with Edith Evans was heaven. It was like being in your mother's arms, like knowing how to swim, like riding a bicycle. You're safe. The late Michael Chekhov said once that there were three ways to act: for yourself, for the audience, and to your partner. Some of the newer theorists say that if it's true for yourself, it's truthful, which is not so. The majority of actors act for themselves or for the audience. I believe that the only way to act is to your partner. As a partner Edith Evans was like a great conductor who allows a soloist as much latitude as is needed, but always keeps everything strict. It's strict but free. Never is anything too set, too rigid. The stage relationship always leaves enough room to improvise. For the first time in my life, acting in *As You Like It*, I felt completely unselfconscious. Acting with her made me feel, oh, it's so easy. You don't start acting, she told me, until you stop *trying* to act. It doesn't leave the ground until you don't have to think about it. The play and our stage relationship in it always had the same shape. It was entirely well-proportioned and yet, in many respects, it was all fluid. In the forest scenes between Orlando and Rosalind, she would encourage me to do almost anything that came into my head. Yet, if I had done anything excessive she would have stopped it by the simplest means. Somehow it didn't occur to me to do anything excessive. For the first time, onstage or off, I felt completely free.

After *As You Like It*, we saw each other only infrequently. It was Edith who ended it. Rachel and I, for what reason I forget, had had an argument and I, in a fit of temper, stayed out all night. Rachel rang Edith in desperation. She came round immediately and spent the night with Rachel, comforting her. Days later she wrote me a letter of farewell. She was incapable of jealousy and hated deception. And she was very fond of Rachel. She would always write, at the end of her letters, 'My love to your two ladies.'

The other lady, of course, was Vanessa, who was born towards the end of my first season at the Vic. It was the last Saturday in January 1937, a matinee performance of *Hamlet* in its entirety. I, as Laertes, could hardly put one foot in front of another. In the wings the other actors whispered, 'Any news?' I shook my head.

'If it's a girl, we can't call her Sarah,' Rachel had insisted. 'She'll end up being called Sally.' We had been sitting up late at night in our flat. Outside, it was snowing heavily. We were waiting to see whether the pangs which Rachel had felt an hour or two before should prove, yet again, a false alarm. From the bookshelf I picked out at random *Men and Memories* by William Rothenstein and, flipping through the index, I came upon the entry 'Bell, Vanessa'. That would do, we decided, and immediately, as if in answer, the pangs came with redoubled force, and we bundled off to Blackheath. There, as the night wore on more or less sleeplessly and the pains subsided, it seemed we were in for another delay.

In the duel scene at the matinée, Olivier placed his foil against mine with infinite care and we pit-patted our way through the fight as in slow motion. Then, between the shows, came a telephone call from Blackheath, and the evening performance flew. When it came to the duel, though Laertes was far from steady on his feet, the fight was fast and brilliant. Larry at the curtain-call made a speech, as was the custom at the Vic on Saturdays, and announced, 'Ladies and gentlemen, tonight a great actress has been born. Laertes has a daughter.' The gallery roared their approval, and from the wings the student actors wheeled on a barrow of flowers with the message 'To Rachel and Michael – Love's Labour's Not Lost.' And after the show, at the Moulin d'Or, a favourite haunt for actors, Larry and Bobby Flemyng cleared a path for me through the tables, throwing flowers to the astonished diners and singing out, 'He's had a daughter.'

X

I N 1928, during my first year at Cambridge, I read that there was to be a performance by the French actor-director Jacques Copeau, founder and creator of what came to be called La Compagnie des Quinze, entitled *L'Illusion*. It was, as its title promised, an exploration of theatrical magic in its simplest and most potent terms, as if a great craftsman, having made a crystal vase, had deliberately shattered it by letting it fall to the ground, and then, with one swoop of his hands, had reassembled the beautiful object in a new and yet more perfect form – the truth, as seen by the illusionist, becoming the truth, at that moment, for the spectator. Actors came forward inviting the audience to a game: 'We can make you believe in anything – and show you it's only an illusion.'

Then, when I was teaching at Cranleigh, came the visit of La Compagnie des Quinze with *Noah*, *Don Juan*, and *The Rape of Lucrece*, followed by a rarefied piece called *Loire*, in which the actors appeared as owls, grass-snakes, and wolves, impersonating the spirit of the great river. It was a revelation: now I knew what I wanted to do.

In *Don Juan*, the actor playing the Don's servant, Leporello, was of a sturdy, pleasant appearance, not so brilliant nor so rib-tickling as Leporellos sometimes strive to be, but fitting with ease into the pattern of a production which was graceful without being mannered, and funny without seeming to ask for laughs. He was Copeau's nephew, Michel Saint-Denis. He was to become, both as director and as teacher, an acknowledged hero of two generations of English actors – that of Gielgud and Ashcroft, and that of his students at the London Theatre School – and a hero of his countrymen, to whom he broadcast daily throughout the Second World War.

I was overjoyed to hear from Guthrie that Michel would be directing Dekker's *The Witch of Edmonton*, the play that was to follow *As You Like It* at the Old Vic, but dismayed to find, when the casting was announced, that Marius Goring, who had acted with the Quinze in France, had been chosen to play the juvenile lead, whilst I had been assigned a thankless role, off the stage almost before I had set foot on it – at all events, nothing to bring me to the notice of Michel. I was so riled at having to play this minuscule part, after my success as Orlando, that in desperation I begged Michel to allow me to swap parts with another actor, Leonard Sachs. It seemed to me that his part, although small, had at least a grain of evil in him. Michel raised an eyebrow at my request, but agreed to the swap, though in such manner as to suggest that there was not a halfpenny difference between the two roles or the two actors.

During the performances I would sit through my long waits with Edith in her dressing-room, with scarcely a thought for the play, neglected for the past three hundred years and soon, I thought, to be consigned once more to well-deserved oblivion. The critics patronized it with faint praise. Something of the quality which the Quinze had shown us in *Loire* kept bursting through, but not often enough. Edith, though praised for her performance as Mother Sawyer, the witch, found it very hard to discard Rosalind. There was always the sense that this old beldam concealed a joyous girl wanting to be out. She wore a bald wig with one sinister raven's feather, seeming one moment to beckon and the next to threaten. She begged me not to look at her.

Michel's first job in London, after the Quinze had disbanded in 1935, had been a production of Obey's *Noah* with John Gielgud. It ran for ten weeks and was respectfully received, but, as with our *Witch of Edmonton* the following year, some of the joy of the Quinze production was missing. There was a *Macbeth* with Olivier at the Old Vic. And then, in the autumn of 1937, Gielgud invited Michel to direct *Three Sisters* for his season at the Queen's Theatre.

John G. had assembled a company which was unique at that time; it not only glittered but was remarkable for being a team. His season was to consist of four plays, *Richard II*, Sheridan's *The School for Scandal*, Chekhov's *Three Sisters*, and *The Merchant of Venice*. I was to play Bolingbroke to John's Richard; Charles Surface in *The School for Scandal*; and last, but least, Bassanio in *The Merchant*. I was to be paid £25 a week, rising to £30 if the box office went above £1,200. So much I knew. But my request to be allowed to play Andrei in *Three Sisters* was stonewalled. Michel, said John, must be allowed to choose his own cast. He would see us working together in *Richard* and then make his choice, and whatever the outcome I should not be too disappointed – all the parts in *Three Sisters* were good.

We assembled for the first reading of *Richard II*. I felt proud to be a member of such a company: Gielgud as Richard; Peggy Ashcroft as the Queen; Leon Quartermaine as John of Gaunt; Frederick Lloyd; Harcourt Williams; Dorothy Green; beside them Anthony Quayle, Alec Guinness, Glen Byam Shaw, and George Devine. Gielgud himself was directing. He was only three or four years my senior, but I was still a comparative newcomer, with only three years' professional experience behind me; Gielgud had been a leading actor for more than a decade. It would be an exaggeration to say that I was in awe of Peggy Ashcroft. She was so thoroughly unpretentious and friendly. But I admired her greatly, from the time when, as a schoolmaster, I had seen her again and again in Komisarjevsky's production of *The Seagull*. (I have seen several actresses play Nina since, and it would be foolish to try to grade them either in technique or personality, though I must add that my daughter Vanessa would not have to fight her way into any list. But the memory of Peggy's performance is indelible.)

It was a nerve-racking occasion. I raced through Bolingbroke's first speech without difficulty, but when I came to his entrance in the lists – 'Harry of Hereford, Lancaster, and Derby am I' – I tripped over my tongue, pronounced 'Hereford' as 'Hertford', and came to a halt. 'That was wrong, wasn't it?' 'Quite wrong,' said John, smiling. I took a deep breath and began again.

John, even at the first reading, was as near perfect as I could wish or imagine. Ninety per cent of the beauty of his acting was the beauty of his voice. To this day I can see no way of improving on the dazzling virtuosity of phrasing and breathing which was Gielgud's in the cadenza beginning:

Draw near,
And list what with our council we have done.

English actors, observed the great French actor Coquelin, have turned into its own defect their national virtue, a passion for originality. Yet Irving, when he was about to play a part made famous by Frédéric Lemaitre, could write to a friend: 'You said you might have a few bits of business of the immortal Frederick. I never saw that great actor, but everything he did would be well worth consideration.' Fourteen years after the Queen's season, when I played *Richard II* at Stratford, some reviewers – amongst them Ivor Brown – found traces of Gielgud in my performance. I do not see how it could have been otherwise.

A passion for originality seized Guthrie, who directed *The School for Scandal*. There was a tendency for a director who wished to impose his mark upon a classical play to set the action in some different era from that in which it was written. Tony set *The School for Scandal* in the 1790s, so that one could almost hear the distant rattle of tumbrils. One thing bothered me considerably: John, as Joseph Surface, was faultlessly dressed in grey watered silk, while I, as his younger brother, Charles, appeared as a 'bumpkin come to town', as one critic put it. And yet Joseph expressly says that he is a fop 'only in his books', and Charles is said to be in debt owing to his extravagance, amongst other things, in his dress.

Once again, as in *The Country Wife*, I found myself at odds with myself. It was on such occasions that I found that, despite what discipline I had learned at Liverpool, my amateur training was still a distinct handicap. I was used to the easy approach of four or five months in which to rehearse.

I was, I suppose, scarcely surprised when John informed me that Michel wanted me to play Baron Tusenbach in *Three Sisters*. Michel, said John, wanted Tusenbach played as a character part. 'Fine,' I said, thinking that Michel obviously did not want me as Andrei and perhaps not particularly as Tusenbach. It would have been absurd to say that I was disappointed with the part. John himself had played the Baron in Komisarjevsky's production. Komis had directed the play with his usual sleight-of-hand, but since he was a Russian, everyone took his word as gospel. His *Three Sisters* was a highly romantic affair, with the ladies in crinolines and Gielgud as a handsome young lover who is killed in a duel.

We gathered together for the first reading. There are certain plays whose beginnings have an echoing quality. I can never listen to the opening of *Hamlet* without a shiver running down my spine:

> Who's there?
> Nay, answer me. Stand and unfold yourself.

'Unfold' has a resonance and depth of meaning which is almost wasted in this opening exchange. The same lambent quality is to be found in the opening few moments of *Three Sisters*. (The very number 'three' has an incantatory magic.) Listening to Gwen Ffrangcon-Davies as Olga that morning, I felt the same authentic thrill as when, a small boy in the gallery at Portsmouth with Uncle Willie, I had glued my eye to my rolled-up programme, waiting for the curtain to rise.

My own reading was rather sentimental and banal. I tried to apply to the part everything I had learned from my reading of Stanislavsky. I wanted more than anything to impress Michel. But as the days went by, I could see that he thought very little of my work. When he gave me a note or asked me a question, I would answer with a show of brightness but with a miserable lack of confidence within myself.

One day, when I came to Tusenbach's speech about migratory birds in Act Two, Michel stopped me abruptly. I had assumed the voice and stance of a lecturer, rather pedantic, beside his magic lantern. Michel gestured at me impatiently with his pipe-stem, bringing me to a halt. 'No, no, my friend. You speak as if the lines were important. You speak as if you wanted to make it all intelligible, as if it all made sense.'

'Isn't that what an actor is supposed to do?' I asked, somewhat tartly.

'No,' said Michel.

I thought, to hell with it, and read the speech again, throwing it all away. At once it came to life.

Michel's reaction was immediate: 'There! You see? You 'ave eet!'

I think I was near tears to have this commendation.

From that moment I seemed to grow in Michel's approval. When we came to the dress rehearsal I had a toupée, and a slight paunch, and a pair of gold-rimmed spectacles, which, besides giving me a slightly owlish countenance, twisted my ears forward. I also painted spots on my face. The effect of this disguise on the company was startling and gratifying. Michel continued to guide me. A week or so after we had opened, he took me aside, pointing out how I had begun to exaggerate certain effects. 'It's beautifully done,' he said, 'but you are underlining, and once you start underlining, it's not art.' No one in the theatre had ever spoken to me like that before.

Rachel had seen an advertisement for a mill and miller's cottage in Essex. We drove down to find a huge tower mill, in about three-quarters of an acre of garden, to be sold for £750. The sails were broken, there were no main services, and the well was not improved by a drum of oil which had fallen down it, obliging us to walk to a pump the other side of the village to fetch pails of water. But we knew we should be happy there.

I had signed the film contract with Gainsborough Pictures, with that all-important clause that I must have six months in every year free for theatre work. During the run of *Three Sisters* Michel had spoken to me about forming a company, mentioning the possibility of *Twelfth Night* and asking what I thought of it. I replied that *Twelfth Night* should be given a long rest. It had been so overworked that that most exquisite of comedies was in need of a holiday. 'Ah!' said Michel. I said I thought it would be impossible to find an adequate cast for the play. Michel smiled and said, 'But what would you think of Peggy as Viola, Ralph as Sir Toby, Larry as Malvolio, Stephen Haggard as Feste, and you as Orsino ... or Sir Andrew?' That, I said, would be an entirely different matter.

I was doing my second film when Michel sent me the script of a Russian play by Mikhail Bulgakov. Called originally *The Last Days of the Turbins*, it was now retitled *The White Guard* in an adaptation by Rodney Ackland, and was to open the season with Michel's company at the Phoenix. It contained a number of excellent parts which might have been written for the company of *Three Sisters* and which perfectly suited Michel's talent for poetic naturalism. There was a wonderful part for Peggy and a fine heroic one for me.

It was a brilliant production but unfortunately it coincided with the Munich Conference and Chamberlain's 'peace in our time', and the play, which dealt with the fortunes and misfortunes of a bourgeois family in the civil war after the Russian Revolution, had to be withdrawn after three weeks. This was a serious setback to our hopes and plans. Bronson Albery had found the financial backing to launch our season. But to convince the backers, still sceptical about the prospects of a permanent company in the West End, we needed the kind of financial success as well as the esteem which *Three Sisters* had enjoyed.

26 October 1937

Michel [I wrote in my diary] came down to the Mill after the matinée last Saturday afternoon. *Twelfth Night*, having to be put into rehearsal so soon, has taken him by surprise and he has not prepared it fully. He prepares extremely thoroughly. A large notebook contains his notes for moves and motives, etc., no random jotting in the margin of a small text, no improvising. His moves and business, though altered sometimes, are nearly always right, very practicable, and never effective at the expense of some other point.

We rang up the Postmistress with elaborate instructions for the invaluable Mrs Brittain [our daily help]. I bought a cheese and some coffee at the French shop behind the Queen's for Michel to take down, feeling that it was important that these things, at least, should be good. Vera drove down with us after the play at night [Vera Lindsay, Michel's friend, a member of the company]. We kept imagining Michel inquiring the way in his delightful and astonishing accent. A very mature and positive person in every way, there is nevertheless something vulnerable about him on which one's affections fasten eagerly, so that one could not bear anything to happen to him. It was a glorious starry night when we arrived.

On Sunday morning it was fine and warm. Michel was in great spirits. I showed him over the Mill. The view from the top door, leading on to the fantail platform, was more stupendous than ever. The clover field opposite the house has been ploughed in the finest straight furrows and looks rich. *Il a un air maritime*, said Michel.

The Sunday papers arrived, which we seized on, to see if Edith's, John's, Sybil's and Emlyn Williams' letter defending *The White Guard* had been printed. It had, but under the heading 'A Helping Hand', which, as Michel said, gave more the impression of what fine chaps the writers were than a leg-up for our play.

Lunch came upon us suddenly. It was all delightful that day. Some time back I should have been so anxious to please Michel that I should have been self-conscious and boring. Now, since quite recently, I feel so much more certain of myself. Knowing his respect for me has helped almost as much as anything.

Vera is the most enchanting creature. In blue trousers, with a sweater and Russian handkerchief on her head, she transforms herself again: she always looks different and always lovely. She and Rachel set each other off like a red and white rose. I thought this when the three of us packed into Michel's car that afternoon. The peace of sitting there with Rachel, whom I have never loved more than these last few days ... '

When we came to rehearse *Twelfth Night*, we found we had a good cast but not a brilliant one. Peggy was Viola. I was Sir Andrew Aguecheek, the part which Jouvet had played in Copeau's famous 1914 production, *Une Nuit des Rois*, brilliantly decorated with business derived from the *commedia dell'arte*. Drawing on everything which Michel remembered of Jouvet, we painted a character who is not simply the butt of all around him, but an ass who knows he is an ass and takes the utmost delight in it. James Agate, the doyen of Fleet Street theatre critics, called me a 'giddy, witty maypole' and spoke of my 'glorious clowning', and then wrote a second review, revising his opinion and saying that, no matter how glorious, my Aguecheek unbalanced the play. Quoting Lamb, Hazlitt, and a great deal of the play, Agate upheld the traditional interpretation of Aguecheek as a butt. I would still defend the perspective we found for the character. But I confess there was some truth in Agate's stricture that it unbalanced the production, if not the play.

Twelfth Night, all in all, was a failure. Michel, a very independent person in all other respects, was still in thrall to Copeau, and his production faithfully followed all Copeau's business. And without the brilliant cast Michel had hoped for – though it was a good cast – his production seemed overloaded and fussy. Audiences were poor; our backers took flight. All our plans for the remainder of the season had to be shelved.

There were several more weekends at the Mill with Michel and Vera. One I remember particularly, after *Twelfth Night* had opened and failed. The plans, the avoiding of excuses, or at least the disguising of them – how happy I felt, underneath my disappointment, to be implicated with such people in misfortune. Or rather I was unhappy, aware that I was unhappy, and content to be so, having good cause, though I had made a personal success and had none of the usual responsibility. Michel, a totally complete and honest character, was neither glum nor dull, as in his shoes I might have been. We only felt he had some secret information about life which he couldn't tell us. That day I remember as clearly in mood as I recall Vera crying and laughing at dinner 'about nothing'. Crying and talking and smiling, and trying to defend herself from Michel's teasing, all at the same time.

With the promise of another addition to the family we left our flat in Bayswater and took a long lease of a house in Clifton Hill, St John's Wood, with a garden in the front, and in the back a magnificent pear tree. I was now being paid well for films, and spent far too extravagantly on satin curtains and fitted carpets, not to mention two chandeliers.

It was here, in the spring of 1939, that we gave a party for the cast after the first night of T.S. Eliot's *The Family Reunion* at the Westminster. Michel was there, and of all the opinions to be voiced that night, it was his I valued most. All our guests having arrived, I took the opportunity of walking him into the garden to hear what he had to say about the production and of my part in it.

Michel had first brought Eliot's play to me, one weekend at the Mill, during the run of *Twelfth Night*. I told him how, after he and the others had gone to bed, I had stood reading the play, tears of fright pouring down my cheeks, so excited that I wanted to wake him up there and then.

> It is possible you are the consciousness of your unhappy family
> Its bird sent flying through the purgatorial flame . . .

It was, to say the least, a difficult play, not the least of whose difficulties was the hero's first entrance. As Lord Harry Monchensey, a modern version of Orestes, I was required to enter into the drawing-room of Wishwood, the family seat, where my family were assembled, not having seen them for eight years, and immediately be transfixed with fear at the sight of the Furies, who have pursued me. Eliot himself has written amusingly about those damned Eumenides:

We tried every possible method of presenting them. We put them on the stage, and they looked like uninvited guests who had strayed in from a fancy-dress ball. We concealed them behind gauze, and they looked like a 'still' out of a Walt Disney film. We made them dimmer, and they looked just like shrubbery outside the window. I have seen other expedients tried: I have seen them signalling from across the garden, or swarming onto the stage like a football team, and they are never right. They never succeed in being either Greek goddesses or modern spooks. But their failure is merely a symptom of the failure to adjust the ancient with the modern.

And their problem, it might be added, is also the problem of the actor who is haunted by them. Only once, late in rehearsal, did I manage to get this extraordinarily difficult entrance right, to convey the fear and the suffering which are necessary without being merely melodramatic. But the harder I tried to recapture the emotion I had experienced at that rehearsal, the more difficult it became. I religiously got myself ready for the entrance well ahead of time, keeping as much as possible out of earshot of the actors playing the preceding scene. I scrupulously followed Komisarjevsky's tip about examining the texture of some object: he had advised his pupils, before they went on stage, to feel very carefully the texture of something – a piece of wood, some canvas – or the temperature of some metal object to achieve that 'circle of concentration' which the actor requires to master his nerves and alert his senses. But the harder I tried, the more completely I failed. Where I should have looked tragic, I looked merely worried. The reason was, quite simply, that I was trying too hard. Michel had told me during the run of *Twelfth Night*, 'You have both comic and tragic possibilities, but at the moment mainly comic.' There and then I had decided that I would be a tragic actor even if I died in the attempt.

I mentioned all this to Michel. He spoke kindly of my performance in *The Family Reunion*, and said that my difficulties were not all of my own making. The director, he felt, had made a great mistake in underlining the Greek origins of the play by the use of white Ionic columns and other stylized allusions to the Greece of Aeschylus and Sophocles. And, especially in the latter half of the play, there was a failure of imagination on Eliot's part. Where do Lord Monchensey and his chauffeur go at the end of the play?

I had wrestled with this question in rehearsal for some days before daring to broach it to Eliot himself. 'Well,' he said, 'I think they would probably go off and find jobs in the East End.' They might, but from the tone of his reply it was apparent that he wasn't at all sure.

Eliot had been present throughout our rehearsals. Very occasionally he glanced at the stage, but most of the time his face was buried in the text, as if it were a musical score. Not a word or a line was changed or cut. Once, I ventured to suggest to the director, Martin Browne, that a certain line might sound more human if it were turned around. 'Michael,' he said, with a forgiving smile, '*everything that man does is human.*'

It was at Clifton Hill, in July 1939, that our son, Corin, was born – Corin, the shepherd in *As You Like It*, and (another link with the same play) William, in case Corin should seem too fancy and because William is the most euphonious of all masculine names. We talked of calling him Cornelius, another sweet-sounding name, after his great-grandfather, Roy's father. That Cornelius had a tobacco shop in Drury Lane, and sold tickets for the two licensed theatres. When the authorities tried to stop this anticipation of Keith Prowse, Cornelius gathered his cronies in the stalls of Drury Lane, where at an appointed signal they all raised their newspapers, thus obscuring the stage and nearly causing a riot. Wisely, the authorities gave in.

Monday, 17 July

I got home earlier from the studios [Twickenham, *The Stars Look Down*] on Saturday, and found Rachel not so well, saying she thought she had a chill, feeling 'stopped up' and aching. She went to bed shortly after and had bread and milk for supper. After dinner, with 'Mac' [the nurse who looked after Rachel at Stonefield when she had Vanessa], I went up to her, brought the wicker chair down from the nursery and read her two chapters of *Lark Rise*, an enchanting book which Edith was reading when I saw her last. We said goodnight at 10.30, but I was some time getting to bed and not inclined to sleep, having a free day the next day for the first time for a fortnight.

At about 11.15 I went in to see Rachel again as her light was still on, and she said she thought she had started, as she had had pains, tightening and definite, twice since 10.45. We waited and talked, wide awake and now full of excitement, until about twenty minutes off midnight, when the pains recurred, regularly. So I called Mac, who had been asleep about three-quarters of an hour. She and I arranged the room, with oilcloth one side of the bed. I stayed up till one. Mac dressed, in uniform now.

Then I thought I'd better sleep a little, expecting I'd be woken within the next few hours. But it was 8 by the time I woke. Rachel had had pains regularly all night, dozing between, but increasing in power. We decided to ring for Dr Broadbridge. He came just before 9, a jolly little man in Wellington boots and a tennis shirt under his mac.

I had some breakfast. Shortly after, he came down and said it was all going fine and would be over in about an hour. At first I heard nothing but feet moving about, but when I went into the hall I could hear my darling Rachel crying with pain, not loud, high and suppressed. I wandered about, looking out into the garden, thinking the silliest thoughts, including the observation that I was watching myself, which I detested. I kept being sure it was a girl coming, to forestall my disappointment. Then I heard Rachel's voice groaning, very low and hoarse, like an animal. Then she said, in the middle of a cry, 'I'm so sorry,' which wrung my heart. The housemaid kept going up and down the stairs, as about her job. Each time I heard her coming down I thought it was the doctor or the nurse, and went into the hall. Then there was a lull, and I heard the baby crying, and thought, they know what it is, but I don't, I must know, they must tell me.

There was no sound from Rachel for some minutes, and I stood in the hall. Then I heard her voice, no longer in agony, and began to go upstairs. At last I couldn't wait any more, and hearing her say my name, called out, 'Rachel.' Then again. Then the doctor came to the door and said I could come in: 'It's a fine boy.'

Rachel and I hugged each other, crying with happiness and relief. And I saw him in the cot, wrapped round in a woollen sheet, wrinkled and ugly and matted with the thick paste he had been lying in. Rachel couldn't see him from the bed and we lifted the basket down for her.

Later I saw him bathed for the first time, saw his cord tied a second time, and wrapped up in a little package on his tummy. His little tongue was bright red like a wood strawberry, and his parts seemed enormous compared to the rest of him. He weighed 8 pounds less $\frac{1}{4}$ oz.

XI

FROM THE moment of my arrival in London I had been pursued by the films. But for a time I had resolutely refused all temptations from that quarter. Not that I had any objection to films as films. Quite the contrary; I had been addicted to them ever since the days when I was taken to see Annette Kellerman, the aquatic actress, emoting under water in a stuffy bioscope which had formerly been Terry's Theatre in the Strand. Towards the end of the First World War I saw *Intolerance* at the Stoll Opera House in Kingsway and walked home with Mother whilst searchlights picked out the German aircraft overhead, which somehow seemed much less real than Griffith's masterpiece. *The Rink*, *The Tramp*, *Shoulder Arms*, *The Kid*, Rod La Rocque, Laura La Plante, and the early Garbo pictures which, later as a schoolboy at Clifton, I saw at the cinema in Whiteladies Road – all these and many others I saw and loved.

As an undergraduate film critic on *Granta* I solemnly predicted that talkies would never last or, if they did, that they would be the ruin of the cinema. It was here that I came into contact with two good friends, Humphrey Jennings and Basil Wright, later to become great names in the documentary films of the 1940s. I remember vividly certain scenes of what must have been Wright's first film, which he shot himself – with, I suppose, some help, for he was also the protagonist – in sixteen-millimetre. It was a naïve little story of a young fellow from the country who came up to town for the day and got so confused by the London traffic and the noise and all the rest of it that he lost his nerve, his reason – represented by a taut frayed string which broke – and finally his life, when he was knocked down by a motor vehicle of some sort – a bus, I fancy – somewhere near Hyde Park Corner. I wish this piece of juvenilia still existed. I remember the general impression vividly, and it had a few of the lyrical touches which distinguish some of Wright's mature work, such as in *The Song of Ceylon*.

As Mr Horner to Edith Evans's Lady Fidget in *The Country Wife* at the Old Vic (1936).

With Edith Evans in *As You Like It*, at the Old Vic. I can think of one prescription only for any young actor who is to play Orlando: fall in love with your Rosalind (1936).

Edith Evans as Rosalind. 'You don't start acting', she told me, 'until you stop *trying* to act. It doesn't leave the ground until you don't have to think about it' (1936).

As Laertes, duelling with Olivier's Hamlet, under Tyrone Guthrie's direction (1937).

With Peggy Ashcroft in *The Three Sisters*. My chief emotion when acting with her was the same as when acting with Edith: a feeling of great safety and great freedom (1938).

With Margaret Lockwood in my first film, *The Lady Vanishes*. I, who believed that in good acting there must be a continual stream of improvisation, began to think that this business of hitting chalk marks was a very mechanical, second-best thing indeed. From Hitchcock I learned to do as I was told and not to worry too much (1938).

As Charleston in *Thunder Rock* at the Globe Theatre (1940).

In the Royal Navy. I'm the troop leader, sitting in the first row, centre (1941).

With Anatol de Grunwald, Paul Sherriff, Anthony Asquith, John Mills, Terence Rattigan and Basil Radford on the set of *The Way to the Stars* (1944).

The Redgraves.

Being welcomed to Hollywood by Fritz Lang. There must have been a dozen or more photographers who had made the journey out to Pasadena to photograph Fritz in his camel-hair coat and off-white fedora and me in my brand-new suit from Saks Fifth Avenue (1947).

In *Secret Beyond the Door*. Even Fritz Lang couldn't make a silk purse out of a sow's ear, and this was a sow's ear and a half. I could never bring myself to see it (1947).

Around the corner from Wright's rooms, the Cambridge Union Film Society showed us some of the great Russian silent-film classics, and I think I saw most of these. I remember an especial fondness for *Turk-Sib*, a documentary about the creation of the Turkestan-Siberian railway, with its remarkable shots of the irrigation of the desert and the steady push forward of the iron way across the barren wastes. Before this, as a student at Heidelberg, I had seen, several times, *The Student of Prague*, *The Golem*, the Fritz Lang *Nibelungen* saga, the early silent films of the demonic, elegant Conrad Veidt, and the astonishing, unforgettable young Elisabeth Bergner.

I do not wish to give the impression that I was solely addicted to the great Continental silent classics. If I mention them more than the *Ben-Hurs*, the *Big Parades*, the Clara Bows, which I devoured just as avidly, it is simply because, in some aspects, they are more memorable.

With all this it may seem a little odd that when at last I decided to become an actor, I should have been so aloof towards the cinema.

But I was a stage actor, and at that time there was a gulf between the stage and the screen. Not an unbridgeable gulf: Olivier and Ralph Richardson made films, but only Charles Laughton took films, especially English films, seriously. Films, Ralph wrote to me when he heard that I'd been offered a contract, 'are where you sell what you've learned on the stage'. And besides, the actors I most admired – Edith Evans, Peggy Ashcroft, John Gielgud – had either done no films at all or only one or two, and those one or two had done nothing to enhance their great reputations.

I was playing in *Three Sisters* when at last I agreed to do a test, for *The Lady Vanishes*, which was to be directed by Alfred Hitchcock in a few weeks' time at Islington Studios. Having taken my decision, I spent a sleepless night on it. With the proviso that I should have six months a year free for stage work, I succumbed and signed a contract.

Of course, to do this I had to have Gielgud's permission, since it would mean leaving the company before the last play of the season, *The Merchant of Venice*. I asked Peggy Ashcroft whether she thought John would mind. She begged me to think again. John cautioned me that it might be thought that I was leaving having played my best parts. (True, only Bassanio was to come, and I didn't relish Bassanio.) But the more that they and other members of the company sought to make me change my mind, the more I thought I had the right to go ahead, provided Gielgud should not positively say no. Edith lamented, 'I'm disappointed only because you do not see that *all that* [films] will come later,' and she thought there was no sense in rushing things. Michel was not so censorious. The French cinema, after all, had its great directors – Renoir, Ophüls, René Clair – and great actors like Jouvet had given many fine performances on film. But he warned me to be careful. He had seen many actors, he said, who had signed film contracts grow to expect a life of luxury and accept parts which were not worthy of them.

All of this was good advice in its way, and I have repeated it myself to younger actors many times since. But I stuck to my decision. I must resist the temptation now to justify it overmuch with hindsight. To say that *The Lady Vanishes* became one of the classics of the screen; that the British cinema was soon to enjoy a renaissance; that the theatre in 1938, with honourable exceptions, of which the Queen's company was undoubtedly one, was at a low ebb, and that for years to come it would continue to suffer for want of an infusion of new creative writing – all this would be true, yet I felt at the time, for all the stubbornness with which, having made up my mind, I stuck to it, that I had made a mistake.

Having at last succumbed to the blandishments of Gainsborough Pictures (1928) Ltd, I found from reading my papers that I was to be 'teamed' with a very popular actress who was soon to head every annual popularity poll for the cinema and to acquire the sobriquet of 'the first lady of our screen'. This was somewhat alarming to me and, I dare say, to Margaret Lockwood.

We were introduced at a charity film ball at the Royal Albert Hall, where we danced together and were photographed in a tight embrace which suggested that, to say the least, we knew each other quite well. My first day's work at Islington consisted of a scene which was designed to show how boy meets girl and, as everybody who has ever seen Hitchcock's films knows, boy must meet girl in a way that is unusual and, if possible, 'cute'. The girl, a rich heiress stranded in a Middle European hotel, has been arrogant enough to persuade the manager to turn the young man out because he, a student of folk music, and his companions have been making far too much noise dancing in his room, which is above hers. The young man is evicted and, in revenge, makes his way into the girl's room, announcing, with a degree of arrogance and bad taste which certainly caps hers, that he is going to spend the night there.

Cinema-goers today are much wiser in the techniques and mysteries of film-making than we were then. I had no idea how fortunate I was, on my first day's work in the studio, to be given a scene from the beginning of the film and not to have to plunge into some climactic adventure three-quarters of the way through the film. What I did discover that first morning was the want of that quality essential to good acting on the stage: the rapport between artists who have worked together for at least as long as the rehearsal period. From the actor's point of view, it is possibly the gravest disadvantage of acting for the camera that one must do an important scene with someone one has never acted with, perhaps never even met, or, as with Margaret Lockwood and myself, met only briefly and in somewhat artificial circumstances. After some initial parrying, Margaret and I got along well, though we remained suspicious of each other for some time. She must have understood, though she was too kind to reproach me for it, that my mind and my feelings were a long way away from acting in films. I respected her professionalism, as I respected Hitchcock's, yet secretly I saw little to praise in it.

The next thing I learned on this my first morning was rather surprising to me; indeed, I expected the very opposite. It is generally supposed that acting for the stage involves a number of artificial gestures and movements which the actors cannot conceivably use in everyday life, but that is not so. In the theatre it is not only possible but essential for the actor to find a sequence of physical movements which – allowing for certain conventions such as raising the voice when playing upstage – seems completely natural to him. Indeed, a break in the flow of his physical movements can destroy the stage actor's sense of inner reality. It was not at all the same in front of the camera. I soon learned that one was frequently obliged to stand much closer to one's partner than one would ever do in ordinary life, or balance one's voice to a more even level because the microphone could not 'take' a sudden change of volume. Not only that, but every movement and every position, from one camera angle to the next, was subject to a series of slight variations, or 'cheats', to compensate for the disorientation which the spectator in the cinema would otherwise feel as the camera shifted from one place to another. Again, this would not be news to a generation of film-goers who take it for granted that if Alan Ladd kissed Sophia Loren he would be standing on a box, or if Robert Ryan shook hands with James Cagney he might be half-buried in a trench. But it was news to me, and rather disconcerting; I fancy that the amount of such 'cheating' which the camera requires in practice would surprise even the most experienced film-goer.

No one, on that first morning, bothered to explain to me the elementary grammar of filming. On my second morning I felt inspired to give a little lift to one of my takes with some improvised business. 'Cut,' said Hitchcock; and then, when the camera had stopped rolling and the scene had frozen to a halt, 'You can't do that.'

'Why ever not?' I asked. I had thought my business was rather a happy invention. But, it was explained, it would not match the business of the previous take.

So this is filming, I thought, schooling myself to try to repeat exactly what I had done before. I, who believed that in good acting there must be a continual stream of improvisation, began to think that this business of hitting chalk marks, adjusting one's gaze to right and left of camera in order to get the 'eyeline' right, and all the rest of the paraphernalia of filming, was a very mechanical, second-best thing indeed. Today, after many films, good and bad, I would no longer find these constraints inhibiting. I would seek, and on happy occasions I would find, within these necessary conventions, the freedom to improvise and find the creative mood. Then and there, however, I thought, Just say the lines and get on with it.

I have learned most of what little I know about film through my directors. From Hitchcock I learned to do as I was told and not to worry too much. Towards the end of *The Lady Vanishes* there is a short scene in which a foreign agent mentions that his perfect command of English is due to his having been educated at Oxford. Whereupon my character picks up a chair and crashes it down on the unsuspecting agent's head. 'Why did you do that?' exclaims an onlooker. My reply – 'I was at Cambridge' – seemed to me so utterly hackneyed and puerile that I should have dearly liked to ask Hitch to cut it. It was perhaps the biggest laugh in the picture.

Being the brilliant master of the technical side of his script that he was, he knew he could get a performance out of me by his own skill in cutting. He knew that mine was a very good part, that I was more or less the right type for it, that I was sufficiently trained to be able to rattle off my lines, and that, mercifully, since I was aware that not even the cleverest cameraman in the world could make me look like Robert Taylor, I was never particularly camera-conscious. But he also sensed that I found the whole atmosphere of filming uncongenial, to say the least, compared to the theatre, where I was playing every night with a remarkable cast. Besides his trick of casting against type, which he managed often with great success, he would use 'shock' tactics, believing, not always correctly, that actors take themselves too seriously, and that those who have an infinite capacity for taking praise will sometimes perform better if they are humorously insulted. He evidently thought I had a romantic reverence for the theatre, and he could see that I had the newcomer's disdain for the working conditions of the studio. I do not know whether his famous 'Actors are cattle' remark was coined for my benefit, but I well remember his saying it in my presence. In time I grew to like him, though I confess I never warmed to the peculiarly dead-pan humour which was his hallmark, on screen and off.

By general consent *The Lady Vanishes* is the masterpiece of Hitchcock's English period, possibly of all his films. Yet I confess I saw it through mud-coloured spectacles. The melodramatic touches – a hand pushing a flowerpot off the edge of a balcony, so that it lands precisely on an unseen person's head, the lifting of a nun's skirt to reveal a pair of shoes from the Rue de la Paix – all this seemed . . . no, I had a prejudice against Hitchcock.

I was sitting in the make-up chair on my third morning, brushing the sleep from my eyes, when a voice behind me said, 'They tell me this is your first film. I have made fourteen in Hollywood, and boy! is it a grind!'

It was Paul Lukas, an actor I greatly admired and liked, and in the long waits between each set-up, he and I discussed the horrors of film-making.

One morning when the film was well-advanced, Paul found me again in the make-up room. He came towards me with a severe frown on his face and then, with elaborate courtesy, took my hand and kissed it. English actors are not accustomed to kissing hands at seven-thirty in the morning. The gesture arrested me, as did, even more so, his next remark.

'You're a real actor! Why did no one tell me? I saw you in *Three Sisters* last night, and boy! you're a great actor. But here, my friend, you're not even trying.'

'No,' I said, 'as a matter of fact I find it intensely boring.'

'But, my dear boy, it's all going in the can. Once the director has taken the last shot of a scene it's too late to wish you could do it again. It's all in the can!'

From that moment I started to act. I could not bring myself to see the film until fifteen years later, but when I did I could detect, even at that distance of time, the moment when Paul had pulled me up and I had started to try.

After the disenchantment of working with Hitchcock, I was almost drowned in the milk of human kindness proffered me by Paul Czinner. Remembering those happy hours in the dingy little cinemas of Heidelberg, I could hardly believe that his wife Elisabeth Bergner, one of my goddesses, should be there beside me on set. Paul sensed this and did everything possible to put me at my ease, flattering me in a thousand subtle ways to make me believe I was good enough to play opposite my adored Elisabeth. It was Gainsborough Pictures, when they leased me out to Paramount for *Stolen Life*, that insisted I should have equal billing with Bergner, even though not a single foot of film on me had been yet shown in public. To my embarrassment Paramount agreed. To my even greater embarrassment they agreed to Gainsborough's other stipulation that I should be paid a huge sum, almost ten times my salary with Gainsborough, the difference to be shared between Gainsborough and me. This almost wrecked the deal. I was so shocked by these manoeuvres that I told Paramount I wasn't interested in the money, I simply wanted to do the film, and I should be returning my half of the ransom which Gainsborough had extracted. This I did for several weeks, until someone pointed out that I should still have to pay income tax on it and might find myself at the end of the year regretting my gesture. It was my first introduction to the sometimes lunatic economics of the cinema.

Czinner was an imperfect perfectionist. He explained very carefully to me his view of the relationship between the actor and the camera, which was, roughly speaking, that if you shot sufficient feet of film, some of them must be in the right direction. He printed all the takes, and there were usually a great many, of all the shots. He said that by frequent close cutting and the selection of a look from one take, a line from another, and a particular, though perhaps quite irrelevant, expression from a third, a performance was very often much richer than the actor felt it to be, even in his best take. He personally directed the editing of the film, and no editing was begun until the entire shooting was completed.

Most of these feet were, quite naturally, focussed on Elisabeth. In common with most great artists, she demanded excessive consideration. In her case this meant above all the right not to face the camera until the sun was well over the yard-arm. Those brimming eyes and childlike features demanded many hours of lying in bed. Such conduct made her the subject of much exasperation, as it did years later with another great Hollywood actress. But not from me.

The publicity and the huge posters linking my name in letters ten feet high with this goddess went to my head. It is hard to describe the impact of a large poster on a little conceit. I know that in my case I was first flattered and then alarmed to find fans fighting in the gutter for my cigarette stub when I went to open a new cinema in Slough. Not one of my pictures had yet been shown. Perhaps not much harm is done if one retains a sense of humour. It was Sam Behrman who remarked – he, Rachel, and I were driving into Leicester Square for the gala opening of my picture *The Years Between*, and as we rounded the corner a frenzied cheering began and the full force of a searchlight hit me square in the face – 'Wonderful the way they get so much on the head of a sixpence.'

XII

THE OLD VIC in the autumn of 1939, on the eve of the Second World War, was to present its programme in 'a new repertory system', alternating its plays on different nights throughout the week. Not only that, but – was there no limit to Guthrie's experiments? – the same leading part would be played on different nights by different actors. I was to share the main parts with Robert Donat and would be, said the *Evening News*, 'the youngest star ever to lead the company at the Vic'.

The approach of war brought with it the finest summer we had enjoyed for years. Donat and Constance Cummings were to open the season in August. I was to join the company in January, having completed my film commitments. Meanwhile I was eager to begin my preparations.

I remembered that Michel had told us how, when he was preparing *Three Sisters*, he had consulted Stanislavsky's widow in Paris. One of my parts was to be Uncle Vanya, and I decided to follow Michel's example by making a pilgrimage to Paris to consult Idyanova.

I had become a disciple of Stanislavsky by chance some two years before. Opposite the Victoria and Albert Museum was a bookshop which specialized in theatre books and magazines such as the American *Theatre Arts Monthly*. It was there that I stumbled on a copy of Stanislavsky's *An Actor Prepares*, which was to light my way for many nights to come. The effect was instantaneous.

I was playing the part of a doctor at the time – it was May 1937 – in *A Ship Comes Home* at the St Martin's. It was the second of three plays I did in quick succession after *As You Like It*, and I felt I was having to learn the art of making bricks without straw.

The single set of the play represented the doctor's consulting room, which the director had dressed with a clutter of objects strewn about in profusion. I was half-way through a matinée performance, in the middle of a love scene, when I looked at the mess around me and thought, this won't do, a doctor should be tidy, and set about tidying my room, to the consternation of my leading lady. I was, without knowing it, making the mistake of certain 'Method' actors who say, 'If it's true for yourself, it's true.'

Stanislavsky's widow, I had been warned, spoke very little French and no English, so I took Michel's friend Vera Lindsay, who was Russian by birth, to act as interpreter. We found Idyanova in what was left of Stanislavsky's apartment, sitting by a small table near the window, with her back to the light, which streamed on to me. She had been told that I was to play Vanya at the Vic, and was said to be very excited at the prospect of *un comédien célèbre anglais* coming to ask her advice. Her reaction was immediate. With a kind of sob she put both hands to her cheeks, a gesture much favoured by actresses of all nationalities, sobbed again, and then, with the utmost force, cried out, 'No! No!' My heart sank. 'No! No! No!' she repeated, 'No Vanya!' She approached me, and for a moment I thought she was going to lunge at me. Then her face unclouded and she stretched out her arms towards me, and with even greater force repeated, 'No Vanya! Astrov!'

Then all was laughter and tears. Astrov, the young doctor, after all, had been *his* part. For the next three days I took my interleaved copy of *Uncle Vanya* to work in Idyanova's apartment, or to walk in the Bois de Boulogne. I would ply her with questions: 'Why in Act One does Astrov say . . . ?' 'What does he mean by . . . ?' And Vera and she would go into a huddle, and after a great deal of talk to and fro, Vera would extricate some meaning, as often as not sibylline in its simplicity: 'Because he is bored.'

However, not only did I not play in *Uncle Vanya*, but the whole season turned out to be a season that never was. As devised by Guthrie, Donat was to have played Macbeth and Romeo, and I, besides doing Richard II and Vanya, should take over one of Donat's parts for the second half of the season. Uncertain which to choose, I asked Michel's advice and he plumped for Romeo. Edith thought I should take the more difficult choice and play Macbeth.

War came and put an end to my indecision. The nearest I came to playing Romeo was in a much-cut version for television at Alexandra Palace, with Jean Forbes-Robertson, and later, in 1940, at a charity matinée at the Palace Theatre, when Peggy Ashcroft and I flitted across the stage to the satisfaction of James Agate, who wrote, 'Michael Redgrave, with his swift turn of heel, may well turn out to be the Romeo of his generation.'

It was Peggy who suggested me to John Gielgud for Macheath in *The Beggar's Opera*. Rachel and I used to sing at Peggy's house in Campden Hill Road in Kensington, and hearing that John was thinking of an actor-singer for the lead in the Glyndebourne production of Gay's ballad opera, she said, 'Why don't you have Michael? He sings.' It was the winter of 1939. The war had started and no one would go to Glyndebourne, so Glyndebourne was coming to London, to the Haymarket. John agreed to Peggy's suggestion. Glyndebourne, however, needed convincing.

Rudolf Bing, who was to direct the production, came to Southport, where I was touring in *Springtime for Henry* with Rachel, Roger Livesey, and his wife, Ursula Jeans. It was the period known as the Phoney War, and theatres in London, which had closed overnight when war was declared, had now reopened. But there was little chance of our play, which had already had a big success in London and Broadway, coming to the West End.

So I stood on the stage, with an accompanist in the pit, facing Bing and John Christie, the founder of Glyndebourne Opera, in the stalls, and launched into Schubert, then Brahms, then some English folk-songs, and finally Macheath. 'Yes,' said Bing at the end, 'I think you can sing it. But could you sing it eight times a week without losing your voice?' I hadn't considered that. Bing continued, 'I'd like you to work with our voice coach, Jani Strasser.' I thought of Fothergill Robinson, and Munich, and Beibig, and said, 'Well, but I've known people with "natural" voices who ruined them by too much coaching.'

'We won't do that,' said Bing.

And so Jani stayed with me for the remainder of the tour. I took to him tremendously. 'You must have a continual flow of air,' he explained, 'like a waterwheel.' Jani taught through metaphor. His principle was breathing, that you must never sing on a dying breath. When you were getting to the end of a breath, and before you had exhausted it, you deliberately expelled the remainder. In other words, in order to breathe in properly, you had to breathe out. 'Amateur singers,' Jani would say, 'often think a volume of sound must come from the throat. Quite wrong.' He demonstrated. Like some teachers, he had a rather harsh, grating voice, though he would never admit it. 'It's as if you were fishing. You cast your line and start to fish. That's where your note comes from, the end of your line.'

I found Jani's metaphors illuminating, though they were not everyone's cup of tea. Years later, when Olivier was to sing Macheath in Peter Brook's film of *The Beggar's Opera*, I recommended Jani to him.

'That chap you sent me to,' complained Larry, 'says I've got a palm tree growing out of my forehead.'

Macheath has what is known as a well-built-up entrance at the end of Act One. For almost forty minutes, the other principals do little else than sing about him and talk about him, and to top all this expectation John had devised as sensational an entrance for me as anyone could wish: from a cupboard high on the landing, where I was concealed, pistols cocked, I took a leap over the banisters on to the counter of Peachum's shop, another jump to the stage, and straight into the duet 'Pretty Polly say'. This was followed by a short spoken scene, a solo, and then Polly and I sang what may be termed the show's hit number, 'Where I laid on Greenland's coast'. Then, with a few strides to the window, I looked out, tossed a huge red rose to Polly, and blew her a kiss. Exit. Curtain.

We were in our third week at the Haymarket and I was sitting in my dressing-room in the first interval, thinking how lucky I was to have 'got away' with Macheath. I had been too much preoccupied with the singing to lay the proper foundations for my character. John had muddled me in rehearsal, giving me one direction one day and countermanding it the next. On tour I had burned the candle at both ends, sitting up night after night with Ivor and friends from the cast of *Perchance to Dream*, tiring my throat and, against all advice, staying up when I should have gone to bed and called the doctor. And then, to cap it all, I had heard from Rachel that Edith Evans had said my work was suffering. This rumour, I thought, could only have come from John, who had dropped in to see a particularly bad matinée. Why, I wondered peevishly, did he have to choose that matinée?

Never mind, I thought, for the past ten days my acting had been truer and freer than ever before. Preparing to go on for Act Two, I gave myself a quick last-moment appraisal in the mirror: eyes slightly slanted, the corners of my eyes pulled back by two pieces of transparent gauze glued to my temples, joined to a piece of strong elastic beneath my wig.

The Second Act curtain goes up revealing all Macheath's accomplices. Very picturesque they look, too. I come in. They go out, singing 'Let us take the road'. As they go I seize a chair, and sitting astride it in that beloved old swashbuckling posture, chair back to front, with an amber in the fireplace to light me, I peel off my gloves to sing Macheath's best-loved solo, 'If the heart of a man'. It is at such moments, when an actor feels he has the audience in the palm of his hand, that his concentration slips and he hears things which at other times he would ignore. In that split-second pause between the last note of the orchestra's introduction and the first note of the verse I heard a voice from the Circle say, in a stage whisper worthy of Mrs Pat, 'And *who* is this?'

It was a Sunday early in May 1940 during the run of *The Beggar's Opera*:

As I had breakfast in the dining room, Van was playing by herself in the garden. First she would rearrange the two bald dolls sitting in the dolls' pram, then wander round the pear tree in a rhythmic sort of way. She bounced a ball, found two sticks, came up the steps to the dining-room window, and asked to be let in.

When I had to go she wanted to be taken to the nursery, and cried a little at being told to stay in the garden. I had to say a firm 'no'; any attempt to compromise brings on a real temperamental fit of tears.

Rachel and I catch the 10.50 train to Great Missenden, to see Andy and Mother at Chapel Farm. We had got up after being telephoned by Cochran, who rang to say that Shaw had recommended me for a part in a musical version of *The Importance of Being Earnest*. Flattering indeed. I had woken very cross and tired, partly because Rachel had cried when we woke, and partly because we had sat up till 3 or so in the morning, talking things out. For two nights before I had not been home, and though I imagined that Rachel knew where I was and accepted it, I find that I have caused her two days of agony. I felt in despair with myself at my cruelty.

I told Rachel all about Roy and his end: always it returns to this question of a split personality, and I cannot feel that it would be right – even if I had the will-power, which I have not – to cut off or starve the other side of my nature. I complained, weakly, but with some sense, that whereas people go to see plays like *Mourning Becomes Electra* and *The Family Reunion*, they nevertheless think a person morbid who feels as those characters feel and I felt last night, and have felt obscurely before, that

It is possible you are the consciousness of your unhappy family
Its bird sent flying through the purgatorial flame . . .

Chapel Farm is looking wonderful. The skyline of the Chilterns – a great gentle bowl – is now all the tenderest green. Some fruit blossom is still out; there are smells of woodsmoke from the chimney, and sturdy wallflowers in the front beds.

Andy and Mother are very glad to see us. We walk and sit in the brilliant sun, with cocktails, before lunch, and afterwards sleep in deckchairs in the rose garden, while Andy retires indoors. Presently Rachel, Mother and I walk down the lane to a favourite gate. The hedgerows are full of violets, speedwell, bluebells, yellownettles, and pretty things I know no name for.

The winter here was intense, Mother says, they spent all their energies keeping fires alight and themselves warm. Each has been ill in turn. She says that a week or so ago Andy looked very shaky. Two friends, Nellie and Joan, died recently. The house in Edinburgh has been sold.

Peggy's child John is very timid. He needs to be left alone more, and less notice taken of him. His eyes are a beautiful agate colour and his hair pure gold. Mother spoils him and tries too hard to amuse him. He is very fond of her, though. I thought of myself as a child in her arms, and oddly enough I don't remember her being especially affectionate, though always calm and gracious and beautiful.

I sit on the lawn behind the house writing this, and the shadow of the yew hedge round the rose garden has rolled itself like a dark carpet across the lawn. 6 pm. I don't dare face the wireless news. The others have been listening to it, and now Andy, with hat and stick, sits far away at the other end of the lawn. An impressive character.

One Sunday, later in that May of 1940, I was at the Mill by myself, recovering from a bad cold which I had tried and failed to shake off, losing my voice. I used the time to read a play that Herbert Marshall had sent me, Robert Ardrey's *Thunder Rock*. Marshall had worked with Stanislavsky in Moscow, and was now the director of The Neighbourhood, a tiny theatre in South Kensington.

The play's hero, Charleston, has secluded himself in a lighthouse on Lake Michigan, disgusted with a world he sees being helplessly driven towards a catastrophic war. His isolation is invaded by the ghosts of men and women who drowned ninety years before when their ship foundered. Immigrants to America, fleeing from hunger and persecution in Europe, they died believing that all they longed for had been lost. Their despair rouses Charleston. He shows them how, since their death, the battles they fought against exploitation, prejudice, and ignorance have been won, and, in so doing, he discovers new courage and hope. Marshall warned me that *Thunder Rock* had closed in New York after a week, having failed dismally. I thought it one of the most exciting plays I had read.

The air raids had begun, and for a while London's night-life almost came to a stop. All but two West End theatres were 'dark' in the week we opened in June. Crammed into The Neighbourhood's two hundred seats, beneath a perilous glass roof, our audience found a play which seemed perfectly to catch their mood. The critics heaped praise on us, as a sort of national asset. 'A tonic to the mind, and a bath to the spirit,' said the *News Chronicle*. Diana and Duff

Cooper came, and urged that *Thunder Rock* be transferred to a larger theatre. I said that we should like to transfer, and that I would put up my own money if necessary. Duff Cooper said he would see if he could use his new post in the Ministry of Information to help.

Next day came a call inviting me to the Treasury. Two officials met me, and assured me, 'Mr Cooper is very interested in your play.' They would make enquiries to see what could be done to help in the way of finance, though, 'Mark you, if this comes up in the House, we should simply deny it.' Their enquiries proved fruitful; and *Thunder Rock*, transferred to the Globe, was so successful that the Treasury was repaid.

The Blitz began in earnest. The sirens would sound, and we would stop the play. I would step down to the front of the stage and explain to the audience where they could find the nearest shelter if they wished to leave; we would resume the play when the raid was over; meanwhile, for those who wished to stay, we would have a sing-song. I would sing and lead the audience in the choruses, with the indefatigable Kitty Black, Binkie Beaumont's secretary, at the piano. Soon these interludes became almost as popular as the play itself, with audiences from the other theatres round about coming to join in.

Who's Who wrote to me for the first time, asking for an entry. A well-known hostess invited me to her luncheons. *Picture Post* put me on their front page. I felt I had arrived.

XIII

EARLY IN 1941 I was sitting under the pear tree in our back garden at Clifton Hill when I opened what appeared to be a circular. It was a manifesto of sorts against the War, and two slogans caught my attention (as well they might): 'a people's war' and 'a people's peace'. These were points 9 and 10 of what was an appeal to rally the forces of common sense to 'a People's Convention'.

I thought, Here's a good socialist document. I had no idea of being a pacifist. My first reaction to the War had been, 'What a nuisance, what an interruption', but I expected to be called up when my age group was due and I was intending to join the Navy. I thought of myself as a socialist, though an inactive one. I signed the manifesto.

I did not have long to wait before I was put to the test. I learned that it was rumoured that all signatories to the People's Convention would be banned from broadcasting by the BBC. Sure enough, I was bidden to present myself for an interview at Broadcasting House, where two very polite gentlemen met me in the lobby.

I recorded our conversation, and the events of the next few days, as fully as I could in my diary. The affair itself was short-lived, but for some years to come I was haunted by the words 'People's Convention'.

Tuesday, 25 February

Day off. [I was filming *Atlantic Ferry* at the time.] I called at Bentinck House, an annexe of the BBC, where I was met by a Mr Streeton and another official, a lawyer presumably. I knew what they wanted because Lew Stone, who is also a supporter of the People's Convention, had already been to see them. They said that the Governors had decided that the People's Convention was not in the national interest and would like to know where I stood regarding it; that I need not answer at once, could have time, etc.

I replied that I didn't need time, and that I took the view that since the People's Convention is not suppressed by the Government, but is a perfectly legal, constitutional method for the People of England to express themselves, it was not for the BBC to censor it. The official thanked me for making my position so clear.

I said, 'I take it that that being the case, you do not wish to use me as a broadcaster?'

'Yes.'

'And how does that affect my contract on Sunday to sing?'

'Oh . . . I was not aware of any outstanding contract – but *that* will be *quite* all right, Mr Redgrave.'

We shook hands very amicably and I was seen to the lift.

I had a moment or two of regret afterwards that I had made the going so easy for them, and as usual a crowd of things came into my head that I might have said. But perhaps it was best so.

Rehearsed with Berkeley Fase [composer, supporter of the People's Convention] at Weekes. Actually we talked indignantly most of the time. Then lunch, then Marlene Dietrich in *Seven Sinners* and, after dinner at Scotts restaurant, to *A Long Voyage Home* [film] with him and Geoffrey Parsons. Then to a drab little nightclub, the Nightlight, with subdued light, subdued talk. The proprietress, who used to run the Torch, made much of me. Told me that Barbara Mullen had been in, who had said that the revival of *Thunder Rock* was awful. She didn't think Walter Hudd would be good in my part, as he was 'too political to be an artist'. I was almost too bored with this old theme to argue and knew that she'd only said it because it was the sort of thing she thought I'd like her to say.

Wednesday, 26 February

At the studio. The opening sequence, launching the *Gigantic*. Read Lenin's *Socialism and War*. My eyes, already strained by those two films yesterday, look very bloodshot under the arcs.

Thursday, 27 February

With Marione Everall [later married to Feliks Topolski] to lunch at Café Royal, where we sat with Lionel Fielden and his Indian friend, whose name, even after asking twice, I cannot get. We talked of the People's Convention. Both Lionel and friend were very scornful of anything that had to do with Pritt [D.N. Pritt, K.C., one of the leading sponsors of the People's Convention, and a well-known fellow-traveller with the Communist Party]. They were very interesting on India, but it was quaint to notice that the Indian, who seemed a great advocate of democracy, became almost feudal on the question of servants. He despised the English for asking their servants, 'Would you please do this; might I have that,' and said that at home he ate when he liked, even if it were in the middle of the night, and no questions asked. They talked of Nehru as the only man who could unite India, of Ram Gopal, whom I've never seen, and Uday Shankar.

Lionel said the BBC ban would make no difference, and that I must do some records for him. But it was depressing to find him, with all his knowledge, initiative, and I am sure, guts, apparently believing that nothing could be done to get us all a bit straighter. . . .

Marione and I went to some bookshops. She wanted *Socialism and War*, but Collet's was closed. Then to the National Gallery to see the exhibition of war paintings, monstrous for the most part, though some of Topolski's are superb. He compares very well with most, and noticeably well with Ardizzone, whose pictures in the mass – and there were a mass of them – show how slickly he composes. No life or movement. It is painful to see such an accomplished artist struggling to express movement. Amidst the general Royal Academy level I found the right perspective for the Henry Moore shelter pictures, which I couldn't 'get' before.

Sunday, 2 March

Rehearse at the Scala, broadcast at 12.30 (farewell!) with Debroy Somers, etc. Sang 'If the heart of a man' and Berkeley's 'Smile from a stranger'. A good reception.

Monday, 3 March

Work again. Only two days' work last week – when will this picture end? Paper (*News Chronicle*) rings up about the People's Convention.

Tuesday, 4 March

News of the BBC ban! The *News Chronicle* gives it front page top headline with a photo of me, pushing Moscow's warning to Bulgaria into second place. A bit breathtaking. There's no mention in the *Telegraph*, though they rang after midnight, wanting confirmation of the *News Chronicle* story and expecting Rachel to wake me up.

The phone goes all day. A meeting is arranged at the Workers' Music Association at 6 o'clock for a protest. Larry Olivier rings up – not having seen the papers – to ask if it's true. He says, 'I thought that sort of thing was what we were fighting against. It's certainly what I came home to

137

fight against.' Benn Levy [playwright, author of *Springtime for Henry*] also most sympathetic.

Silence on the subject at the studio. They had been sufficiently worried by Jonah Barrington's article in the *Express* some weeks back which foreshadowed the ban, written in that good *Express* style that by ellipsis made it sound as if one were both pacifist and communist.

Now I can see them whispering about it, but not one person except Culley Forde [wife of Walter Forde, *Atlantic Ferry*'s director] speaks of it to me. Rachel goes to the meeting in my stead, and says it goes well.

Wednesday, 5 March

Front page again, with picture of Rachel at Workers' Music Association meeting. The Council for Civil Liberties is to hold a protest meeting.

Jack Dunfee [my film agent] says that Black and Ostrer [producers of *Atlantic Ferry*] are 'wild' and don't know what to do. He suggests that I meet them at Claridges for a drink this evening, but there, in Jack's room, I found only Marcel Hellman [Hellman was to produce my next film, *Jeannie*].

I make my position clear, that I know what I'm doing. Black and Ostrer have said it's like the Gracie Fields case. [There had been a great patriotic hue and cry against Fields in the press when she went to live in America with her Italian husband.] Hellman doesn't agree. He says I have the chance to become 'the most popular man in England'. Every one of them says, 'They are using you.'

Hellman is very nice on the whole. I offer him back the *Jeannie* contract. He says he would hate to have to think of such a thing. He says, 'We must do something.' Suggests drafting a statement, getting Oscar Deutsch [part-owner and managing director of the Odeon circuit] to invite the press to a cocktail party on Monday to tell them about my joining the Navy, etc. I don't think this will help but I agree to let him go ahead.

Dinner with Rachel at Café Royal. David Henley, Rank's press officer, most sympathetic – says he will organize Donat, Olivier, [Leslie] Howard, Vivien Leigh, etc., not to broadcast. Somehow I doubt this also.

Thursday, 6 March

A late call for the studio. I attempt to go to the *Star* office in Bouverie Street with my letter, but the driver has no idea of the direction and I'm afraid of being late, so I phone the letter from the Post Office in Euston Road.

At the studio I find I'm not wanted (of course) till after lunch. About two shots, of *Anne of Liverpool* deck scenes. Someone has chalked 'Make Peace' between my names on my canvas chair. I laugh this off, but do not sit in the chair. Presently it is wiped off.

The *Star* contains my letter in full, with photo and large heading: 'Michael Redgrave replies'. Nothing in the other papers – no mention of the ban at all.

Call at Grosvenor Square to see Carol Reed [he had just directed me in *Kipps*], who is kind and sympathetic. Collette Harrison, Rex's wife, is there, also Harold French, who is to direct *Jeannie*. I explain how sorry I feel for Carol, because of possible bad publicity for *Kipps*, and that I know I'm committing a sort of professional suicide.

To the Ivy, to meet Rachel and Marcel Hellman. I find them outside in the dark as the Ivy doesn't open in the evenings nowadays. With them is Joseph Pole. Dinner at Hungarian Czardas. Pole – who handles publicity at United Artists – talks at great length about the Communist Party and the People's Convention. He's worked in the Labour Party – I think – for years, and was a Conscientious Objector in the last war. He says that he and his wife knew, just as everyone in the Labour Party knew, when first they saw the list of signatories, that it was a C.P. affair. He explains how they always use another organization, and then drop it when it suits them. I listen with alarm, he obviously knows what he is talking about. He shows me a letter he has drafted. Although very tired I take it home and rewrite it.

Friday, 7 March

Telephone the *News Chronicle* to hold my letter, similar to the one I wrote to the *Star*. Rachel takes the new letter to be typed at Marcel Hellman's office.

Meet Geoffrey Parsons and Berkeley Fase at the Nightlight, where I am not so well received as before, but maybe I'm imagining this.

I tell Geoffrey that I must make my position clear, and explain about my letter to the papers. He talks more or less convincingly. Says that it all looks hopeless, but these things so often do until the moment comes when they change. I charge him, as a member of the C.P., with their being liable to drop the People's Convention when they have no further use for it. He says, 'So what? Aren't the Government "using" the Labour leaders, and won't they drop them when it suits them?' These sorts of arguments and parallels exhaust me and I begin to distrust them.

Saturday, 8 March

My letter in the *News Chronicle*, beneath a protest from 40 M.P.s, J.B.Priestley, Harold Laski, etc.

In the afternoon to studio for tedious and tiring post-synching. Culley Forde very angry about the 'Make Peace' episode, about which Rachel had rung her up.

I was becoming more and more irresolute about the stand I had taken. At first I thought, I'll see this through, and for all the studio's anxiety about my future – and their investment – I was inclined to stick to my guns. But the more I thought about the People's Convention, the more ambiguous it seemed. What was its attitude to the War? What would it advocate supposing we were invaded by Germany? How could one answer the charge that it was a C.P. front, on orders from Moscow, following the line of the Molotov-Ribbentrop pact?

One of those who tried to reassure me was the famous geneticist J.B.S.Haldane. A great big burly man, he arrived one afternoon unannounced at my dressing-room at Denham Studios and asked if we could talk. He told me about his experiments on the human body, using himself as a guinea-pig, to determine how far and under what conditions it could withstand temperatures of extreme cold. I knew Haldane was on the board of the *Daily Worker*. I didn't know then, and neither did anyone except the War Office, that he was their leading expert on submarine escape. As to the People's Convention, of which he was also a signatory, I remember little of what he said, except one thing: 'People will soon forget what it was that you put your foot down about. The main thing is that you put it down.'

Another who tried to answer my doubts was D.N.Pritt, who wrote that he had read my letter in the *Chronicle*, and suggested we meet to talk it over.

Saturday, 15 March

To Reading to lunch with Pritt, who meets me in a smart yellow and black car. Reading very peacetime-looking. Pritt very amiable, rather like a schoolmaster. A pleasant drive to a lovely house. Mrs Pritt is warm and friendly, with a rosy face like a nice winter apple. She knows a lot about gardening – they have a beautiful garden with a stream and pond.

We sit in the open, drinking Cinzano. Cold breeze but warm sun. Then lunch, lovely Russian plates on the walls, 'biscuit' from the old Imperial potteries, with Soviet designs. Then coffee in the drawing-room (Russian picture papers with views of marble Metro, Mayakovsky, etc.).

After coffee Pritt and I walk in the garden, including many times round the lawn, talking of the People's Convention. He quotes some alarming rumours of Churchill saying, 'There'll be a few people after this war who'll need machine-gunning,' and says it is thought the Canadians and Poles are being kept for this.

I raise my position re films. He says there's nothing he can do to help. I suggest that the People's Convention must make clear where it stands on the war effort. He agrees, and says the Dean of Canterbury has raised the same point and been convinced. Says it will be good if he can say that the Dean and I are reassured on this point and still staunch.

I quote Geoffrey Parsons' answer when I said that it was held that the C.P. were using the People's Convention as a blind – which was 'So what?' 'So what indeed?' says Pritt. On the way back to the station, referring to actors and politics, and to my present position, he says, 'Well, never mind – perhaps you'll one day be an honoured Artist of the Republic.' Significant remark. Of course it's just the sort of daydream which flatters and pleases me but I think, even at the time, 'No, this is England, not Russia, I think you have got Russia on the brain.'

At home, I confess to Rachel that I'm not much clearer than when I started. In the evening to the Convention dance at the Royal Hotel. A friendly, jolly, atmosphere. . . .

I sing a song, and give the prizes, and there is much applause whenever I am mentioned.

Home, and the 'all clear' goes before twelve to absolve us from fire-watching. A mercy.

Sunday, 16 March

To the Royal Hotel for Convention. A long depressing day, full of disappointment and dismay. I can see very well why the movement is charged with revolutionary defeatism. Everyone who speaks, airs a grievance. . . . I long several times to get up and say, 'But what about the War? What is our attitude to the possibility of defeat? Friendship with the USSR certainly – but England must do better than that.'

The chairman makes a snarling speech, referring obscurely to my letter to the press. At the collection I foolishly give a cheque for 15 guineas, I cannot now think why, but not until the next day did I see the necessity of leaving this false set-up.

My singing record for the Workers' Music Association is played about a dozen times, and I sign about sixty copies.

After dinner I write my speech for tomorrow.

O a sad day.

Monday, 17 March

Lunch at Claridges with Marcel Hellman and Harold French, who express surprise at the 15 guineas – it's all over the front page of the *Daily Mail* – and I can't explain. Black and Ostrer are in the other restaurant but we avoid them. From Marcel's hints of what they have said, I'm furious with them. Ostrer had tried to scare Marcel out of using me for *Jeannie*, really in order that I should do *Spitfire* for him, and *Spitfire* is now off anyway.

Then to Conway Hall for the Council for Civil Liberties meeting. E.M.Forster speaks, Beatrix Lehmann, the Archdeacon of Westminster, and myself. My speech goes well, especially the crack about, 'I've searched hard for a precedent for a politically-conscious actor, and the only one I can find is John Wilkes Booth, who murdered Lincoln.' Both the Ediths – Evans and Hargraves – are there, Rachel, Roger Livesey and Ursula, Benn Levy and Connie Cummings, bless them.

Wednesday, 19 March

Bromyard. [The children were evacuated to Bromyard in Herefordshire to stay with Rachel's cousin Lucy Kempson.] Vanessa calls on me in bed very early, and recites and sings long verses of a hymn, something about 'precious blood', which occurs a lot. Corin wakes me up at 7.30 and yells at his potting. Rachel leaves by the early train for a film test at Ealing Studios, and I get the children up. Corin won't eat much breakfast. He likes everything to be 'in order' and can't understand why I'm there.

We go for a walk, and Vanessa insists on taking her tricycle down into town, which is far too steep, and then up the old road to Mrs Ware's, also too steep. I sing 'Daisy, Daisy', 'Lovely to Look at', and 'Old Man River', vaguely thinking this may counteract 'precious blood'.

Lunch, and Corin consents to eat a jam pancake on my lap. Then to play in the garden, where Vanessa keeps saying she is getting a cold too. I say 'Rubbish' very firmly. She also insists she has something in her toe. I say 'Rubbish' to this, too. After about the fourth complaint, I say, 'All right then, take your shoe and sock off and see what it is.' It is a large thorn. A cold, rather windy day. Nurse Dulcie arrives back just as I am beginning not to cope.

After dinner I persuade Lucy to go to a Spencer Tracy–Hedy Lamarr film, which I know will be bad, by saying that he is always interesting. He is, too. He does some remarkable things.

To study to write letters, to Adams and Pritt, asking that my name be withdrawn from the list of People's Convention supporters.

Churchill made a speech opposing the BBC's broadcasting ban, and it was dropped. The careers of those of us who signed the People's Convention were, so far as I know, unaffected by all the fuss and consternation. The film *Kipps*, about which I had expressed alarm to Carol Reed for fear that its chances of success might be ruined by so much adverse publicity, was well-received. (Years later I detected an echo of the furore which attended my participation in the People's Convention. I was playing Hector in Giraudoux's *Tiger at the Gates* on Broadway in 1956, when I received a request for an interview with someone from the State Department. Obliquely I was given to understand that the subject of our interview would be politics. Somewhat amazed, for the matter had never been raised before on any of my previous visits to the States, I heard myself refer to my C.B.E. 'Was it really likely,' I wondered aloud, 'was it really likely, that Her Majesty would confer membership of such an Order on an *untrustworthy* subject?' This, and a wounded voice, seemed to dispose of the matter.)

Kipps was the third film I made with Carol Reed. He was the gentlest of directors, so quiet that his 'Action!' was almost inaudible. Yet underneath that gentle touch was an iron will which eleven times out of twelve would have its own way. I found that admirable. With Reed I learned for the first time how subtle the relationship between an actor and a director could be. The theatre and acting were in his blood and he was able, with infinite pains and care, to bestow on his actors the feeling that everything was up to them and that all he was doing was to make sure that they were seen to their best advantage.

I cannot say that I became aware of this all at once. Our first film, *Climbing High*, which I made in 1938, a few weeks after *Stolen Life*, had been intended as a song-and-dance vehicle for Jessie Matthews. But the Studio had lost money on her previous film and were looking for economies, so somehow the dances and most of the songs got lost, and what was left could hardly have been redeemed by the combined charms of Cary Grant and David Niven. Certainly my presence as the young millionaire hero didn't help much.

The Stars Look Down, which we shot in the summer of 1939, was much more suited to both our talents. A warm and friendly feeling prevailed, and Reed encouraged me to feel that I had assisted him in the preparation of the film.

He often asked for my suggestions and usually, I think, adopted them in his own fashion. One such occasion was when we were shooting in a narrow street of miners' cottages in Cumberland and I noticed a child sweeping a puddle in the road with a look of rapt determination in its face and sensuous pleasure in every sweep of the broom. Whether this detail is in the finished film I cannot now recall, for by the time the camera came to turn on her the girl's mother had changed her out of her grimy smock into her Sunday best and put ribbons in her hair. I do remember Reed being infinitely tactful about this. He was inordinately considerate and attentive to people's feelings. He had a way of plying you with questions and watching as you answered, his big blue eyes as wide as a child's. His seeming ingenuousness and his repeated exclamations of surprise or incredulity – 'Do you really?' 'That's fascinating!' 'How true!' – would strike one as naïve to the point of absurdity if after a short time one did not become aware that these simple and direct questions were not so simple nor so direct as they seemed. Unwittingly you had supplied him with an answer or a clue to a different question.

Carol ate, drank, and slept cinema. *Kipps* was shot at the Shepherd's Bush studios throughout the 1940 Blitz, and for the duration of the shooting we both took flats in a solid, steel-girdered building, Number 20 Grosvenor Square (now part of the American Embassy), so that we could meet and talk in the evenings. It was a time I remember above all, for its divorce from any reality except that of imaginative work for to face the cameras each morning as a younger man than myself I was obliged to take sleeping pills each night in order to sleep through the noise of the bombardment. And there in the morning on the set would be Diana Wynyard, who had driven through the tail-end of a long raid to have her hair washed and be made up, ready to appear at eight o'clock, ravishingly gowned by Cecil Beaton.

Carol and I sat up late one night discussing Diana, then at the height of her mature beauty. Carol maintained that she had yet to come to terms with her looks, that she was at arm's length from her beauty. 'She needs some man to wake her to the realization of her glorious self. You could help her do that. Why don't you have a shot, Michael? Go on, wake her up, wake her up!' The next day Diana casually informed me that she and Carol had been married a few days before. It was not I who woke her up, if, indeed, such a thing was necessary. But we began a long friendship.

In the evenings we left the Studio ten minutes before blackout and, as we drove home in the dusk, the sirens would start. If they did not, I remember, we were faintly worried. No wonder that my memory of the Blitz is largely of a fictitious Folkestone in Edwardian dress.

It was on one such evening at the end of a day's shooting that my film agent, Jack Dunfee, appeared with a briefcase full of papers. He wanted 'a few signatures', he said, and as we drove home he explained what these were all about. There had been a flourishing British film industry at the start of the First World War, he said, but during the war we had lost the initiative to the Americans, who had snatched the opportunity to swallow up the home product. The

Government was determined not to let this happen again, and wanted to put key actors and technicians under contract.

The papers were to do with a contract for me whereby my call-up would be indefinitely postponed provided I made myself available for whatever films might come my way. I told Jack that I was about to undergo my medical. He pointed out that, at my age, it might prove more useful to make films than mark time in one of the Services. He urged me to accept the contract, and was rather surprised when I insisted that I intended to join the Navy when my age group was called.

'But,' I said, 'I'm not going into the Army.'

'You are, you know,' said the officer, scanning my papers. 'You expressed no preference.'

'I wasn't asked.' And here I stamped my naked foot. Stamping one's foot is always an ineffectual gesture, but to stamp it when starkers is the height of folly. 'It's not too late to change, is it?'

'Why don't you want to join the Army? What Service do you favour?' he said, with heavy sarcasm. 'You're a bit old for the RAF.'

'I know that.'

'Why the Navy? Any special reason?'

'Yes, my wife's family are naval. Her father is the Headmaster of the Royal Naval College at Dartmouth.'

He was clearly a bit impressed by this, so I followed up with 'One of her brothers is a naval lieutenant' – I could see him weakening – 'My wife and I were married in the Royal Naval College chapel at Dartmouth.'

That shook him. 'Were you really? Look,' he said, pointing to the other end of the drill hall, 'you'd better have a word with the Colonel over there. Better put your clothes on first.'

I dressed and looked around for the Colonel. He turned out to be a Colonel of the Marines, and was civility itself. He seemed amused about something.

'You look frustrated,' he said. 'What is it you want?'

I told him, briefly.

'Yes, well,' he said, 'that's simple enough. Only, my dear fellow, you ought to learn that it's one thing to put your foot down, and another thing to stamp it.'

When my call-up papers came, in June 1941, I was in the middle of another film, *Jeannie*. Rachel and I had taken a short lease of a farmhouse owned by the director Gabriel Pascal near Denham

Studios in Buckinghamshire, where I was filming, so that I could spend as much time with the family as possible. Various friends came and stayed with us a few nights. One of them brought news that Paddy Railton, one of my closest friends from Cambridge days, was dying of tuberculosis in a sanatorium in North Wales, and that weekend I took the opportunity of going to see him. His death would leave a dark shadow.

I took the train to Manchester and arranged for a car to take me on to Ruthven the next day. I had asked the Studio to book a ticket for whatever was on at the theatre that night, and was delighted to find that I was to see the second performance of Noël Coward's new comedy, *Blithe Spirit*.

I was on my way to my hotel room when I heard a familiar voice. I did not know Noël, except from one meeting of The Actors' Orphanage committee, of which I was a member and he was President, but now he invited me to join him and the actress Joyce Carey that night in his box. He disappeared during the first interval, and when he came back he seemed rather highly-strung. I ventured to remark with special praise on the actress who played Madame Arcati. Apparently it was the last thing I should have done. Margaret Rutherford was not yet the almost national figure she later became. Noël slaughtered her in one clipped word – 'Amateur!' The house lights went down. A merciful eclipse.

Afterwards we went backstage and Noël introduced me to his other guests. When I told him that I was going into the Navy his manner became suddenly serious and he said that I must come and see him at the Savoy before the Navy swallowed me up. I promised to do so.

XIV

On the night train to Plymouth I slept most of the way. I wondered if I should shave, but decided that my shipmates would almost certainly do no such thing. As I stepped out of the station the sun hit me forcibly as if it were midday, and I blinked as I looked around me. My throat was parched and I longed for a cup of tea. I could not see a café, so I peered inquisitively through the windows of a pub, the Royal Standard, but the blackout curtains had not yet been drawn.

Just as I turned away, a woman appeared at the door with a cup in her hand. 'Want something?' she asked.

'Do you know where I could get a cup of tea?'

For a second or two she looked at me as if trying to identify me. Then she tapped her cup and shot the tea-leaves into the gutter. 'Come on in.'

Inside the dark bar she said, 'I don't make a habit of this, as you can *well* imagine.' I started to say something, but she cut me short. 'Don't tell me,' she said abruptly, 'I know you. I *know* you, very well. It's your face. Well, fancy seeing you. You been on leave?'

'Not exactly. It's my first day.'

'Well ... fancy that.' She moved to where a kettle was boiling. 'They won't believe me when I say I had Michael Redgrave ... There! That's the name, isn't it? ... That I had Michael Redgrave to tea at seven o'clock on a nice fine morning.' She suddenly burst into a short gale of laughter. 'My husband'll have something to say about this.' There were sounds of footsteps coming downstairs. 'Here he is. Bert, look at this gentleman. He's a bloody film star. It's his first day over the road.'

I peered past the blackout curtain and saw a sailor going through the gates of the barracks. 'I think I'd better go and present myself.'

'That's right. We mustn't keep you waiting, must we, Bert? Finish your tea, don't worry, the first four days are the worst, so they say. Then they'll send you to HMS *Raleigh*. Why do some of them call it "*Rawleigh*"?' she added.

'Pleased to meet you, Michael,' said Bert.

Once inside the gate I was given over to a nice young Ordinary Seaman, who told me cheerful details of the air raids as he took me over to the kitting-up mess, a sort of hut building, where about fifty or sixty young men, stokers-to-be, sat about playing cards and reading papers, while at a table two very affable Petty Officers were taking down particulars.

'Oh hello, Michael,' said one, 'sit down and put your bag over there. Have you got a little gas mask? Well, take it out.' He handed me a copy of the Regulations.

'Just arrived, did you?' one of the stokers asked me. 'We've been here three weeks and there's still no clothes.'

The other Petty Officer came up with a Wren on his arm, whom he introduced as his young lady.

'Here's Michael.'

'I know,' she said, 'I wrote to you.'

I thought she meant a fan letter.

'Yes, she sent you your call-up papers.'

'Oh. thanks.'

'I like your pictures,' she said.

That afternoon, and almost every day for the next two months, I wrote to Rachel.

1 July

An extremely nice rating called Siddall took me for a stroll around. The noise and the general confusion . . . it doesn't look as if one would ever make sense of it. Have intimated to a Petty Officer that I don't want to be a coder. He's told me the procedure.

I was warned that unless I fought for it I should find myself without anything to eat at lunch. But this wasn't so, or at any rate I seemed to do all right. Lunch was in fact pretty much what I'd expected.

Afterwards I was introduced to one Needle, who is not a very nice piece of work. Interesting, though. Full of dodges, has a secret hoard of sugar and cigarettes, and warns me to beware of scroungers. Except that Gilbert and Sullivan is the height of his culture, he's like Chester Coote in *Kipps*.

I can sleep out any alternate night (being over 21) – except that in Plymouth there's nowhere to stay. But Needle knows all the places round about where you could come and stay.

Now I'm sitting outside the kitting-up mess and it's very nice and hot. Some of the lads go bathing at Plymouth Hoe in the evening. Not a bad idea at that. The dreaded continual wireless has started. The first four days, as the lady in the pub warned, seem likely to be the worst.

2 July

I leave the kitting-up mess today to go to HMS *Raleigh*, a training barracks across the water. I had been entered as a coder, but got that changed yesterday to an ordinary seaman, which is a tougher job but will lead to a commission eventually. (I put in a request for one yesterday – you have to put in a request for everything, including leave, in the Navy, or else you don't get it.) *Raleigh* is said to be a picnic compared to *Drake* where I am now. Certainly the kitting-up mess is no picnic (though I've had no actual *work* to do as yet). But it's funny, I already feel sentimental about leaving it. The friendliness is indescribable, it could make anything bearable. The ubiquitous, the unfailing Needle goes with me. I begin to like him a lot. An amazing character – a Jew, and I think I told you a Russian by descent – he had been a soldier in the Grenadiers for nine years, and for many years since then a cab driver. His general knowledge astounds me and puts me to shame. Still, I learn quite a lot.

Yesterday we went ashore to the Hoe. Plymouth is beyond belief. London may have greater areas of square feet of devastation, but Plymouth is almost entirely *flat*. But, incredibly, there are still people about, and singing in the pubs, and bathing at the Hoe, and in the evenings dancing on the Hoe.

The attendant at the beachpool told us they no longer hire trunks and towels so we had to watch, and watching soon made us thirsty, so we went for a drink at the Grand. Into the very quiet bar came two lieutenants RNVR, and presently when I went to get an evening paper one of them spoke to me:

'What are you doing in these parts? I didn't know there was a theatre open.'

When I told him, he said, 'Oh, God! how ghastly,' and promptly invited me aboard his ship, which is some sort of motor launch. Name of Bailey.

Yesterday the PO in charge of the kitting-up mess took me aside during a little diversion which consisted of everyone putting on gas masks for half an hour – (an ideal day for it, really 'brillig'. I was reading Pushkin and feeling sorry for the poor buggers who were doing work) – and told me to be careful at *Raleigh*. Because of my height and reputation, he said, I'd be watched more carefully than the other lads, and Newton's example (don't repeat) had to be lived down. Everyone in barracks, it seems, knows about him. But I'm inclined to think it will be easier to follow him than some sort of shining model – by contrast I may

149

seem quite serious and efficient. [Bobby Newton had earned himself a thoroughly black mark, at least in the eyes of the officers. He had managed to gatecrash an officers' party, and when they asked him what he was doing there, he slapped them on the back, saying, 'It's all right, I'm Robert Newton.' Apparently it wasn't all right.]

8 July

Yesterday and today we started in earnest and it's at first quite tough going, especially on the *feet*! I really love most of it, though my new job as class leader takes some of the freedom to enjoy it all away. It's hard to have so much new to learn, as well as getting used to new surroundings, and also to have to assume responsibility for thirty others. I have to see the mess is kept clean, appoint cleaners and cooks (not real cooks – just blokes to hand out the stuff and stow away the plates, etc.), keep order in the mess and also, which is what plagues me most at the moment, relearn all the parade words of command of a section leader so as to march my class past in Divisions. I suppose it will be all right 'when I know the lines'. And the thirty are so mixed, from Needle, who is thirty-six and was in the Grenadier Guards, to some rather half-baked youngsters who don't have any idea of discipline yet. But what is wonderful is to see the classes who have been here only three or four weeks, and which were obviously as mixed as mine, and who are now really very trim and smart.

13 July

Today is the first day I've felt really low since I came here. It's partly thinking of you being so near at Dartmouth, and so disappointing that we can't meet. And it's raining, after a fortnight of brilliant sunshine.

I'm supposed to compère and sing in a foc's'le concert on Thursday, which would be enjoyable if only one had time to do it properly. As it is, we can only hope. I've spent part of the afternoon coaching a very earnest seaman to do 'All the world's a stage'. He wanted to do Richard II and Richard III also, but I dissuaded him.

I had not long been in barracks when I was approached by the Entertainments Officer. From my first morning I had found that attitudes to me fell broadly into two categories: those who were naïvely flattered to meet me, and those who made it clear that whoever I was I could expect no special privileges. But Lieutenant Green, the Entertainments Officer, was in a category of his own.

'We shall *have* to organize a ship's concert,' he said, looking at me with a gleam of hope. 'Could you do anything?'

'Everything, if you like.'

'Splendid.' He seemed very relieved. 'I can leave it to you, then?'

Which he did, entirely. I wrote to Noël asking if he had any new songs which I might sing, and by return post came a package containing three or four songs copied out in manuscript, including one – 'Could you please oblige us with a Bren Gun?' – which seemed to fit the bill perfectly. The trouble was there was neither time nor place during the day where I could learn the words quietly by myself. I was obliged to learn them in the lavatory after lights-out:

> Colonel McNamara who/Was in Calcutta in ninety-two
> Emerged from his retirement for the war.
> He wasn't very pleased with what he heard and what he saw.
> But whatever he felt,/He tightened his belt –
> And organized a corps . . .

It was a 'patter' song and very difficult to learn. I had just about mastered it when a telegram arrived from Noël: PLEASE CHANGE MCNAMARA TO MONTMORENCY STOP THERE IS A REAL AND VERY ANGRY MCNAMARA IN THE WAR OFFICE.

The package that contained the songs also carried a letter which told of a meeting between Coward and Mountbatten, where Noël had praised the beginnings of my nautical career so warmly that 'Dickie' had 'requested' me for his new command, the aircraft carrier *Illustrious*.

30 July

Didn't tell you of my interview last Friday with the Divisional Commander [Jeremy Hutchinson, Peggy Ashcroft's husband]? He told me he was going to relieve me of being class leader as Menzies had to be tried. He said, 'I'm thoroughly satisfied with your performance and have put you down as commission-worthy. It's just that Menzies, you see, is secretary to the Duke of Atholl and we have had a little pressure!'

10 August

Your letters are more lovely to get than you can imagine. I love your news, and of Van and Corin. 'V for Vanessa' it certainly shall be. I hate this 'V for Victory' nonsense. Did you ever hear the like of the press now that Russia is 'on our side'? Disgusting.

Did you hear my broadcast last night? I do hope you did. It was the greatest fun to do. Edith [Edith Hargraves, my voluntary secretary] and I – Edith, as I think I told you, has been taking her holidays at Crafthole – went round on the Friday and saw the Henry Hall Variety Show at the Palace from the wings. You can imagine with what nostalgia. Oh, the smell of those old provincial theatres! Actually I don't think I've ever been backstage during variety before, except once at the Coliseum during the last war when Mother was playing with Potash and Perlmutter. I always remember the thrill of sitting on a skip and revolving with the stage.

At the Palace there is a serving-hatch in the wings through to the stalls bar, which makes it delightful for a stage-door Jack who can drink himself silly while watching the show. A rattling good show it was, too. A marvellous man called Owen McGiverney played *all the parts* in the scene from *Oliver Twist* where Nancy is murdered. He did complete changes in less than two seconds. A gorgeous ham of an actor – but you could learn something from watching what can be done in the matter of quick changes if you've a mind (and muscle) to do it.

I didn't actually know Henry Hall but shamefully pretended we had met and knew that we'd see the show somehow that way. (All the best seats were sold – he's done record business at the Palace this week. In 1941, think of that!) He was really charming. He asked me to go on and take a bow, but I, wisely I think, thought not. I need hardly tell you it was Edith who suggested to him that I should sing in his Guest Broadcast the following night. Actually, as I guessed, and as he confessed afterwards, he'd no idea I sang at all and was a bit doubtful in his mind.

I was very nimble the next morning, and got permission to go ashore in the afternoon, having found a substitute for my duties. (All very formal. A request, an interview, etc.) I also wired Noël for permission to sing 'London Pride'.

So I got into my tiddly suit in a lavatory at the Grand and went along to rehearse at 2.30. Then Edith and I had tea. Then I slept in the lounge of the Grand. Then a sherry. No smoking. It was like old times. I wasn't a bit nervous, but very keyed up. I knew I'd get a good reception, the uniform would settle that if nothing else, but I must say it was terrific. Did you hear it? I long to know. I sent a wire to Mother and another to Noël. The band had already played 'London Pride' and performed really well. It's the first time I've had proper support from a dance band. Usually they're very scraggy.

Commodore's inspection this morning. About an hour standing rigid on the parade ground, while the Marine Band played 'Roses of Picardy', 'Because', etc., plus their own special derangement of 'Bitter Sweet'. You can't imagine what Ivy St Helier's 'If Love Were All' sounds like when played by a Marine Band on Church Parade. Or perhaps you can . . .

That September I was on my first leave in London when Noël called me to his house, where I found him in a serious mood, talking to a Colonel Buchanan of the Marines. Noël introduced us and said, 'Buchanan has something to tell you.'

'You'll be very disappointed,' said the Colonel, 'if I tell you that Mountbatten has now been appointed C.-in-C. Joint Ops. So I'm afraid you won't be able to serve under him.'

I had a choice, he explained, between joining HMS *Illustrious* where she lay refitting in Norfolk, Virginia, or waiting to be drafted elsewhere. If the latter, it might mean a long wait. Mountbatten had suggested I might join a Commander Morrison, but his destroyer was still at sea. 'You could be kicking your heels about in barracks for several months,' said Buchanan. On the other hand, I could join *Illustrious* almost immediately.

I chose *Illustrious*. It *was* disappointing that Mountbatten would no longer be commanding her, but, besides the fact, as the Colonel had pointed out, that I could join her within a few weeks, and so put in the three months at sea which were needed before one could be trained for a commission, there was another enticing factor: New York!

It was no secret that *Illustrious* was being refitted in the States. There were pictures of her on the front page of *Picture Post*. But how were we to get there? If you're an Ordinary Seaman, the Navy never tell you anything. I went with a small draft of seamen, accompanied by a Master-at-Arms, to Birmingham, where we stopped for something to eat, and then on to Gourock, on the west coast of Scotland, which seemed a very hot, busy, bustling place, the September sunshine making our kitbags and ditty boxes unbearably heavy. We were directed to the SS *Pasteur*, newly-painted in camouflage. She had been designed for the South American luxury trade, we were told, and now, crammed to many times her normal capacity, mainly with RAF troops bound for training in Pensacola, Florida, she was making her first transatlantic voyage.

Once again my film face was noticed, and amongst those who sought me out were some of the stewards of the White Star Line, who invited me to their mess. The *Pasteur*, it seemed, was a 'dry' ship, but not for them. Their company, and the two ship's concerts I organized, helped to pass the time.

'What kind of a climate is it?' I asked my companion, an American Air Force man. We were in calm waters now, sailing down the

St Lawrence River to Lake Erie; the same route, I thought, as the refugees in *Thunder Rock* had taken when escaping from the oppressions of Europe. The *Pasteur*'s deck was once more thronging with passengers, after the rolling in the Atlantic which had driven all but a few of us below.

'Virginia? Well, let's see. It's kinda damp.'

'Oh, dear.' I had hoped, I said, to have left that sort of thing behind in England.

'Well,' he said, 'it's not like English damp.' And here he paused for reflection. 'It's a kind of a *dry* damp.'

'I see.'

'Yes sir,' he said, warming to his theme, 'you get all kinds of damp there, *and* all kinds of sunshine.'

And then, the longest train ride I had ever taken, from Montreal to Norfolk, Virginia.

I was in a deep sleep in our coach [I wrote to Rachel] when I was woken by a PO who said there was a party forrard in the Pullman with some Air Force and other worthies and that I was requested to come and sing. I looked at him sleepily, but the next word I caught was 'whisky' and was on my feet in a flash (you know the Redgrave flash) and we found one very pie-eyed Air Force bloke and an assorted Pullman full of people, all moderately fried. I was introduced, whereupon instead of saying howdo they did what I always thought was a convention of Hollywood and clapped my entrance in a polite, if as I say slightly-fried, fashion. So hey presto I sang 'London Pride', of course, and several others.

My overriding obsession was to visit New York, and at about noon the next day that truly fabulous skyline came into view, as if hurling itself out of the ground. A night in New York, perhaps, or even a few hours? The Navy, as was the Navy's practice, had told us nothing at all about our movements. And then, while I was still gasping and craning, the train suddenly took to earth, and we changed trains underground. Twenty minutes later we were on our way again, with one last tantalizing glimpse of Manhattan. I almost wept. The train rumbled on all day. By nightfall we arrived at Cape Charles, where we disembarked, exhausted, and then changed trains to a local which took us through the streets of Norfolk, uttering that strange wailing that goes with American railways.

2 November

Well, this is a ship, and some ship. There seems at first glance no chance of ever getting to know one's way about, it's so vast and complicated. But I have tried to learn various routes systematically, and can find my way unaided to the lavatory and the washplace, and with great concentration to the foc's'le (I am a foc's'leman), and the flight deck. And by dint of walking about at an angle of forty-five degrees I have so far avoided braining myself.

The first morning after Divisions I was dispatched with a clutch of other ratings to a remote place where we were issued with paint cans and brushes, and an Able Seaman (as distinct from the Ordinary kind) was put in charge of us and our cans. 'How many cans of paint does she require?' I asked facetiously. No reply. We halted by the forward end of the flight deck and were detailed into pairs. I followed my companion to a porthole tucked away under a flange of the flight deck. Nimble as a squirrel, he leapt through the porthole to where a board some four feet long and a foot wide was slung, bumping against the ship's side. I attempted to copy him, but as I looked down I could see that we were slung not over the water but the concrete paving of the pier, scores of feet below.

'Don't look down,' shouted my companion. 'There's no hurry. You can take the whole morning if you want.'

The days extended into weeks, and still *Illustrious* was not ready to sail. Her refitting was taking longer than predicted. I began to regret my decision at Noël's house that morning, and to wish I could have my choice over again. None of this time at Norfolk would count as time at sea, and for me it seemed a waste.

Norfolk, Virginia, one might think, was not so bad a place for a sailor. It was so clean, so smooth, so shipshape . . . but so dull. And the damp which my companion on the *Pasteur* had promised – 'you get all kinds of damp there' – turned out to be a very damp damp, sticky and rather enervating. No liquor, of course, which did not make for gaiety. Norfolk at that time was a quiet town indeed, a far cry from Devonport, or from the Portsmouth of my childhood – where, in the pubs, so Uncle Willie told me, especially on Saturday nights, merry hell was apt to break loose. True, the cinemas were free, but one had the feeling they were subsidized only to keep the boys off the streets. And yet in this dear, dull town I made some dear friends.

A note from the ship's padre had suggested I might like to meet some people he knew, natives of Norfolk. And so I made the acquaintance of the Masyngylls. They had an old-fashioned wooden house, very simple, furnished with a nice conservative taste. Harold Masyngyll was one of those few people of whose goodness one is immediately and utterly convinced. But then he was so charming, so courteous and kind, that one wondered if it could be true. And then again, after a short while, one came back to one's first conviction: he was just plain damned good. They had a son of eighteen, Harold junior, known as 'Bud', very bright, healthy, and rather artistic.

The first evening I went to the Masyngylls', Harold's wife, Carole, said, 'You just come any time, there'll always be a place laid for you.'

And so I believe there was, though I never tested it, but always telephoned first.

We'd play the piano, or talk, and Harold would mix his mysterious 'Old-Fashioneds' quietly and powerfully, and by the end of each evening we'd be a little stinking, and pulling out photographs, and albums, and chatting about our children.

When Manhattan's skyline had disappeared from view on our train ride down south, I had made up my mind that, come what may, I would not let New York slip through my fingers again. But there were all kinds of difficulties. I found out that you had to get a letter inviting you there. That part was simple enough. Letters of invitation from Paul Lukas and Ruth Gordon arrived by return of post. And then by adding the name of Rachel's aunt, Nora McMullen, who had married Andrew Mellon, and laying it on thickly that Ruth had offered to take Vanessa and Corin, I got 'relative's leave'. We had only been allowed to take £10 out of England, which was just enough to get an aeroplane ticket. The train would have been cheaper, but I was determined to enjoy as many moments in New York as I could, and counted on someone lending me money when I got there.

Over the marshes and broad rivers of Virginia to Washington, D.C., changing planes at the most beautiful airport I'd ever seen, like some highly-dramatic modern temple, and then taking off for New York – it seemed the most gay, enchanting, and improbable journey of my life. Ruth Gordon met me at the airport and said, 'Darling, I'm not just going to show you New York, I'm going to show you *theatrical* New York.' And so she did.

In those three days Ruth and Paul and Daisy Lukas took me to all the smartest restaurants and clubs and we had a whale of a time. Ruth had asked what show I wanted to see and I'd said *Watch on the Rhine* which Paul is in and is a fine play, and Helen Hayes in the new Maxwell Anderson play, *Candle in the Wind*. I'd always longed to see Helen Hayes. The play was awful, as I thought it would be – I don't like Maxwell Anderson – but I loved Helen, saw her afterwards, and drove with her to her rehearsal at the broadcasting studio. She asked me to broadcast with her the next day in *The Last of Mrs Cheyney*, but I didn't know how that would go down with my Captain, so I thought it best to refuse.

Then we saw the new Garbo picture, *Two-Faced Woman*, which Ruth is in. She had MGM run it for us. And the people I met! Ronald Colman, Edna Best, Jack Warner, Rouben Mamoulian [head of MGM], Gaby Pascal – who wanted me to go to Hollywood and act in an episode of the British War Relief film, with Charlie Chaplin of all people – tea with Robert Sherwood and his wife, oh, and hosts of other celebrities!

On Sunday night (the shows can open Sunday if they want to) we went to *Pal Joey*. I've never seen a musical so well done, except when I visited New York two weeks later and saw *Let's Face It*, the new smash hit.

The second visit was even more amazing than the first. I came to do two broadcasts, one for British War Relief and the other for 'Bundles for Britain'. The first was a bad play with Flora Robson, the second a terrifying quiz programme called 45 *Questions on Broadway* with Ruth, Jessie Matthews, and that marvellous, eccentric character actor Mischa Auer. We were sat at a table, and there was a large and very excited audience who backed their favourites and who were very pro-me, mostly on account of my uniform, of course, but also because I had fans there, which I'll tell you about in a minute. Ruth won, which pleased Jones very much – Jones is her son, aged twelve – because, he said, 'she never wins anything'.

Well – the fans! It started the first evening of my second visit. No, before that, because a popular columnist had written in his column the time before that I was in New York, and some of the fans had written to *Illustrious*.

The Stars Look Down had only just been shown here, and was still playing at what they call the neighbourhood theatres. Also, *The Lady Vanishes*, which is always being revived here – it's just about the most popular English picture in New York.

Well, as I said, on the first evening of the second visit, Mr and Mrs Tyrone Power had given Ruth four seats for the new Cole Porter musical, *Let's Face It*, which is such a hit that I doubt whether even Cole Porter could get in. And as we were coming out some 'standees' recognized me and asked for autographs. I told them I was broadcasting and they said, 'We'll be there!' I thought they meant they'd listen in. But no, they found out the times of rehearsal, and next day at Radio City about six of them were there when I went in, and slightly more when I came out. And at the broadcast that night they were about a dozen strong. They'd gone off and bought stills of *Stolen Life* and *The Lady Vanishes* and gave me notes and walked along with me until, in self-preservation, I got into a taxi and said, 'Go to the Alvin,' where Gertie Lawrence is playing in *Lady in the Dark*. I heard them take up the cry, 'The Alvin!' And off I went, gaily waving and thinking I'd seen the last of them. I went into the Alvin and stood for about twenty-five minutes of Gertie's show, which although everyone says they loathe it, is a big hit. Came out – and there were the faithful, massed across the street, and now about two dozen of them, including a huge coloured woman who with overwhelming sincerity told me that *The Stars Look Down* was etc., etc. I went from the Alvin to see the last two acts of Ethel Barrymore in *The Corn Is Green* and damme if they weren't still there when I got out of that. After that I had the sense to say I was going home to bed.

But they turned up again on the Sunday at the quiz programme, and whenever I got a question right, which I did very occasionally, they cheered me lustily.

Well, I'd always heard that in England you have to fight to get publicity, and in America fight harder to avoid it, and I guess it's true. The moment I landed in Canada someone from the press came aboard. And at Norfolk whenever I gave a concert, they'd make a great song and dance of it and there'd be a two-column story about me.

It's taken rather longer to describe than I meant to, but I thought you'd like to hear it. Together with meeting all the stage folk and hearing the gossip and everyone [then, before Pearl Harbor] carrying on as if there wasn't a war, it made me homesick to act again.

The other play I saw was *Life with Father*, which I stood for and would stand on my head to see again. It came in quietly in November 1939 and no one thought it would be much to write home about, with no stars and taken from a book by Clarence Day, very popular but with not a shred of plot in it. It has become almost an American institution. I laughed and cried and have since reread the play twice. You shall read it when I get back. It's just about the most human, funny, touching and enjoyable thing I ever did see.

I met lots more people this second trip of course, but I shall chiefly remember the Saturday night, after seeing *Life with Father*, when Ruth gave a dinner party for Ludmilla Pitoëff, Lillian Gish and Thornton Wilder. That was a real actor's evening.

And so was my last evening in New York. Guthrie McClintic had asked us to dinner, but I had to fly back that night to rejoin the ship. So he said come along as soon as we'd done the quiz broadcast. So about six o'clock we went to his lovely house in Beekman Place, overlooking the East River. Katharine Cornell, his wife, was on tour with *The Doctor's Dilemma*, so unfortunately I didn't meet her. I had an early dinner on a tray and then, at about eight, when I had to go, the party began to arrive: Ethel Barrymore, Mildred Natwick, Aubrey Smith and his wife and their nephew – a naval commander whom they'd not heard of since Crete and who had turned up suddenly on their doorstep. It was horrid having to leave that party. But next day, very suddenly, we went to sea, so the anti-climax was not so bad.

I had intended to borrow some money from business friends of Noël's, and the hope was not ill-founded. I did not have to ask. Several people would hang on to a handshake long enough to tell me there was money in the hand, and when I left I was several hundred dollars to the good. I was even contemplating a third trip to New York when the gunnery officer called us together to tell us we were going for our gunnery trials off Jamaica.

To my surprise and excitement I was posted to the bridge, where I was to relay commands to the starboard batteries. I had no idea of what these consisted, beyond a recollection of about eight 'pom-poms' and some other very powerful-looking guns. I had been chosen to be on the bridge, I supposed, because it would be assumed that my professional diction would be useful.

And then began what seemed to be a game. Suddenly the sky spat out black smudges against the deep Caribbean blue. I could not understand why we seemed to be firing at American targets. Beside me on the bridge stood the gunnery officer. I could not understand why 'Guns' kept on giving the same command, 'Follow Evershed', which I relayed. We were being mock-bombed by squadrons of American planes. Repeatedly this same command, 'Follow Evershed', rang out, first from the throat of the gunnery officer, and then from mine as I echoed him. I could not imagine what or who Evershed was. Some daredevil Errol Flynnish pilot, no doubt. Though of course I knew that this was only practice and that Evershed would live to tell the tale.

And then came news that out there in the Pacific the *Prince of Wales* had received a mortal hit. I knew that Rachel's younger brother, Robin, was on board.

XV

REFITTING ACCOMPLISHED, *Illustrious* sped home. After the excitement of the gunnery trials, the night watches in the Atlantic seemed almost dangerously uneventful, the most imminent danger being to fall asleep. To prevent this catastrophe, I found a remedy. I would take some point in my life – say, 1921, the season at Stratford. Usually at such an hour my thoughts would run or rumble around any old how, but standing up there on the bridge in the dark, during the long middle watch – midnight to four a.m. – I trained my mind deliberately to follow certain sequences, trying to fit each detail and development to the next. Stratford, 1921, when Mother was a member of the company. . . . I started with my sister, Peg, and me arriving at the station. It was a hot, sunny day. Near the station there were posters of the Festival. . . . Mother wearing a hat with a broad brim: 'It's *The Wives* tonight [Mistress Page was her favourite part], you'll be able to go.' . . . The little house she had taken, with a piano in the front room, where the dining-room was redolent of lime juice and a-buzz with wasps. . . . Marion Phillips, a young actress, coming to stay and saying she was an atheist, which shocked my conventional mind very much at the time, not so much because of her atheism as because she should want to tell me about it. . . . Percy Rhodes's son and I fishing up the Avon . . . a wonderful night when we lashed the punts together by lantern-light. . . . I tried to visualize the geography of the theatre, the stage door, bicycles stacked outside it, Mother's dressing-room . . . an all-woman production of *Henry V* which cracked a few breastplates . . . the last night of the season after *Antony and Cleopatra*, when we carried the flowers home and the stars were so bright that the Milky Way looked newly-spilt across the sky. . . .

When I had pursued these recollections as far as I could, I tried a different tack. I made a list of all the places I had always wanted to visit but had never had the opportunity, and chief amongst these loomed, for some reason, the Ritz Hotel in London.

I had developed a severe ache and stiffness in my right elbow. No one could say for sure how I had come by it, but it was thought that it was perhaps due to some injury sustained whilst ammunitioning ship in Norfolk, and our ship's doctor promised to send me to the Liverpool Hospital when we landed. My view was that I was suffering from a surfeit of bananas. When we left Jamaica, where we had anchored during our gunnery trials, a local banana merchant, to show his appreciation of *Illustrious* and all who sailed in her, presented the ship with as many bananas as could be hung on the cable deck. The ship's company was encouraged to eat as many as they could swallow, and they tucked in with a will, but they very soon grew satiated with bananas, which then began to rot. I was one of the party, stripped to the waist and armed with huge shovels, which was detailed to jettison the evil-smelling debris.

Once back at Liverpool, I went to the David Lewis Hospital for treatment to my arm. I was expecting some brilliant manipulation or some radiant heat, at least an X-ray. But after some rather limp massage I was told to return next morning and was then turned loose on the streets of Liverpool.

Liverpool without the Playhouse company was like a foreign city. I treated myself to lunch at the Adelphi Brasserie, where the woman who served me failed to recognize me. In the afternoon I started by browsing in a bookshop, but I found myself very tired and, for the first time, allowed the thought that I was too old for a sailor's life to come uppermost in my mind. There was a 'flea-pit' cinema up the hill from the Adelphi. Indeed, Liverpool was rich in its number of cinemas, and I think I must have fallen asleep in each one of them in turn. I really must be tired, I told myself. I took myself back to the Adelphi and booked a room for a rest. Every morning, after Divisions, I presented myself at the hospital for massage, and every afternoon I repeated, with minor variations, my aimless wanderings about Liverpool, punctuated at some point by a snooze at the Adelphi. It was a far cry from the young Lochinvar who was to have served under Mountbatten.

My arm was showing no signs of improvement. I saw myself spending the remainder of the war in barracks in Liverpool, and the rest of my career playing Richard III. I requested to see the Captain, and was told he was on leave and would not be back for some weeks.

The ship's doctor suggested that as I myself was due for leave in a week or two, I should have a specialist in London look at my arm. I began to yearn for London.

The Head Porter at the Ritz greeted me warmly. 'What do you want, mate?'

'A room.' I advanced towards the desk. It was eight in the morning. I had just got off the train from Liverpool and was still wearing my Ordinary Seaman's uniform and carrying my kitbag.

He must have thought I was drunk, or joking. A few minutes later I found myself across the road, trying a slightly different tack at the Berkeley. But my polished posh accent failed to do the trick, and I found myself on the pavement again, walking towards Jermyn Street.

I seemed to recollect a pleasant evening at the Cavendish Hotel with Dick Green and some painter friends, Robert Beulah and his wife, Eric O'Dea, Lucien Freud – now there, I felt sure, they would let me have a room, if only for the night.

'What do you want?' said a voice, seeming to belong to a pair of legs: it was Rosa Lewis, legendary proprietress of the Cavendish, caricatured as Lottie Crump in Evelyn Waugh's novels and post-humously commemorated as 'the Duchess of Duke Street', half-hidden in her famous wicker chair, 'having her feet done', as she put it. Very pretty feet, too.

'Good morning, Mrs Lewis,' I said.

'You're early, aren't you?' she replied. 'Sure you've come to the right place?'

'Quite sure, if you've got a room I could have for a few nights.'

She hesitated a moment, and then called into her office, 'Edith, show the sailor into – you know the room I mean.'

The room she meant was at the end of a long, dark corridor. There was no running water, only an enamel jug and a china basin. The bathroom was at the other end of the corridor. I returned to the lobby to find Mrs Lewis casually glancing at the label on my kitbag. Still, her manner betrayed no particular interest in who I was or what I was doing.

'It's all I've got for the moment,' she said firmly, 'Will you take it?'

'It'll do for the present,' I said, 'and perhaps, when I've had a bath, say round about eleven o'clock, you'll help me crack a bottle of the Widow?' (Despite all wartime shortages, the Cavendish somehow maintained a fairly well-stocked cellar. Rosa showed it me one night.

'These,' she said, gesturing at thousands of empty champagne bottles, 'are my *ruins*.')

Later, over champagne, she became less guarded. Soon she was calling me by my Christian name, and by midday she had corralled some more guests who were about to leave, and more champagne was opened. It was clear she had taken a shine to me. 'Think of it,' she said to the assembled company. 'Here's Michael, with a wife and two children, and has to pay for all of this' – and here she made a sweeping gesture, as if to embrace not only the Cavendish Hotel but all of Jermyn Street as well – '*all* of this on two and sixpence a day.'

I made my headquarters at the Cavendish Hotel for the next three months. Rachel was on tour; I was on leave. Our third child, Lynn, who was born in March 1943, was already on the way. I had seen a specialist within a day or so of my arrival in London, he had indicated that the injury to my arm might be a permanent disability, and had undertaken to inform the Admiralty. And then a telegram arrived from that quarter informing me that my leave was to be indefinitely prolonged.

Bill Linnit, who had been so helpful in forming my stage career, sent me a play to direct. It was called *Lifeline*, and depicted the voyage of a tanker in wartime across the Atlantic. The four leading characters had already been cast, and I thought to myself that if I could direct Wilfred Lawson, Frank Pettingell, Arthur Sinclair, and Terence de Marney, each one of them a good actor, but collectively four of the more eccentric actors in London, I could direct anything.

I set about trying to put the play's rather loose script on more solid foundations. I practically rewrote the play. The authoress seemed grateful. I obtained permission to spend several days in the London docks. I got to know Wilfred Lawson and something of his pattern of self-destruction. It was after the first run-through, and we had adjourned, as was our custom, to a neighbouring pub in Drury Lane, when Wilfred with his perennial grin casually informed me that my ambitions as an actor were doomed. He had been at a midnight performance of *Three Sisters*, he told me, and my performance as Tusenbach was not worth talking about, *but* – this was said with great candour and sincerity – 'you really ought to take up directing, you have something of a talent for that. *Not* acting.'

'Not acting?'

'*Not* acting.'

Lifeline opened and closed within a fortnight, and any lingering hopes I had had that the notices would proclaim a triumph of realism proved ill-founded. Still, most of them were respectful, and meanwhile Linnit had other plans for me: a play by Patrick Hamilton, *The Duke in Darkness*, a costume melodrama, with a bravura part for Leslie Banks as the Duke and for me as his tailor, Gribaud. I enjoyed playing the tailor and, best of all, I could take real satisfaction in the production. Yet this play, too, despite our good notices, failed. Perhaps it was too sombre for its time.

Meanwhile I had received another telegram from Their Lordships at the Admiralty, requiring me to present myself in uniform at Chatham Barracks at eight-thirty in the morning. Not in uniform, I thought, they'll keep you for good. I wore a suit, trusting to luck that no one would notice.

I was on the point of jumping on to the train to take me down to Chatham, when I felt a hand slap me on the back. I turned round to find Needle.

'Mike! Where are you off to? No, don't tell me, let me guess. Chatham?'

'Yes ... '

'Oughtn't you to be wearing your uniform? You naughty boy, you've been up to something. Am I right?'

'Not really ... '

The whistle blew and we climbed in. I had reconciled myself to the thought of sharing the compartment with Needle for the journey, but instead he dived off past me down the corridor, pausing only to explain in a stage whisper, 'I suppose you heard I was married? No? Terrible mistake!' – leaving me to rehearse my coming interview.

I had guessed right about the uniform. No one so much as asked me why I wasn't wearing it.

The interview with the Surgeon-Admiral, X-rays included, was brisk and business-like.

'Well, it certainly seems that you would be of more use making films than giving ship's concerts. Rather a pity, but there it is. What do you think?'

'Well, sir, I don't want to sit in barracks till the end of the War running messages. I've had enough of that.'

'I dare say. Could you scramble down the side of a sinking ship?'

'I doubt it, sir.'

'I doubt it, too. Very well. Thank you.'

An awful thought occurred to me: 'They won't call me up into the Army, will they, sir?'

'Frankly,' he said, with a ghost of a smile, 'I doubt if they will. Don't you?'

A few weeks later, in November 1942, a year almost to the day since I had boarded *Illustrious* in Norfolk, Virginia, I was discharged from the Navy. I began to look around me.

I first made acquaintance with Turgenev's 'summer' play, *A Month in the Country*, at the Cambridge Festival Theatre, where it was played in a sad, though very effective, key. I had always wanted to see its comic side, and now plans were afoot for me to do it with Peggy Ashcroft. Everything was set – the cast, the theatre, the designer, the director (Emlyn Williams) – everything. And then, on the first day of rehearsal, Peggy trapped her foot in a taxi door; the doctor said it would take several weeks to recover from her injury; and we were without a Natalya Petrovna.

Valerie Taylor's name was suggested. The only part I could remember seeing her play was Nina in *The Seagull*. Binkie said he would release her from *Watch on the Rhine*, in which she was playing at the time, and the general opinion seemed to be that Valerie would be ideal. It was arranged that I should see *Watch on the Rhine*, and, when I did, two things happened. One, Valerie gave a beautiful, tragic performance, and two, she missed her first entrance, causing Athene Seyler and the rest of the cast to improvise innocuous lines – 'Whatever can have happened to the girl?' 'Darling, are you coming?' and, finally, 'It's getting late, dear!'

If I mention Valerie's missed entrance in *Watch on the Rhine*, it is to remind myself how everything, within the picture frame that dominated our theatre for two centuries, is done to sustain an illusion. And yet the very completeness of that illusion, or suspension of disbelief, can numb the audience, and can induce in the actor a false sense of security. It was in the course of a matinée performance of *A Month in the Country* at the St James's, half-way through our long run, and I was settling down to the first undisturbed duologue between the heroine and myself, looking up at Valerie with eyes brimful of affection and love, when I heard a lady in the stalls whisper to her companion, 'I like *her*.' I was noticeably quicker on my cues after that.

There are those who think that the advent of films, and then of television, where the reactions of the spectator cannot affect the spectacle, has made audiences more insensitive and noisier. Personally

I doubt this. For what it is worth, I have noticed throughout my career a marked increase of concentration in audiences. Perhaps a part of this is due to the general prohibition on smoking. And the deplorable custom of drinking tea off trays on the lap, which was so prevalent in the English theatre, especially at matinees, has now – so far as I know – disappeared.

It was thanks to a tea drinker in a matinée of *A Month in the Country*, when we were on tour in Liverpool, that I lost my temper and shattered the illusion by addressing the audience. After a fifteen-minute interval during which teas were served, the Second Act began with its long soliloquy from the heroine, after which I had to enter for an impassioned scene between us. I could hear, as I stood in the wings, the rattle of teacups, and this annoyed me, more particularly as I had recently complained that fifteen minutes was surely long enough for people to drink a cup of tea and the manager had promised to do something about it.

As I waited, my irritation mounted, and I forced myself to remember what Edith Evans had once told me. She recalled how, when she once was playing *The Way of the World*, the local Hammersmith boys would come and bang on the metal scene-dock doors out of pure mischief, which used to throw her out of gear, and Robert Loraine, seeing her distress, had advised, 'If there is a disturbance which you can stop, have it stopped. If you can't stop it, take no notice.' I reminded myself of this and said to myself that I must make my entrance and be especially good and that then the audience would forget about their teacups. I entered and, as it happened, the noise of teacups ceased for several minutes – how fatal it is to be pleased with oneself! – but suddenly a noise that sounded as if three trays of tea had been dashed to the ground echoed round the theatre. I was about to take Valerie in my arms when the incident occurred. Instead, I dropped her as suddenly, if not as noisily, as the tea-trays and, turning to the audience, said with the kind of frigid authority of which, amongst actors, Coward alone was the master, 'When *you* have all finished with your teas, *we* shall go on with the play.'

Of course, far worse things have been said by actors to audiences. It was in Liverpool also, I believe, that George Frederick Cooke, when playing Othello, was hissed by an audience probably more versed in the ways of melodrama than in Shakespeare, though it is also possible that in Cooke's production there was not so great a distinction between the two. He stopped in mid-sentence and turned on them in fury, saying, 'So ye hiss George Frederick Cooke, do ye? Let me tell you that every stone of your damned city was cemented by the blood of a Negro.' One would dearly love to have seen the audience's reaction to that.

In my own case the audience's response was instructive. My rebuke reduced them to such a cowed silence that although the play is termed a comedy, and our production – as I fondly hoped – had succeeded in bringing out its comic side, no one, least of all myself, succeeded in getting another laugh for the rest of the Act. As another actor in the cast, Michael Shepley, said to me afterwards, 'I rather admire you for having done that, but you'll never want to do it again, will you?' He was right.

At the back of my mind, since Liverpool days, was the ambition to work with a permanent company. Kindled by the visit of La Compagnie des Quinze, it had flared up during the Gielgud season at the Queen's and blazed like a meteor after working with Michel. Wartime was no time to start such a project. But one could make plans for the future, and I began to think about forming a company.

Rachel and I had seen Sonia Dresdel in *Hedda Gabler*. 'There's your leading lady,' whispered Rachel. There are certain people who have what we please to call 'star quality', which compels you to look at them whether you want to or no. Sonia was a highly-talented actress. She was also, I discovered, her own worst enemy.

I outlined to her the sort of work I had in mind. One of the plays I wanted to revive was Goldoni's *La Locandiera – The Mistress of the Inn* – in which Duse had had one of her greatest successes.

'Oh, I could never play that,' said Sonia, handing me back the script.

'Why ever not?'

'I haven't the charm.'

I was very shocked by this remark. I did not then believe, as I do now, that nine-tenths of a good performance lies in good casting. I believed that a strong director could always wring a good performance out of his actors. I thought that all my geese were swans.

I wanted to get as much varied experience of directing as possible. During the year-long run of *A Month in the Country* I directed three plays: Henri Becque's *La Parisienne*, with Sonia and myself in the leading parts, for six special matinées at the St James's; Peter Ustinov's second play, *Blow Your Own Trumpet*; and Maxwell Anderson's *Wingless Victory*.

Ustinov's first play had raised great expectations for his second. He had created some memorable character parts for elderly actors, but, in both plays, it was noticeable that his characterization of young, or younger, people was not so effective, and in *Blow Your Own Trumpet* the two young people had a love scene that was positively embarrassing. I decided to ask Ustinov to rewrite it, which he agreed to do, and in due course he came back with his rewritten scene written on the backs of envelopes. I asked the stage management to arrange for the revision to be typed. When I read it I was somewhat puzzled. There was no difference between the 'write' and the 'rewrite'; not a word had been changed.

Blow Your Own Trumpet closed after a fortnight. I was stung by the dismissive reviews of Ustinov's play. With all its faults it had ambition, and I felt it had deserved better treatment from its reviewers.

With eight performances a week of the Turgenev, rehearsals of *Wingless Victory* were bound to suffer. The first time I saw it in performance was at a matinée at Oxford, during the pre-London tour, where a scant and unappreciative house made me fear that Anderson's play would fare no better with the critics than Ustinov's. Perched on someone else's suitcase in the crowded corridor of the train going back to London, I started writing a piece which I labelled 'An Actor to the Critics'.

Wingless Victory had some of that strain of thin high-mindedness – the legacy of Ralph Waldo Emerson – that I had so disliked in *Winterset*. But it had a worthwhile theme. Its setting was almost the same as in Arthur Miller's *The Crucible*. The heroine and hero, a woman from the Fiji Islands and her rich white husband, incur at sight the wrath of the citizens of Salem, amongst whom is the hero's mother.

Unknown to me, though guessed at, forces were at work that almost guaranteed the failure of Anderson's play. I had been obliged to fire the first actress who played the racist mother when, during early rehearsals, I could see that, like many an older actress, she was not prepared to be totally unsympathetic. I told her that the play simply couldn't work unless the citizens of Salem displayed their bigotry without reservation. The actress had been at the Savoy with my mother in H.B.Irving's company, and my feelings can be imagined when I had to tell her to go. Another actress was approached, and I explained to her the need for the villainess to be a villainess. She nodded and said she could quite see what I meant, and set about giving a serviceable interpretation of the role. Yet the matinée at Oxford had revived my fears. She simply could not help trying to ingratiate herself with the audience.

On the first night in London, as soon as the curtain was down on the Turgenev, I skipped with a heart of lead over to the Phoenix Theatre to hear how *Wingless Victory* had gone.

The actress who played the Fijian heroine was almost in tears, and it was confirmed by other members of the company that it would have been almost impossible for the audience not to take sides against her when her opponent was all sweetness and light. I raced up the stairs to the dressing-room of the actress playing the mother, but she had fled. I called the company for notes the next morning, but their hearts were not in it, nor was mine.

Meanwhile, 'An Actor to the Critics' had been published in the *New Statesman*. So that it should have extra impact, I arranged that a copy should be sent to critics of all the leading newspapers. I was invited to address the Critics' Circle, which I did, and spoke heatedly and badly, and a journalist named Beverley Baxter rounded off the debate by praising me for taking the theatre seriously but begging me not to take myself too seriously. And that seemed to sum up the general reaction: I must not take myself too seriously.

As to the points which my article proposed by way of improvement to the general run of theatrical criticism – that newspapers should reserve space for their reviews at the end of the week, so that a critic would not be obliged to dash off his review by telephone, sometimes even before the curtain had fallen on the first performance; that critics should sometimes avail themselves of a study of good dramatic criticism, such as Hazlitt's, or G. H. Lewes's (again a note of frigid authority, I fear) – these were accepted with good grace but dismissed as impractical. 'Mr Redgrave,' wrote Harold Hobson, 'can write most of London's critics off their heads and into the middle of next week,' but he doubted whether my outburst would have much influence.

(Some years later, when I published a second book of essays on acting and the theatre, *Mask or Face*, Mr Hobson – whom we referred to in the family circle as 'Handsome Harold' for a good notice and 'Horrid' or 'Hobnailed' for a bad one – reviewed the book in terms so lavish that all the actors in the profession could have been forgiven for sending me to Coventry for bribery. I had asked my secretary to send advance copies to some of my friends in the theatre. I had jotted down a list of names, with a suitable dedication attached, including one addressed to 'Harold, from whom I have learned so much'. I had recently been playing in Giraudoux's *Tiger at the Gates*, and I could truthfully say that I had learned a lot from the American director Harold Clurman, for whom the copy was intended. It would have been churlish, of course, having discovered the mistake, to have attempted to correct it. One does, after all, in the long run, learn something from one's critics.)

When *A Month in the Country* finally closed at the St James's, I was looking for a play to take on tour for ENSA, the Entertainments National Services Association, and the Turgenev was considered too heavy for consumption by the troops. Meeting Beatrix Lehmann outside the theatre, I asked her about the melodrama *Uncle Harry*, which for some reason had folded on the road the previous year. Beatrix was not only a good actress; she had – as might be expected of John and Rosamond Lehmann's sister – an incisive mind. I trusted her judgement. She said it was a fine play and Eric Portman a fine actor, but that Willie Armstrong had misdirected the play. The central character was an amateur painter, a facet which was overstressed, making Harry into an artist *manqué*. Moreover, the play needed two sets, and a revolve to make the two sets work. Beatrix gave me the script of the play, and that evening, having read it, I rang her up and asked her if she would be prepared to do it again in a different production.

Beatrix was very well cast as the younger sister. As Lucy, the girl who jilted Uncle Harry, I cast Rachel. She and I had planned to act together whenever possible, but after our season at Liverpool the plan had met with a set-back. No statistics can convey how many gifted young actresses have suffered such set-backs with the birth of children, set-backs from which their careers never quite recover. At Stratford, before we met, Rachel had had a great success as Juliet, and after Liverpool she was to have played Ophelia to Larry Olivier's Hamlet at the Old Vic, and Viola. She had not, of course, been idle since Vanessa's birth, but she had not had the chances she deserved. Now, she and I would have the key scene of the play.

We did the customary six weeks' ENSA tour, which with a lesser play might have been a chore, yet it was evident even at the beginning that *Uncle Harry* was going to be a huge success.

On the morning of the opening night in London, 29 March 1944, I woke, terrified by a sore throat. At lunch, at the club, Leslie Banks wouldn't sit next to me: 'Because you have a first night.' Then, in the afternoon, I tried to sleep at the Garrick Theatre in my dressing-room, which was filled with telegrams and flowers, without success. That flat, deadly calm, my form of 'nerves', invaded me. And then the temperamental member of the company threw her tantrum, which gave me a dose of adrenalin, and I started the First Act angry. The lights were wrong; there were no bar bells to summon the audience back for the Second Act; the house lights were left on too long. It was not, could not be, as good a performance as the dress rehearsal had been, when I had said to myself, This is your best performance, *don't* try to repeat this tomorrow – which, of course, was exactly what I did, all the while thinking of the critics in front.

At the end, a great reception. James Agate came round 'to pay his respects'. He said, 'Now you can stop being an intellectual and start being a real actor,' and wrote in his review: 'Here and now I take the opportunity of advising him to give up the intellectual drama and devote himself to the profession (the secret of intellectual drama is that anyone can do it).'

'Algebra in wigs,' John Mason Brown called it, referring to the ingenuity of *Uncle Harry*'s construction. After ten years in the theatre, I had my first 'commercial' success in the West End. I had intended to play in *Uncle Harry* for three months, but I agreed to extend the run, and by the end of the year I felt close to a nervous breakdown. Harry was an unnerving part, not only for the audience but for the actor. I would take to delaying my arrival at the theatre as long as possible, rushing in at the 'quarter', leaving myself just sufficient time to make ready for my entrance. At the end of the performance I felt fit for nothing. It was a year of hurly-burly, Benzedrine, and colonic irrigations: illnesses real and imaginary.

The air raids suddenly became intense, and the theatres began to close. Binkie was determined not to let a little thing like that stop the progress of *Uncle Harry*, and he booked us for a long tour of the provinces, playing mainly the big Northern towns where the bombing had almost ceased.

We were in Hull on the second week of our tour when Anthony Asquith and Terence Rattigan appeared on the scene. They were about to make *The Way to the Stars* and wanted to offer me a short part in it if matters could be arranged with Binkie. Flight Lieutenant Archdale was killed in action so early in the story that one was tempted to dub it 'One of Our Actors Is Missing', but the part was well-written, with the promise of enough distinction to make his presence felt even after his departure. Shooting was to begin on location at Catterick, in Yorkshire, the following week and, amazingly, within forty-eight hours it had been agreed that the cast of *Uncle Harry* would be retained on full salary – an almost unheard-of arrangement then – while I took three weeks' leave of absence for the location scenes.

At Hull station the following Monday, Rachel and I parted, she to join the children in Herefordshire; I to catch the twelve-twenty to York. 'A right *clever* train,' said the porter, '*if* it comes.' I had my Everyman copy of *Doctor Thorne*. I had become addicted, during that short tour, to the novels of Trollope (and am so still), an admirable antidote to the high tension of *Uncle Harry*. No hurry, I thought. This will be a holiday.

And so it was. Rattigan's story commemorated a way of life that was vanishing while the film was being made and was past by the time it appeared in July 1945. His script was superb. Not that there was anything so exceptional in his characters, but the ingenuity, the contrast of characters and situation were masterly. And his story contained a strong, clear idea, one to which the makers of *Yanks* returned recently: the conflict of temperament between the British and Americans in time of war.

Our location at Catterick was a real, though no longer operational, RAF camp, its corridors spotlessly painted in regulation cream, its narrow beds hard and yet unbelievably comfortable, like the bunks of my dormitory at HMS *Raleigh*. To tumble into such a bed at night after an evening spent in the Sergeants' Mess, or with the WAAFs in the village pub, was to be transported back two and a half years to the first few weeks of my naval training at Plymouth. The same indescribable friendliness, the same wartime atmosphere of living for the moment, yet without the underlying anxiety because now the end of the war was in sight and I was no longer an actor having to prove myself as an Ordinary Seaman.

Shooting proceeded in fits and starts. Hours of enforced leisure, waiting for the sun to appear; playing snooker with the C.O.; taking driving lessons with Johnnie Mills round and round the perimeter in an old Aston Martin, and discovering that I was only slightly more incompetent than on my honeymoon nine years before; bicycling down long, straight Yorkshire roads, criss-crossed by one-track railway lines. Days of anxious waiting for my moustache to arrive. (I had decided, reluctantly, that Archdale must wear a moustache. It makes one look and feel older than one's years, as

RAF pilots tended to look.) It was to be flown direct to Catterick – no, it was awaiting collection in the parcels office at York. And then, while all eyes were turned to York, it appeared mysteriously blowing along the platform at Darlington.

At half past five in the afternoon the sun would put in an appearance and we would scramble into activity. After three weeks at such a tempo the actor began to feel he had earned his uniform, if not his medals.

The success of *The Way to the Stars* was largely owing to the atmosphere of those three weeks at Catterick, which could never have been created in a studio. I remember 'Puffin' Asquith calling at my room at the end of the second day's shooting and lending me Donald Tovey's book on the Concerto, which has the following: 'One of the first essentials of creative art is the habit of imagining the most familiar things as vividly as the most surprising.' I cannot now recall whether it was he or I who underlined those words, but they sum up rather well what he did and what made the film memorable, as did John Pudney's poem, written for my character, with its strong socialist undercurrent:

> Do not despair
> For Johnny Head-in-air,
> He sleeps as sound
> As Johnny underground.
>
> Better by far
> For Johnny-the-Bright-Star
> To keep your head
> And see his children fed.

Before we had finished shooting *The Way to the Stars* I was approached by Ealing Studios to play in an episodic film about the supernatural called *Dead of Night*. It was to be directed by Alberto Cavalcanti, and I was to play a schizophrenic ventriloquist. It was not an easy part. For one thing, the ventriloquist has to remember to keep his mouth open. I managed that all right, but still I wanted an entirely different voice, though my own, for the dummy. I asked a friend, Diana Graves, to help. I would speak the dummy's lines; she would copy me, following as closely as possible my inflections and timing; then I would copy her copying me.

For the dummy itself I enlisted the help of the ventriloquist Peter Brough, who was, strange to say, an almost national figure on radio. Cavalcanti's first idea was that the dummy should be modelled to look like me. I wanted a figure which would look as different to me as possible, a caricature of a cheeky overgrown schoolboy, like Brough's Archie Andrews. Some people think this is my best film – especially on the Continent, where for a time the success of *Au Coeur de la Nuit* meant that I was greeted by total strangers as a long-lost brother.

XVI

I T WAS Jean Gabin, I believe, who answered when someone asked
him what he looked for in a film, *L'histoire! L'histoire!* I might have
done well to consider this before accepting *The Secret Beyond the Door*. It
had a story, to be sure, a mystery of sorts, pseudo-pathological and
pretentious. But it was to be directed by Fritz Lang, a hero of mine since
those far-off student days when I watched the *Nibelungen* in a dingy,
smoke-filled cinema in Heidelberg. And it was to be made in
Hollywood.

It was not that I had ever been especially keen to visit Hollywood *qua*
Hollywood. When I began making films in the late 1930s, at a time
when our home-grown product was considered almost a laughing-
stock and most young English actors eager to make their way in the
cinema looked towards the States, I frequently had to rebut rumours
that I had a one-way ticket to Hollywood in my breast pocket. And my
love affair with the States, which began, I think, in boyhood, with the
arrival in London of those fabulous American musicals like *Hit the
Deck*, was principally a love affair with New York.

But I loved travel. And sunshine. As I motored back and forth from
our home in Chiswick to the film studios at Denham in the first week of
January 1947, anxiously surveying each day's schedule to see whether
we should complete *Fame Is the Spur* in time for me to catch Saturday's
sailing of the *America*, Hollywood seemed infinitely far away and
infinitely attractive. The pea-souper fogs (long since swept from
London by Clean Air regulations) were so dense that the short distance
from Chiswick to Denham was frequently stretched out to a two-hour
journey. At times the fog was so thick that I was obliged to walk on the
pavement a pace or two ahead of my car, holding an open book in my
hands, its white pages guiding my driver like a beacon.

Fritz Lang met me off the *Super Chief* at Pasadena station, an act of old-world courtesy not lost on me as I blinked in the Californian sun at eight o'clock in the morning. I tried to arrange my face for the photographers. 'Now in Hollywood they understand the value of publicity,' I remembered Margot Dempster saying. They did, too. There must have been a dozen or more photographers who had made the journey out to Pasadena to photograph Fritz in his camel-hair coat and off-white fedora and me in my brand-new suit from Saks Fifth Avenue. (Clothes, like everything else, were still rationed in England. I had spent all my clothing coupons before I left London, thinking I ought to look the part of a visiting English 'star'. But in New York I was met by someone from Universal International and whisked to a suite in the Sherry Netherland. I was given a fistful of dollars for expenses. My navy blue chalk-stripe suit and ill-fitting dinner jacket were jettisoned and I acquired an entirely new wardrobe.)

We drove from Pasadena to Bel Air, our chauffeur pointing out the sights along the way: 'This used to be John A.'s place.'

'Oh? Whose is it now?'

'John B.'s.'

Hollywood seemed to be changing hands with bewildering speed.

'That's Cromwell's place,' Fritz told me, pointing to a ramshackle old house in the middle of the Sunset Strip. Richard Cromwell, he explained, was a long-standing member of Hollywood's English colony, a successful feature player who had had the good sense, before he retired, to buy himself an avocado orchard in what was soon to become one of Hollywood's most expensive pieces of real estate. He lived there still, tucked away amidst the expensive restaurants and the bright lights, half a dozen avocado trees all that remained of his orchard now.

'Take in the church, Joan honey. Give a glance at the ceiling. You're waiting for Michael – be a little apprehensive!'

We were shooting our first scene, in a Mexican church. Joan Bennett seemed a little distressed, I thought, as Fritz kept up a continual running commentary from behind the camera.

'Don't close your mouth, Joan. No, *don't* close your mouth! I said *don't*. Cut! Do you think you could leave your mouth a little open, Joan honey?'

'He treats me like a puppet,' muttered Joan as she walked off the set to her caravan after the shot. But he must know what he's doing, I thought. In his two previous films she had given very polished performances.

Lang had proved with his first Hollywood film, *Fury*, that he, like Renoir in his *Swamp Water* and *The Southerner*, could successfully absorb material which was not native to him. But neither Lang nor Renoir could make a silk purse out of a sow's ear, and *The Secret Beyond the Door* was a sow's ear and a half. I could never bring myself to see it.

I learned from Lang what it is like to be caught up in the Hollywood machine, working in studios where even your personal telephone calls might be tapped. He would often ask me about working in England. I urged him to come and direct Dylan Thomas's *The Doctor and the Devils*, which I had persuaded the Rank Organization to buy for me. He never came, unfortunately, and Thomas's script was never made. I tried hard to have it filmed, but was told it was impossible because a 'B' movie on the subject of the body snatchers had been made a year or two previously.

Hollywood produced its share, perhaps more than its share, of eccentrics, most of whom seemed, in my short stay, to be of the imported variety. I was lying by the hotel pool one day when I heard the clatter of heavy feet approaching, making a considerable noise. Their owner was dressed in high boots and a trench coat. He smoked a pipe, and I noticed he conspicuously avoided taking a shower before jumping into the pool. It was Evelyn Waugh.

As it happened, we were both invited to the studio that afternoon, where they were running a preview of Carol Reed's *Odd Man Out*. More by accident than by design, we sat next to each other.

'Who is that young man wearing a Guards' tie?' asked Waugh. It was Greer Garson's husband, Richard Ney. He repeated the question in a rather louder voice. 'Who is that young man?'

'I don't know,' I said, making as if to get up, but there was no other seat.

'Surely that is a Guards' tie?'

'Probably,' I said, weakly.

The lights went out. The picture had been running about a quarter of an hour when Waugh nudged me. 'What did you say the name of this film was?'

'*Odd Man Out*.'

'Do you think we've missed something at the beginning?'

'No, I don't think so.'

'But it doesn't make sense.'

'It will,' I said, rather flustered.

Another five minutes elapsed. Suddenly we heard a delicate high-pitched chiming sound, and a few heads turned round from the rows in front. Waugh had pulled out his repeater watch. 'This is a very *long* film,' he said.

'Now in Hollywood they understand the value of publicity. ... ' Yes, but not always how to get the best value for their money. For the Lang film, Universal's publicity department worked hard to promote me as the clean-limbed, all-weather type of Englishman. 'He's tall – he's rangy,' began one of their handouts.

For *Mourning Becomes Electra*, which I began in April 1947, RKO set about restoring the image of the English classical actor, pipe-smoking, reclusive, deeply philosophical. Nothing is so serious as Hollywood when it takes itself seriously, and when it tackles a Great American Classic, it takes itself very seriously indeed. There had been several attempts to put Eugene O'Neill's play on the screen, but he had refused them all. But at last, with the promise that it would be filmed with the utmost fidelity to the original, and that the direction would be entrusted to Dudley Nichols, a fine scriptwriter and a personal friend of O'Neill's, RKO had finally secured the rights.

The production was unique in one respect, I believe. The film was shot in strict continuity. No doubt this was in deference to O'Neill, though whether he had actually requested it, I don't know. It meant that all the sets – and they were very heavy – had to remain standing throughout the shooting period, which must have added considerably to the production's costs. It also highlighted what was wrong with the film : it was simply too faithful to the original. O'Neill had ransacked Greek myth to make a modern American myth, based on Freud's incest wish. By the same token the film needed to take some of the liberties with O'Neill that O'Neill took with Aeschylus. But Nichols's script scrupulously avoided all temptation to take his camera beyond the walls of the New England mansion which is the play's setting. Though it shortened the play's four hours' traffic to two and a half hours' screen time, it was very faithful to the text. The camera remained fixed on the face of whichever actor was speaking, often in very long close-up, as if hardly daring to look beyond for fear that the audience might not concentrate on the speech.

These were minor problems, however, compared to the problem of casting. Rosalind Russell was an excellent comedienne, but the very qualities of sanity and wholesomeness which lit up her comedy worked against her as Lavinia / Electra. Mourning did *not* become her. On the first day's shooting she greeted me with 'Hi, Michael! I hear you dig deep into your part. Not me, I'm afraid. I like to have a laugh with the boys in the gantry, know what I mean?' I thought it wiser not to pursue this too far.

Leo Genn, another English actor, with a very fine voice and a soothing manner, was a pillar of rectitude as Adam/Aegisthus, the raffish sea captain who is adored by mother and daughter. To the part of the heavy father, Ezra/Agamemnon, Raymond Massey brought all his personal charm, which was considerable, but made nonsense of the plot, so that his part of the story – like Leo's – was, as it were, scuttled. But the biggest disappointment was Katina Paxinou, the Greek actress who had won an Oscar for her performance in *For Whom the Bell Tolls*. As Hemingway's peasant woman Pilar, she had been splendid, but as Christine/Clytemnestra, with O'Neill's dialogue to speak, she was bowled out by the very thing which had helped her before, a heavy Greek accent and a very imperfect command of the English language.

Why, I wondered, should such a multi-accented cast be assembled for a story about a New England family at the end of the Civil War? I was concerned on my own account to manage the New England accent. I consulted George Cukor, who opined that I had a 'lazy upper lip', and sent me to a well-known studio dialogue/accent coach. She listened to my upper lip, but told me that New England English must have been as close as dammit to English English seventy years ago, so I should carry on just as I was. The one piece of casting I could not quarrel with was that of a sturdy young American with a corncrake voice, Kirk Douglas. He and I got along well until the end of the film, when I made a bad blunder. Browsing in a Los Angeles bookshop I came across a theatrical pamphlet published some time in the 1840s, which offered advice to the aspiring young actor on how to behave towards his older, more experienced colleagues. I bought it for a joke and gave it to Kirk. My idea of a joke was obviously not the same as his. He shot me a glance which more than justified his casting in his next picture as a boxing champion.

Mourning Becomes Electra didn't reach England until five years later. It hadn't done good box office in the States, though it won me an American award, from the National Board of Film Review, and a nomination for an Oscar. The English exhibitors cold-shouldered it altogether, until in 1952 BBC television broadcast the play and to everyone's surprise it proved very popular. Whereupon an independent exhibitor in Manchester booked our film for a screening and the notices in the national newspapers were so good that the exhibitors in Wardour Street rather shamefacedly dusted it off their shelves and screened it in London, where it was publicized as 'the film they didn't want you to see!'

George Cukor was on the telephone. He was organizing an 'English Lunch' and, since Ethel Barrymore was getting too old and frail to go out to lunch, it was to be given at her house in Pacific Palisades.

It was arranged that Katharine Hepburn should give me a lift. She was playing tennis at the Beverly Hills Hotel when I called there to pick her up. She appeared to be beating the bejesus out of her opponents. When she had finally disposed of them, she disappeared to take a shower, and emerged about five minutes later looking as fresh as a daisy. I had met Miss Hepburn before, in London. She asked me if I could see Fanny Brice anywhere. This lady was, as usual, pretty easy to see, and hear.

Katie drove and Miss Brice listened. But not for long. In about five minutes both ladies were talking at the tops of their voices, the only difference being that Hepburn gesticulated somewhat more than Brice. This seemed to unnerve the latter.

'Do you think it would help if you occasionally took hold of the wheel?' she demanded.

Hepburn did not hear this, and we continued to hover between life and death until we reached Pacific Palisades.

Some of the guests had already arrived. Ivor Novello was the guest of honour. Bobby Andrews, Dorothy Dickson, Beatrice Lillie, Gladys Cooper, and – surprise, surprise – Miss Greta Garbo.

Cukor was an accomplished host, subtly steering the conversation from one guest to another. I was so overcome by meeting Garbo that I did not venture to produce my camera, which I had left in the hall. At one point in the afternoon there was a lull in the conversation. Cukor's voice quietly put an end to this with a remark that woke everybody up: 'What do you suppose would be the combined salaries for this afternoon?'

Someone coughed discreetly.

Garbo had never seen Bea Lillie perform, and Cukor persuaded the *diseuse* to do 'I've been to a marvellous party'. She went through what must have been half her repertoire. It was a joy to see Garbo laughing with the same abandon as in *Ninotchka*.

When the time came for the guests to leave I found that by a stroke of luck I was in the same car as Garbo and sitting directly behind her. Cukor was driving. There was a pause. Suddenly he addressed himself to me. He asked when Rachel was arriving. Before I had time to answer, Garbo turned round in her seat and, smiling as if in great wonderment, said, 'Ooh, you are married?'

The question caught me unawares and I do not remember how I answered. I tried to think of something to prolong the conversation. She continued to smile, and all I could think of was her astounding eyes.

After a few long seconds she spoke again. 'How is Mr Rank?'

'Blooming,' I answered.

She continued to look in my direction as if wishing to help me say something. She spoke again. 'Is there much Buddhism in England?'

Everyone who knows anything about the lady knows of her interest in Eastern religions. I was quite ready to worship at her shrine. What, then, was the matter with me that I should have said the one thing that would make her drop me like a hot brick? 'Not a great deal, I think. And what little we have, we have exported to the States.'

The great blue eyes turned to ice and she returned her gaze to the Californian landscape.

News came that Andy, my stepfather, had died. Towards the end of his life he had become almost blind. I had overcome my childhood resentment of him, and had come to like him and respect him increasingly ever since the time when, as I was leaving Cambridge, he said one day, 'You know, Michael, you and I don't speak the same language.' An admirable man.

I invited Mother to come and stay with us. Rachel, who had joined me in Hollywood at the beginning of March, was busy preparing a film she was to do with Charles Boyer. Mother had rather a dull time. The O'Neill film was in full swing. The few amongst the English colony who knew her would invite her to tea or drinks, and she would regale them with an endless flow of theatrical gossip from the distant past. I found it was almost impossible to persuade her to go to bed, and what with early calls to the studio nearly every morning, I found myself snapping at her. Both my films were turning out to be disappointments. Rachel and I had reached a turning point in our marriage, and all things seemed aggravated by being in Hollywood.

At last, in July, the end was in sight. J. Arthur Rank was in Hollywood for the christening of a grandchild, and we were invited to the christening party. There was something rather dynastic about the event, as the newcomer to the Rank empire gurgled happily alongside a replica of himself and his cot modelled in ice. Rank introduced me to one of his henchmen and instructed him to acquaint me with the situation: audiences, it seemed, were not yet responding as they should to all the talent and money which J. Arthur was pouring into British films, and as for the Common-wealth, no one had heard of us. J. Arthur thought it regrettable that so many fine English actors and actresses who had made films in Hollywood simply bypassed Canada. I was returning to England shortly, was I not? Would I consider returning via Canada, to do some personal appearances?

Why on earth did I succumb to this proposition so easily? True, Rank was the leading British producer and I was under contract to him at the time, and had made several films for him; but I was under no obligation to undertake this kind of publicity venture. But Rachel was still filming *A Woman's Vengeance* with Boyer. Mother had already returned home. I accepted, with the proviso that I should have two weeks in New York before setting off, and that I should have someone who would accompany me and look after me every inch of the way in Canada.

We started at Niagara Falls. An irritating lapse of nature. In addition to the humid summer climate – no one had mentioned to me that Eastern Canada in summer was renowned for its humidity – the spray from the Falls could be detected for miles around. After half an hour or so, one would be soaked. 'Shirts for Mr Redgrave.' Someone was sent to purchase a quantity of shirts, and I would be ferried to my hotel to put on a clean dry one, and then back to the Falls again.

Next stop, Belleville, Ontario, where I had my first real check. I had asked that someone should get me a drink and was told that it just wasn't possible unless I bought a bottle from a licensed liquor store. Canada's liquor laws – another thing they had forgotten to mention. I began to feel rather irritable.

And on to Hamilton. 'Michael Redgrave drives a Buick in Hamilton,' proclaimed an advertisement in the local daily paper. They evidently didn't realize that I couldn't drive (still can't). I glanced at a copy of the tour itinerary. 'Mounted Police,' it said, 'to guard back door of hotel.' I was to be taken in by the back staircase, hold a press conference, and, at the conclusion, address the crowd from a first-floor balcony. The hotel was opposite a new Odeon cinema. 'What makes you think', I asked my guide, 'that there are going to be crowds? We didn't see anything like that in Belleville.'

'You're forgetting', said my guide, 'the power of local radio. We've been putting out on this for three days, and I can tell you the interest in you is quite something.' He said this very seriously.

'We'll see,' I muttered.

He was right. I stepped out on to the balcony, to find a huge crowd filling the square. I spoke for ten minutes; heaven knows what about. They clapped me politely, and I set off for Toronto. A visit to a veterans' hospital, three personal appearances, and then I was in Montreal. Three more personal appearances, this time in French.

In all these capers I was accompanied by a young American, Bob Michell, who offered to come to England with me in the hopes of working there. Try as we might, a work permit couldn't be arranged. But Bob stayed with us, a dear friend to me and to the whole family, for nearly twelve years. Then he went home, married, and had two delightful children. He died in 1975 while I was touring America in *Shakespeare's People*. Shortly before his death I flew to see him and his wife and children at their home in Reno. As I entered the departure lounge to leave, he scribbled on the notebook that he used, lacking the power of speech: 'I won't stay to wave you off. I know I should start crying.'

XVII

FOR THE latter part of my stay in Hollywood the studio had rented a house for me. Its walls were lined with books and a priceless collection of magazines and periodicals – copies of the *Illustrated London News* dating back to the first issue. The owner, John Balderston, had been a distinguished war correspondent in the First World War. He had also collaborated with J.C. Squire on the play *Berkeley Square*, a very successful adaptation of Henry James's *A Sense of the Past*. It was there that I began to think about James and the theatre.

The following year, holidaying with Rachel and the children at Bexhill-on-Sea, I began an adaptation of James's story *The Aspern Papers*. It had been a busy year. I had played Macbeth on Broadway in the spring of 1948, an enterprise which takes some nerve, as other actors have discovered. I had translated and adapted, with Diana Gould, a French play by Georges de Porto-Riche, *Amoureuse*, which we called *A Woman in Love*. I had introduced Diana to Yehudi Menuhin, whom she later married. I needed a rest and a change. In the mornings I worked on *The Aspern Papers*, letting James's words transport me from hydrangea-besotted Bexhill to the Venice of the 1880s. In the afternoon I dug sandcastles and 'waterworks' with the children on the beach.

Eleven years and many versions later, *The Aspern Papers* reached the stage, with Flora Robson as Miss Tina, Beatrix Lehmann as Miss Bordereau, and myself as H.J., the story's narrator. Some surprise was expressed by reviewers that James, whose long and notorious courtship of the theatre had been so unsuccessful in his lifetime, should find success posthumously with an adaptation of such an 'untheatrical' story.

No such thought occurred to me at Bexhill. Here, I thought, were at least half a dozen capital scenes which could be lifted almost straight

As Macbeth at the Aldwych Theatre in London and the National Theatre in New York (1947–48).

On holiday with the children at Bexhill, Sussex (1948).

With Nancy Coleman, Kirk Douglas and Katina Paxinou in *Mourning Becomes Electra*. Nothing is so serious as Hollywood when it takes itself seriously, and when it tackles a Great American Classic, it takes itself very seriously indeed. I won an Oscar nomination (1951).

With Brian Smith in *The Browning Version*, directed by Anthony Asquith. Rattigan's script was a marvel of its kind – one of those scripts where every line seems so right that you do not have to learn them. For Crocker-Harris I won the prize for best performance at the Cannes Film Festival, the first English actor to do so (1950).

As Antony in the Shakespeare Memorial Theatre Company's *Antony and Cleopatra*. There is no plain sailing in Antony, no point of rest where the words will carry you along. It is a part that calls on all the strength one possesses and tests out every weakness (1953).

The Redgraves at Chiswick, our home for
twelve years. Vanessa was fourteen, Lynn
eight, and Corin eleven (1951).

As Hector in *Tiger at the Gates* at the Apollo
Theatre (1955).

With Diana Wynyard and Vanessa in *A Touch of the Sun*. This was Vanessa's first appearance in London, and our first together (1958). 'Be severe, demanding, a person of taste. That leads to success in our work.' No young actress could have taken Bernhardt's injunction more seriously.

The Redgraves in 1962. We were now all on the stage and, as Vanessa once said, 'Ours is a family that rejoices in each other.'

At Angkor Thom, Cambodia, a break from shooting *The Quiet American* in Saigon (1957).

As Hamlet with the Shakespeare Memorial
Company in Moscow. It was the last Hamlet I ever
gave, and the best (1958).

With Maggie Smith in *The Master Builder* at the
National Theatre, London (1963–64).

(*Below left*) As Samson in *Samson Agonistes*, Yvonne Arnaud Theatre, Guildford, and (*below right*) with Ingrid
Bergman and Emlyn Williams in *A Month in the Country*, Cambridge Theatre, London (1965).

As Uncle Vanya. Antony and Vanya are the two performances I am proudest of (1962–63).

In *Hobson's Choice* at the National Theatre (1963–64).

As King Lear, with Vanessa, at the Roundhouse in London (1982).

on to the stage. What was more, two strong Jamesian forces gave promise of holding these scenes together: situation and suspense. The suspense might be finely-drawn, almost imperceptible, but it was there. And where there was suspense, there was theatre.

Snapshots galore. From my earliest experiments with a Brownie box camera I have thousands of snaps of the children. Corin did not take to the camera at first. In a group photograph he can usually be seen shielding his eyes from the sun or looking in a different direction. The Lynn of those early photos is a plump little dumpling: hard to associate with the svelte, out-giving Broadway star, mother of three, now settled in California. Vanessa's joyous smile she inherits in large part from her mother.

This was the time when Vanessa, fending off some interviewer anxious to know if she would be 'following in her parents' footsteps', replied with devastating frankness, 'Good God, no!' Yet it was evident, I thought, that she was bound for the theatre. We took it for granted and seldom talked about it. At the age of about ten she favoured ballet, accepting the fact that she might grow too tall for it. She was almost too tall already. But Marie Rambert, to whom I took Vanessa, said that she would be glad to have her as a pupil. At some point, tall girls stop growing, and if she were to go into the theatre the grace of ballet training would not come amiss.

I pointed out to Vanessa the examples of Edith Evans, Margaret Leighton, and other tall women who had built fine stage careers in spite of their inches. I encouraged her to stand up straight. 'Be severe, demanding, a person of taste. That leads to success in our work.' No young actress could have taken Bernhardt's injunction more seriously.

'Hugh Hunt telephoned while you were out,' said Rachel. 'He asked if you could ring him back.'

'I know what that's about,' I said. Michael Benthall had told me about Hugh's plans for the 1949 season at the Old Vic, in which he was to direct *She Stoops to Conquer*. Hunt had been director of Dublin's Abbey Theatre before the War, and later of the Bristol Old Vic. The next season was to be his first as the newly-appointed director of the Old Vic in London.

I telephoned Hugh, who suggested that we meet for lunch. Was it about the season at the Vic? I asked. It was. Were the plays to be *Love's Labour's Lost*, *She Stoops to Conquer*, *A Month in the Country*, and Molière's *The Miser*? Yes.

'And what's the fifth play?'

'I don't know,' said Hugh, 'but it will probably have to be another Shakespeare.'

'There's no need to take me to lunch. Make the fifth play *Hamlet* and I'll play as cast.' (I remembered meeting Robert Helpmann at a party not long before. 'And when are you going to give us your Hamlet, Mr Redgrave?' 'When someone asks me, I suppose.' 'If I'd waited to be asked, I'd *never* have played Hamlet,' said Helpmann.)

There was a moment's pause.

'Haven't we had rather a lot of Hamlets lately?' Hugh asked.

'No,' I said, firmly.

'I'll have to talk to the Governors.'

Within twenty-four hours it was settled. I would play Berowne in *Love's Labour's Lost*, Young Marlow in *She Stoops*, Rakitin in *A Month in the Country*, and Hamlet.

Meanwhile, I had to earn some money. It was the summer of 1949. We should not be playing at the Old Vic until the autumn, and I knew that my salary there would not go far.

Another unexpected telephone call: Noël Coward.

'They're making a film of *The Astonished Heart* and you've got the part.'

'Oh, yes?' I didn't even know that I was being considered for it.

'Yes. There are only two actors who could play it: you and I.'

In that case, I thought, I wonder that you don't play it yourself. But I put the thought out of mind and waited for the script. Noël, it appeared, was tired and in need of a holiday in Jamaica.

The screenplay, by Muriel Box, was very faithful to Noël's play. One thing troubled me. The hero, an eminent psychiatrist, put an end to his life by throwing himself from the roof of the Dorchester Hotel. Surely, I asked the producer, Sydney Box, a great man in such a profession would choose almost any other exit than that? It was agreed that Noël should be asked if this could be changed. Word came back very smartly: nothing doing. But by then I had persuaded myself to accept the film. Celia Johnson and Margaret Leighton, two of the greatest leading ladies, I thought, were to be my co-stars.

We rehearsed at Denham Studios. Asquith, whom I liked and trusted, was directing. But soon he and I began to lose confidence. I tried changing my words. Noël had insisted that not one word should be altered, but he was on holiday and didn't want to be disturbed. I did not yet know that his contract said that his judgement on any matter of shooting or script was irreversible. I was soon to find out.

On the day after his return from holiday a great commotion could be heard in Denham's corridors, and soon Noël himself swept in like a whirlwind. I had expected him to invite me to lunch, but no such thing.

'What do you look like in a moustache?' he asked. I had decided that I needed a moustache to make me look older. In any case, a moustache was indicated in the script.

'Like this,' I said, pulling out an eyebrow pencil and drawing one across my lip.

'No moustache!' said Noël.

'But it's in the . . .'

'No moustache!'

After a fortnight or so of shooting I was in a quandary, and requested a meeting with the producers. Sydney Box came, and Tony Darnborough, and Noël. As best I could, I explained that I simply couldn't see myself in the part. This seemed to cause a mild sensation. (Afterwards I reflected – and the point is made in Coward's diaries – that Noël himself had probably engineered this situation as the most tactful way of replacing me.)

'We'll have to find another actor,' said Sydney.

I suggested one or two, including Stewart Granger.

'No,' said Noël, very firmly, 'I'd rather have Mike.'

There was a silence, whilst we turned the pages of *Spotlight*, the casting directory.

'I *could* play the part,' said Noël eventually, adding quickly, 'But of course Mike mustn't lose a penny.'

'Of course,' agreed Sydney.

I could not resist seeing the film, nor help noticing that Noël had taken more pains over the script than in the version which had given me such difficulty. Nor could I help the feeling that my doubts about the story had been confirmed in the result, though there was not much joy in that.

Until we came to play it on the Continent, *She Stoops to Conquer* was only a moderate success. But for me it was a second homecoming. Like the arrival of an Albert Finney or a Peter O'Toole from the provinces, my first appearance in London at the Old Vic years before had caused a considerable stir of excitement, not least because it was known, or rumoured, that I had already turned down several glamorous offers to play in the West End. And after the success of *As You Like It* I was praised to the skies, besieged with invitations to play this, that, and the other. No part seemed beyond my reach. Whatever leading role was to be cast, I was every producer's first choice. Once, as I entered the room at the Garrick Club where Seymour Hicks was giving a party, Godfrey Tearle, a most commanding figure in the theatre then, said, in his most distinguished voice, 'And here's the great white hope.'

For all that, I paid a penalty. As Terence Rattigan once told me, 'When you've had three good notices in a row, get ready for a bad one.' This was not by any means an entirely cynical remark; critics will always find ample time to repent their over-enthusiasm. Their reaction to me as time went on was to find my performances too studied, too elaborate, too 'intellectual'. And no doubt there was some truth in this. As Remond de St Albine, an eighteenth-century author of a treatise on acting, puts it: 'The reason why we sometimes discover the study'd action of the player, is not because he has been at pains studying it beforehand, but because he has not studied it enough: the last touches of his application in this kind, should be those employed to conceal that there was ever any labour bestow'd at all upon what he is doing; and the rest, without this, always hurts instead of pleasing us.' This may be simple but it is profound.

Since *A Month in the Country* at the St James's in 1943, I had played very little comedy. For that, strangely enough, the critic James Agate was partly responsible. He had written that I succeeded best in parts that had a touch of the 'morbid' in them, that I lacked light-heartedness. 'For Michael Redgrave to play Young Marlow,' he wrote, 'would be as unprofitable as for Bob Hope to play King Lear.'

Now Agate was dead, and Michael Benthall, our director, had the happy knack of convincing me that I was a great comic actor. Rehearsals for *She Stoops* went smoothly and well. I seized on a fragment of text – 'This stammer in my address' – to justify playing the young man with a stammer. I found that by holding back on the letter 'm', letting the audience attune themselves to the stammer, I could pause as long as I liked before the line 'Madam, will you marry me?' and the longer I paused, the greater the laugh.

The audience reception was warm. Next morning I lay in bed and heard *The Times* and the *News Chronicle* drop like time bombs through the letter-box. Should I, or shouldn't I? Yes, I should read them and face the worst, and to hell with Agate. Had he still been among the living, I would have been neither so eager nor so nervous.

I had no need to quail before his ghost. The notices were excellent. 'A performance accurately pitched on a note of high comedy,' said *The Times*. High comedy!? I raced upstairs to show Rachel the good news. 'What's the matter, darling, why are you crying?' she said. (The reader will have noticed that the Scudamores cry very easily.) We read the reviews over and over. 'The part of Young Marlow,' wrote Eric Keown, 'is a pretty good test of an actor. ... He who plays him must be constantly changing gear. He must be hesitant and tongue-tied, though not quite a boor, and the next moment a warm young amorist still palpably a gentleman. The success of the play depends upon his mastery of these diverse elements, and the success of this production is Mr Michael Redgrave. ... It is a fine piece of gentle comedy, and Mr Redgrave has a way of locking his lips mulishly on an "M" that puts him among the great stage stammerers.'

And to hell with Agate now!

Despite Hugh Hunt's 'Haven't we had rather a lot of Hamlets lately?' there had, in fact, been rather few. There was the Stratford *Hamlet* in 1948, with Bobby Helpmann and Paul Scofield alternating in the part, and Robert Eddison's at the Bristol Old Vic. But in those days *Hamlet*, as befitted one of the peaks – if not *the* peak – of dramatic literature, was not performed as it is now, in season and out. To play Hamlet was the supreme test of an actor's quality.

I think Hugh, who had a military background, appreciated the dash with which I had insisted on Hamlet before accepting the other parts he had to offer. Probably that, more than anything, convinced him that I could play it. At all events, he said something at our first meeting after that telephone conversation which puzzled and intrigued me: 'You are a misunderstood actor.'

'What does he mean?' I asked Rachel.

'He's right,' she answered, 'but for that you have only yourself to blame.'

We gathered together for the first read-through. Wanda Rotha was to play the Queen, at my suggestion. The Queen needs a quality of over-ripe sensuality. This, Wanda had. What was more, she spoke perfect English but with a trace of a German accent, and the Queen's line, 'O, this is counter, you false Danish dogs,' suggested to me, which I had never noticed in any commentary, that she must be a foreign queen. Yvonne Mitchell was to play Ophelia – a very happy choice. For Laertes I had insisted on a good fencer, Peter Copley, remembering how I as Laertes had cut Larry's forehead thirteen years before.

Hugh opened the proceedings with a specially-prepared lecture, as he had for *Love's Labour's Lost*. On that occasion most of the actors, unfamiliar with the play, had congratulated him warmly. For *Hamlet* his lecture was rather longer and the actors seemed restless, feeling that they knew the play and wanted to get on with it. No one pressed forward at the end to thank him except myself, feeling that I had to. Perhaps they were right. The difficulties of *Hamlet* are many, but none so difficult in performance as they are on paper.

'Roy,' says Mother in one of her notebooks, 'could never be bothered with Shakespeare and the poets. He told a story of how he was going to play Hamlet when he was at Mrs Lane's theatre and had not troubled to read it till he heard one of the costers reciting some of it, and then he thought he'd better get on with the words.' Good or bad, Roy's Hamlet was his own. My first attempt, as a schoolmaster at Cranleigh, owed so much to Gielgud's performance in the part in 1930 that I must have seemed like Gielgud's understudy. So much so that I obliged myself not to see any of his later interpretations, knowing that if I were to play the part myself I should want to clear my imagination of his presence.

When we came to rehearse *Hamlet* I brought with me only a few preconceptions, most of them of a negative kind. *Hamlet* was not, I thought, as the Olivier film had suggested, 'the tragedy of a man who could not make up his mind'. On the contrary, he *did* make up his mind, as thoroughly as anyone in his unique circumstances could. To take another example, I so strongly rejected the 'pathological' interpretation of Hamlet, as in some way the victim of an Oedipus complex, that I used every possible occasion to stress his love for his father.

For the actor, the difficulties of Hamlet are those which reveal themselves only when one starts to act him. How, for example, to greet the ghost, when several other characters have already met him twice? Garrick, we know, made great play with his hands, and for years after, his business was copied by successive Hamlets, becoming almost a test of an actor's skill. It seemed to me that the solution was to do nothing. Just as in the cinema Eisenstein showed that by skilful editing a close-up of an actor without any expression will reveal by suggestion what the audience wants it to reveal, so there are moments in the theatre when the actor is able to do nothing, and even feel nothing, and yet the audience will see in him all that they want or need to see.

In the closet scene, I imported a piece of business from William Poel's production of *Fratricide Punished*, in which Mother had played the Queen to Esmé Percy's Hamlet. A maidservant placed the Queen's chestnut-red wig on a block, and the Queen was seen to have grey hair.

(*Fratricide Punished* deserves, and has probably received elsewhere, a chapter to itself. It was a simplified version of *Hamlet* performed on the Continent by English actors in the 1650s, when Cromwell had closed the theatres.)

For 'Look here upon this picture, and on this, / The counterfeit presentment of two brothers,' I drew a coin from my pocket with Claudius's head on it, and holding it side by side with a miniature portrait of Hamlet's father which I wore in a locket, I thrust them at the Queen, almost ramming them in her face:

> . . . Have you eyes?
> Could you on this fair mountain leave to feed,
> And batten on this moor? Ha! have you eyes?

Since the 'rogue and peasant slave' soliloquy brought the curtain down on the first half, I thought some theatrical effect was called for there. The troupe of players had brought on a large theatrical skip, so on the words 'O, vengeance', with the players' sword held in both hands, I did a forward fall as if stabbing Claudius. I spoke the remainder of the soliloquy very quietly until the last two lines. Then, rising to my feet, holding a crown from the players' prop basket at arm's length above my head, and with the other arm swirling a red cloak about me, I gave a joyous shout, as if, for the first time, Hamlet knew what to do:

> . . . The play's the thing
> Wherein I'll catch the conscience of the king.

Yvonne Mitchell had waited in the wings till the end of the Act before returning to her dressing-room, and when the applause subsided, she gave me a radiant smile, as much as to say 'What did I tell you?' As I reached the stairs, my dresser met me. He said he had just been telephoned by Olivier's dresser at the St James's, where Larry was playing with Rachel in Christopher Fry's *Venus Observed*. 'Sir Laurence wants to know how it's going.'

In the scores of times I have played Hamlet, it seems to me that I never gave the same performance twice. Not that the theatre-goer who came on Wednesday would see something very different to what he would have seen on Tuesday, but that I was always open to a new effect. This was not, for me, a matter of pride or deliberate choice. I could admire, if not envy, those actors who prided themselves on repeating in each performance what they had done on previous occasions. I admired Donald Wolfit, who knew exactly how he had mapped his part and would stick to that territory through thick and thin.

'Michael,' he once said to me, 'you've worked with Guthrie. What's he like?'

We were at the Garrick Club. Wolfit, I knew, was going to the Vic to play Tamburlaine, in which he would be very fine, and Lear (though the latter never materialized).

'Well,' I said, choosing my words carefully, 'he's very stimulating.'

Wolfit brushed this aside, as I thought he might. 'Yes, yes, I dare say, but what's he like?'

I was a little nonplussed. 'Did you see – ' I asked, and reeled off some of Tony's productions.

Donald's face clouded. It was clear he had seen none of them, and the bare mention of them seemed to deepen his disquiet. 'Because, you see,' he said, 'I have thirteen effects in my Lear, and *I don't intend to lose one of them.*'

No notices, however good, can ever quite satisfy an actor. No applause is ever quite long enough. At the end of a reception, no matter how tumultuous, one part of an actor's vanity must ask, 'Yes, but why have you stopped?'

Only in Leningrad and Moscow, where, eight years later, in 1958, I gave my last performances of Hamlet with the Shakespeare Memorial Company, did the applause, which lasted several minutes, silence almost all my doubts and questions. I was fifty, an age at which one can start, like Solness, to look over one's shoulder at the next generation pressing on one's heels. The young and brilliant Ian Holm was my understudy. He would watch every scene from the wings, which is right and conscientious for an understudy, but I could not help imagining him saying to himself, 'Yes, but just let me play it.'

Once I came off after the battlements scene and passed him in the wings, as usual, and he whispered, 'What you are doing out there is absolutely incredible.' I flew, I walked on air for the rest of that performance. It was the last I ever gave. And the best.

Something else happened on that tour. When our plane landed in Moscow, from amongst the press corps waiting to photograph us on arrival an English journalist took me aside and said he had a message for me: 'Guy Burgess wants to know if you would agree to meet him.'

'Guy Burgess? Yes, of course.'

I'd not seen Burgess since we had been together at Cambridge. He had designed the sets for a play I was in. I had a general recollection that he was amusing. He had a very lively mind.

On the first night of *Hamlet* in Moscow a rather noisy group of English newspapermen were gathered outside my dressing-room door. Out of their hubbub came one voice I thought I recognized. It could be Guy's – it was. He swept into my dressing-room, extending both arms to greet me. He had been crying. 'Oh, Michael! Those words, those words! You can imagine how they carry me back. Magic!'

His face underwent a sort of convulsion; he lurched past me and, with what looked like practised accuracy, was sick into the basin. An athletic-looking young man who had come in with Guy waved his hands in apology. 'Oh, Guy, you are a *peeg*,' he said, with considerable force.

When Guy had recovered, which he did almost immediately, he introduced the young man: a factory worker, studying ballet at evening classes, whom Guy had persuaded to leave work early to see my Hamlet.

Next day, Guy called for me and we drove through the snowy suburbs to lunch at his flat. He seemed anxious to impress. He was wearing his old Etonian tie; his suit was well worn and a bit shiny; he was stouter than he used to be.

His flat was tidy and comfortable. Placed on the coffee-table in order to catch my eye was the current *New Statesman*: equally eye-catching was a pot of pâté de foie gras from France. Lunch was served by a cook-housekeeper. She appeared to speak no English, though Guy in her presence said that she understood every word, adding as she left the room, 'She reports on me, of course.'

We sat down to eat the foie gras. Or, rather, I sat alone at the table whilst Guy, who was already too drunk to eat, paced up and down the room, talking. The second course was a hare, but the cook-housekeeper had omitted to remove the gallbladder, and it was totally inedible. Guy apologized profusely, but there was nothing else to eat except the remains of the foie gras.

After lunch we walked. We passed a nearby basilica which he said he often visited: 'They have wonderful music.' He told me 'they' had only wanted him to deliver Donald Maclean; he repeated this more than once.

He came to see us several times at the theatre and made friends with Coral Browne, who played the Queen in *Hamlet*. She agreed to order him some clothes at Simpsons in Piccadilly when we got back. He said he still had some money in England.

On the day we were leaving he came to see us off at the hotel. As we drove away, he was near tears. 'Write to me,' he said, 'it's bloody lonely here, you know.'

'And which is *your* favourite film?' A favourite question, this, and a difficult one to answer. Among the fifty or so pictures I have made are some that would hardly appear in anyone's selection of memorable films, yet I loved every moment of making them. There have been times, working with Orson Welles on *Confidential Report* (1955), for example, when even at three-thirty in the morning I have not wanted to stop. And I have seldom been happier than when working with Gene Kelly in Paris on *The Happy Road* (1956).

One thing I learned from working with Fritz Lang – or, rather, relearned, for I think I knew it already – was that not only should a film have a strong central idea, but its idea should be such as can be conveyed in a single sentence. Not all good films, I realize, conform to this criterion. But I have found when answering that other favourite question, 'What's it about?' that if you can awaken the interest of your questioner in a sentence or two – 'It's about a ventriloquist who thinks he's possessed by his dummy,' 'It's about an embittered schoolmaster whose defences break down because someone, unexpectedly, is kind to him' – it's a fair, though not complete, test of the appeal that your film will have at large.

So it was with *The Browning Version*. In 1950 I found myself, unexpectedly, at a loose end, when the money ran out for a film I was making with Anouk Aimée in the South of France. I returned home to another surprise. 'Puffin Asquith wants you for *The Browning Version*,' I was told. Eric Portman had created the part of Crocker-Harris with great success. Now Eric was unavailable for the film, and at short notice I took on the part. (Sometimes two actors' careers become strangely enmeshed. Eric had taken over my part in *The 49th Parallel*, a war-effort movie that Michael Powell shot in the early days of the war.)

The 'look' of a part is always highly important, especially in films, where once the first scenes are in the can it is too late and too expensive to make any substantial changes in one's appearance. For *The Browning Version* I did a number of camera tests. There was the question of spectacles. I was in two minds about this. Spectacles are the first thing that actors lay hold of when they have to play an academic character. So I thought, *I* won't wear spectacles. I tried one camera test without. Then another, with: the first pair concealed too much of the expression in my eyes, so I asked them to make me another without rims to the lenses, and then, when these seemed to suit, a spare pair for safety's sake.

I also asked for camera tests with sound. I wanted a light head-voice for Crocker-Harris, and I knew that when one first assumes a pitch or an accent different from one's own, it is hard to get a true impression of what it will sound like to an audience because the sound in one's own ear at first is often very exaggerated.

I lightened my hair with very strong peroxide, which in black-and-white photography would give a look of hair that was fading and turning grey. I also had the hairdresser shave the crown of my head (though to my annoyance this bald patch was seen in only one shot in the film).

Despite these preparations it was a terrible beginning. We had to do the last shots first, and these last scenes were very emotional. There were none of the scenes of minor importance which one usually did first so as to work one's way into the film. I can still see perfectly clearly in that film where the camera angle changes during a scene, where my make-up changes; even my weight changes from scene to scene. (At that time I could gain weight and shed it almost at will, which was very useful for certain character parts, because even a slight change of weight would show immediately in my face, altering its expression. But in taking on *The Browning Version* at such short notice, I had not had time to lose as much weight as I wanted at the start.)

In the scene with the headmaster at the cricket match, there is another mistake in my playing, which shows if one looks for it. Not many in the audience would spot it, I think, but C. A. Lejeune, the *Observer* critic at the time, who had been bowled over by Portman's performance in the part, noticed it immediately. 'For such a big man,' she wrote of me, 'his performance is wonderfully delicate' – ominous compliment – 'but it is the delicacy of a floorwalker rather than a scholar.' And, as far as the cricket-match scene went, she was right. At the last minute, and to my surprise, Wilfrid Hyde-White had been cast as the headmaster. A very successful actor in his chosen field, but too smooth and urbane, I thought, for this part. I tried to adjust myself, but in doing so I somehow slipped into a manner that was too deferential, almost obsequious, where my character should have stood his own ground more firmly. 'The delicacy of a floor-walker' – how one phrase like that remains in the memory long after recollections of the most lavish praise have faded, and all the more so if one recognizes its partial truth.

Rattigan's script was a marvel of its kind. There are scripts, now and then, where every line seems so right that you do not have to learn them. It is enough to repeat the words a few times for every line to fall into place. Rattigan's script also gave me that rare opportunity, such as I had in *Dead of Night*, and would have again as Barnes Wallis in *The Dam Busters*, to create a character totally different from my own. This is not necessarily the highest achievement of acting. I could equally, if not more, admire a Garbo, who could change her mood in a score of different ways without ever changing character. Nevertheless, it is one of the most satisfying.

It was Barnes Wallis himself, incidentally, who gave me the clue to my performance in *The Dam Busters*, a film which I enjoyed making more than any since *The Browning Version*. We were introduced, and Wallis, who was a good deal shorter than I and rather slim, burst out laughing. We 'clicked' at once. At our second meeting I said, 'I'm not going to mimic you, you know.' His reply was interesting, not so much because he was evidently relieved as for what it showed of the method he would use to tackle a problem, even in the field of acting.

'No, of course. Your problem is not to imitate a person, but to create him.'

It illustrated, I thought, his scientific approach to the very essence of what he was considering. A quality – not at all to be confused with the stereotype of the absent-minded professor – of setting aside everything but the essential, which must have driven him on and sustained him through countless set-backs and disappointments.

XVIII

T HE MEMORIAL Theatre had been expensively refurbished for
the hundreds of thousands of visitors who were expected at
Stratford in 1951, the year of the Festival of Britain. Shakespeare's
history plays were to be produced, from *Richard II* to *Henry V*.
Anthony Quayle, the actor-director of the Memorial Theatre, was to
play Falstaff. The young Welsh actor Richard Burton was Hal. My
parts were Richard, Hotspur, and Chorus in *Henry V*. Also Prospero
– a Stratford season at that time consisted of five productions, and at
my request *The Tempest* was chosen as the fifth play.

Memories of the season when Mother played Mistress Page
buzzed about my head as I bicycled to rehearsal every morning. The
old theatre, where I had been allowed to walk-on in *Henry IV, Part
II* to swell the tiny crowd of extras who cheered Maurice Colbourne
as Prince Hal in the coronation scene, burnt to the ground in 1926 –
set alight by the Flower family, it was said in jest. The Flowers, that
munificent family of Warwickshire brewers whose ancestor built the
first theatre at Stratford in the 1890s, had long wanted a modern
theatre in its place, and built one in 1933, and were rewarded for
their pains by the universal 'ya-boos' which greeted the new design,
red brick upon red brick, 'the Jam Factory'.

Stratford was much changed. The Stratford of my boyhood was a
little market town. Sheep Street in the town centre was memorable for
its tea-shop, where they sold wonderful lemon cakes. The season was
divided into two parts, with nine or ten productions in all. Ten days or
a fortnight was considered sufficient time to rehearse a production,
though rehearsals in those days, when Actors' Equity was only a
gleam in the eyes of a few, would frequently go on till the players
dropped from exhaustion. There were fine actors at Stratford then,
but no one expected to make his reputation or his fortune there.

Nor for that matter were fortunes to be made now, at least not by the actors. The top salary was £60 a week, the minimum £9. But the quarter of a million visitors who would come to the theatre this season would keep the cash tills ringing, and the box office was confidently expected to recoup the £75,000 spent on enlarging and improving the auditorium.

In its own prestige, and the reputation it could bestow upon its actors, Stratford was totally changed. Anthony Quayle had seen to that, almost single-handedly. Since the War, Robert Helpmann and Paul Scofield had played there, as had Godfrey Tearle, Diana Wynyard, John Gielgud, and Peggy Ashcroft.

The 1951 season was the first in anyone's memory when the history plays were produced as a cycle. Quayle and I discussed how this might alter and define our view of the chief characters, for characters and events change their meaning when the plays are seen as a whole. Richard II, for instance, was customarily played as a figure of tragedy and Bolingbroke as a ruthless schemer when the play was performed on its own. Indeed, to Bolingbroke's opponents in the later plays that is how he appears in retrospect: 'Richard, that sweet lovely rose'. Yet it seemed essential that Richard's vanity and cruelty, so evident in his treatment of John of Gaunt, be given full measure if Bolingbroke's usurping the Crown were to be understood not merely as a crime but as a *necessary* crime. Having some responsibility for the cycle (I was to direct *Henry IV, Part II*), I laid some emphasis on Richard's pettiness and hysteria in the first half of the play – too much emphasis, in fact, in my anxiety that the audience should get the point.

Hotspur, says Lady Percy, was 'thick of speech'. That, and some of Hotspur's own lines, suggested to me that he was a rough, ragged rascal, unversed in the ways of the Court. At Quayle's suggestion I had gone up to Northumberland in search of a convincing accent for Hotspur – not the Tyneside 'Geordie' but the Northumbrian country accent. Somehow this had got into the press, and amongst those who came forward offering help and tuition was the Duke of Northumberland, who invited me to dinner at Alnwick and introduced me to Jack Armstrong, who had the honorary title of the Duke's Piper.

So, armed with the cumbersome wire recorder of those days, I acquired something that passed for Northumbrian, with its burred 'r' almost like the French guttural 'r' sound. I found the accent an enormous help. It took me outside myself and made the strongest possible contrast with the tones of Richard II, which I had been playing in each preceding performance. Of course, no amount of argument or textual justification would have carried the day if the accent had not been felt by audiences to come off. On the whole I think it did. Perhaps the greatest compliment paid me on that account was by two Northumbrian friends of Quayle's.

'What did you think of Redgrave's accent?' he asked them after a performance.

'Ooh, right, yes, bang on. Alnwick,' said one.

'Ye-es, very good,' said the other, 'but I'd say more Wooler than Alnwick.' Wooler and Alnwick are less than twenty miles apart.

Traditionally, Hotspur was the romantic hero of *Henry IV, Part I*. But in the cycle as a whole, Quayle and I decided Burton's Hal must emerge as the hero, whose final justification and expiation comes at Agincourt.

I had, I suppose, a slight possessive feeling for Prince Hal, having played him for the Marlowe Society at Cambridge. But I was fascinated by the ease with which Richard Burton slipped into the part without even appearing to try. My Hotspur in the preceding play was, I thought, the best thing I had done. Yet it was overshadowed to some degree by Burton's Hal. He had 'arrived', as I had fourteen years before, and taken everyone by storm.

'You must be more competitive!' Mother used to warn me. But I wasn't. I saw no need to compete. I felt as sure of myself at this time as I had ever felt, secure in the knowledge that those whom I most admired – Michel, Peggy, George Devine – respected my work.

I think I got on well with Burton, and would have got on better had not a caucus of inflammable Welshmen been moved by his mere presence to take sides between the two of us. With so many Welsh members in the company, especially in the Glendower scene, the atmosphere of a Rugby final at Cardiff Arms Park was never far away.

'Would you mind,' asked Olivier, 'if I made a film of *The Beggar's Opera*?'

'Not in the least.'

We were staying at Notley Abbey, Olivier's country house near Thame, one weekend towards the end of my Stratford season. I had a question for him.

'What would you think of a film of *The Importance of Being Earnest*?'

'Who's directing?'

'Puffin.' It would be my third film with Asquith and there were few directors I would have sooner worked for, but, 'Do you think he has the incisive style necessary for such a production?'

'Do you?' Olivier parried.

Edith would recreate her definitive Lady Bracknell. I would play Ernest, Joan Greenwood would be Gwendolen, but ... but ... for the time being I put it out of my mind. And then a week later I thought what nonsense, of course I must do it.

When I saw the first screening five months later in a private viewing theatre in Wardour Street I was very disappointed. The tempo, which it is true must not be hurried, was ponderous, and sometimes the players, as Shaw noted of the original production, were too much in awe of Wilde to give their lines the air of conversation. I missed the response of an audience terribly. Wilde's epigrams demand their tribute of laughter and, without it, both the actors and the story seemed very vulnerable.

Since then I have seen the film three or four times on television, and each time I like it more. I find, in general, with a few obstinate exceptions, that I like my films more the further in time it is from the making of them. But with *The Importance of Being Earnest* time has restored a truer and certainly a more generous consideration of its qualities.

The scenes between Gwendolen and Cecily are the best I have ever seen them done. (I had asked for Dorothy Tutin to play Cecily, her first film part. I later adored her Sally Bowles in *I Am a Camera*.) And, of course, there was Edith as Lady Bracknell. It was not and could not be quite the performance she gave in Gielgud's unforgettable revival at the Haymarket in 1940, but it was unmistakably there.

We had been nervous, she and I, at our first meeting on the set of *The Importance of Being Earnest* and a little shy of each other. Not so, however, for our last film together. It was in Dublin, where we went to make *Young Cassidy*, a film biography of Sean O'Casey. We were on location and the players had been allocated a sitting-room in one of the nearby buildings. I was playing the middle-aged W.B. Yeats. Miss Horniman was played by Edith, no less. The part of O'Casey was entrusted to the capable hands of Rod Taylor, an excellent actor if a trifle too robust for the poet.

I came into the sitting-room and found myself face to face with Edith. I was expecting to meet her in the course of filming, but for an instant I was caught by surprise. Edith rose to her feet and, swooping down on me, hugged me and kissed me. Rod Taylor scrutinized this and remarked, 'I didn't get anything like that when I came in.'

'Ah,' said Edith, and let out a short peal of laughter, hugged me again and said with that famous dive in her voice, 'Ah, but you see Mike and I are *old* lovers.'

Amongst the plays I had been sent whilst I was filming *The Importance of Being Earnest* were Arthur Miller's adaptation of *An Enemy of the People*, Lillian Hellman's *The Autumn Garden*, and a play by Clifford Odets about the theatre. Originally called *The Country Girl*, it was now retitled *Winter Journey*.

A young Broadway director wants, against all advice, to cast in the leading part in his production an older actor whose career is almost finished. The part of Frank Elgin, the actor, had a touch of Barrymore about him which appealed to me. Years before I had been sent a play about Barrymore, *Goodnight, Sweet Prince*, a horrifying cautionary tale, though an unconvincing play. But *Winter Journey* is authentic in its portrayal of actors and theatre people. Elgin is an extreme contradiction. He is said to be a great actor, and whoever plays him must convince the audience of that. He is also abominably sly, vain, self-deluding and an alcoholic.

I couldn't make up my mind. The Third Act, though well written, was sentimental and rather hollow. I asked the young American Sam Wanamaker, who was to play the director and to direct the play, to give me a week to decide. I had spent a year at Stratford and now, after *The Importance of Being Earnest*, I wanted to do a modern part – but I wasn't sure. I had also been offered the part of the Judge in Rattigan's *The Deep Blue Sea*, which had all the hallmarks of a box-office success about it.

Friday came and I was still uncertain of my answer. During a break in shooting I wandered over to another sound stage to pay a call on Alec Guinness. We had been friends since our first season at the Old Vic in 1936 – not close friends, but liking one another and respecting each other's work. We were near neighbours: I at Chiswick Mall, Guinness at St Peter's Square, in one of a terrace of Regency houses built from public subscription for the victorious generals of Wellington's army at Waterloo. Our sons played together. There was very little sense in which Alec and I could be considered rivals. Yet, as I waited for him to appear – he was somewhere in the studio, no one was quite sure where – I had the peculiar sensation that he was avoiding me. And this in turn was followed by the notion that perhaps he wanted to play Elgin in

Winter Journey. He would be an excellent choice, I thought, and at that moment I wanted to play the part more than anything else and made up my mind to do it.

Later that day we shared a car home, and it turned out that I was right. Alec not only wanted the part, he had been offered it. I made some senseless apology and Alec, the soul of politeness, said, 'Not at all. I'm only wondering how much I can sue the producer for.'

It was a strange beginning, but rehearsals went smoothly enough, with no more than their fair share of disagreements. Wanamaker was a devotee of Stanislavsky, more so than I at that time, and suggested that he, I and Googie Withers, who played my wife, should write down the prehistory of our characters, before the moment they are first seen in the play. I thought this a useful exercise for students, but impractical for us, or for me at any rate. I had no wish to commit myself to a definite preconception of Elgin until I'd had a chance to explore him more fully in rehearsal. On the other hand, when the suggestion arose that a certain part of the first scene should be improvised at each performance, I agreed readily. It would not be easy, I thought. In improvisation it is usually simpler to lead than to follow, and Elgin in this scene had to follow. Moreover, I should have to sustain my New York accent, which is harder to do in improvisation than in lines one has learned. But it would help to keep our performances fresh each night.

Late one night, after we had opened at the St James's Theatre and had been playing for about three weeks, Wanamaker rang me in a fury.

'You called me a kike.'

'When?'

'Tonight. On stage.'

'No,' I said, 'I called you a tyke.' This is a Yorkshire term, half insult and half admiration, for someone who is like a bull terrier. Not at all New York, but there it was, I'd used it. Wanamaker would have none of it.

'I've got three witnesses.'

With all the finality I could muster I suggested he should stuff his three witnesses.

From that moment on, for the rest of our six months' run, we were not on speaking terms. Neither of us said anything about it in public, but word got out and each night, as the gallery queue formed on the pavement outside my dressing-room window, I could hear them talking about it. Perhaps it contributed something to the atmosphere of the play and served to neutralize its sentimentality, but it was horrible. I had always loathed quarrelling with those I worked with, and now every performance seemed like a contest. During one of my speeches in the Second Act, I became convinced that Wanamaker was scraping a chair across the floor to upset me, though no doubt in his own mind there was a perfectly adequate reason for it. I glared at him night after night till I could stand it no longer, and the next night, as the scraping began, I grasped the back of the chair with both hands so firmly that we would have stopped the play altogether if he'd tried to wrestle it from me. We obviously couldn't continue doing that every night without an absurd, undignified scramble to see who could reach the chair first. For the next few performances nothing happened. Then the scraping began again. I halted in mid-speech.

'Don't do that!' I yelled.

'Why not?' asked Sam, rather taken by surprise I fancy.

'Because it goes *right through my head*!'

It didn't happen again.

Wanamaker was excellent in the play, and his direction was first class. I owed a good deal of my own performance to him. We've met since then once or twice, and drawn a veil over *Winter Journey*. Like all clashes of personality, it was agonizing at the time and afterwards it is hard to imagine how it happened.

My 'An Actor to the Critics' and other articles which had been published from time to time in theatrical magazines had brought me a number of invitations to lecture or to write a book about acting. I had refused them all. Two considerations held me back, the first being that whatever a player may say about his work, it is by his work, by what he projects on-stage, that he is judged. In England, especially in the English theatre, there is an ingrained prejudice against any attempt at an analysis of acting. Agate's 'Now you can stop being an intellectual and start being a real actor' summed up this attitude.

An invitation from Bristol University to deliver the Rockefeller Foundation lectures on the subject of acting changed my mind. It was 1952, my nineteenth year on the stage – not quite the twenty years that by tradition are said to make an actor, but near enough. I had a strong sense that it was now or never. And besides, Bristol was my birthplace.

I took the opportunity to pay a fleeting visit to Clifton. The paper shop on St Michael's Hill was still the paper shop on St Michael's Hill. The cinema in Whiteladies Road was still 'the flicks'.

I was to give four lectures. The first, in the University's largest auditorium, before an audience of a thousand or so, was open to the public. The last three were for University members only. This suited me rather well, for it allowed me to approach my subject by a discursive, circuitous route, with all the necessary disclaimers. I was aware, I told my audience, that my questions were far more plentiful than my answers, and that my answers, in most cases, were implied far more than they were stated.

As I sat down to prepare a framework for the lectures, which came very readily, and then to undertake the much more difficult task of sifting my material to fill my framework, I was aware of another constraint. Six months from then, I realized, when the lectures were published, I might well be thinking very differently about my subject. An actor can add up many or most of the figures on his professional ledger, but it is in the nature of his work that he should never attempt a final sum. Moreover, as in higher mathematics, where two and two need not necessarily make four, his sums may come out differently on different occasions. The title I chose, *An Actor's Ways and Means*, was itself a kind of disclaimer, for it suggested to me the sort of day-to-day account which in the conditions of the theatre then – the English theatre of the 1940s and 1950s – was very much the way a professional actor had to live and work.

The book sold slowly, but it sold steadily. A quarter of a century hurtled by, and I was asked to write a preface to a new paperback edition. Re-reading it I found, with surprise, that there was very little I wished to change. Something, surely? 'The actor must create his own luck.' That was a statement which had provoked understandable annoyance in some quarters. Yet I believe it to be true. Edith Evans's remark 'You only really begin to act when you leave off trying' annoys some people still. It contains, I think, as much truth as many paradoxes, and more than most. For it goes almost without saying that to achieve that sense of effortlessness which is a hallmark of good acting, much discipline and effort are necessary.

'Unless the actor is on that particular evening wishing above everything else to act, that performance may be reasonably good but it is unlikely to be his best. To act well and to act well repeatedly has to become an obsession.' *There* was something I wished to withdraw. For the actor may and sometimes does give of his best on those evenings when he feels ill, or tired, or even slightly bored. Reading those lines, I remembered a young actor, playing Laertes at the Vic, who discovered that in the 'eternity', or uncut, version of *Hamlet* there are some two hours between his exit in Act Two and his reappearance in Act Four. He tried staying in his dressing-room, keeping in the mood. That lasted for about twenty minutes. He tried sitting in a nearby cabman's shelter, drinking innumerable cups of coffee. That gave him sleepless nights. Then he remembered that at the end of Waterloo Road was Waterloo Bridge, and beyond Waterloo Bridge stood the Gaiety Theatre, where Leslie Henson, one of the great comedians, was playing nightly in *Seeing Stars*. Taking careful note of the time, he set off at a run for the Gaiety – a strange figure, no doubt, in his raincoat, green tights, and flaming red wig. Reaching the gallery entrance door, he slipped inside, climbed the long gallery, and took his seat unobserved in the 'gods', to watch the great Leslie.

That strange tall figure was, of course, myself. At that age I took many things for granted. Yet I dare say I was even then as 'obsessed' as any with the ambition of acting well, and I doubt whether these nightly excursions did any harm to my performance – they may even have done it good.

Edward Thompson, of Heinemann's, who had started the ball rolling by asking me to write a book about acting (an offer I had always refused), pressed me, after the publication of *An Actor's Ways and Means*, to write another. I refused again. I've done enough, I thought. And anyway, that book had grown naturally out of the lectures. But Thompson persisted, and the result was *Mask or Face*, in which almost everything else I had written or lectured about on acting, including the Theodore Spencer lecture at Harvard, was collected into a book of essays, subtitled *Reflections in an Actor's Mirror*.

Three years later, in 1958, I was at Stratford again, playing Hamlet and Benedick. August came round, and with it the annual series of lectures in the Conference Hall given by Shakespearian scholars, directors, and actors. As usual I was asked to lecture, and as usual I agreed. And then I thought, But I've nothing to say. Surely I had said all I wanted to say in 'Shakespeare and the Actors'? Even on that occasion I had found it necessary to fill up my matter with a quantity of art: my lecture had included a monstrously long quotation from *The Tempest*. It had pleased my audience, for I had spoken it with much feeling, but on paper it looked like padding, which it was.

Going for a walk in the country, I began to ruminate on the question 'What makes an actor "tick"?' and realized I might put it into fiction. By the end of my walk I had the outline of my story. Two weeks later I read it at Stratford in the Conference Hall, before an audience surprised, and then delighted, to find themselves listening to a story instead of a lecture. That winter I read it in Vienna to an audience in the Auditorium Maximum, having prefaced it with a speech in German to soften them up. A year later it became a short novel, *The Mountebank's Tale*: 'Joseph was a classical actor in the unusual but real sense of the word. He never altered the balance of a part, consciously or unconsciously, to suit his own style or personality. He scrupulously measured each part in relation to the text and the author's meaning.' Joseph, I might add, is not myself. But he is the type of actor whom in *An Actor's Ways and Means* I dubbed 'protean' or, in Jouvet's terms, a *comédien*. The novel says as much about acting, I think, as either of my two previous books. Like them, it ends with a question.

It is 1953. At Stratford again. We assemble for the first read-through of *Antony and Cleopatra*. It is the third play of the season. We know that, whatever its success or failure, nearly every performance will be sold out for the next three months. Stratford is *still* the unofficial national theatre.

Do I detect a hint of nervousness in Peggy's reading? Perhaps. A trace. In my own? No, having reluctantly agreed to play the part, I go for it hammer and tongs. It's *not* a part I would have chosen to play. Come to think of it, of my three parts this season, only Lear, which is yet to come, accords completely with my own choice. Shylock, they said, was a question of money. If I wouldn't play Shylock, another leading actor would have to be engaged, and the annual budget couldn't stretch to that.

But Shylock was easy. Antony is another question. I declined the part two years ago when Peggy invited me to play it with her at the Vic. 'Do you really want to play Cleopatra?' I had asked her.

'We-ll . . . ' She thought, and after a moment said, 'It would be a *challenge.*'

'In that case, Peg,' I replied, 'I don't think so.'

And the idea had been dropped.

Of all the plays of Shakespeare's maturity, *Antony and Cleopatra* is the least often performed. There had been only two major productions since the War: Godfrey Tearle's with Edith Evans, and the Oliviers' at the St James's. Neither was notably successful. Indeed, looking back, since the days of Benson no actor's reputation had been enhanced by playing Antony. Now, reading through the play, I think I can see why. There is no plain sailing in Antony, no point of rest where the words will carry you along, no safe haven until the very end, at Antony's death. It is a part that calls on all the strength one possesses and tests out every weakness.

No creative artist is complete without a fatal flaw. In life, as in art, he is paradoxically only at full strength when his spirit grapples with this flaw. He may not be aware of it – indeed, he must not be too aware of it. But the battle has begun.

I make a stupid mistake. I allow myself to become convinced that Antony is difficult to learn. I ask Godfrey Tearle over lunch at the Garrick Club whether he, too, found the text of Antony peculiarly difficult to commit to memory. He tells me that he learned all the great Shakespearian roles by watching his father play them – all except Antony. 'It's the very devil,' he says.

I compound this mistake by asking Olivier the same question. 'Difficult? You must be joking,' he says, with a wry smile.

I have never had any difficulty in learning a part until this moment. Now, every evening I sit with Glen Byam Shaw, the director, who hears me the lines, and by the end of the evening I know them; but the next day the difficulty returns. At the dress rehearsal I hesitate, fluff, and dry with mounting panic.

On the first night I wait for my entrance with my usual feeling of deadly calm, hearing rather than listening to the opening lines: 'Nay, but this dotage of our general's o'erflows the measure . . . ' A typical opening, this, for one of Shakespeare's great tragedies. A note of doubt or questioning, conversational in tone, almost conspiratorial, as if deliberately to counterpoint the splendour of the chief charac-ters' first appearance. At each dress rehearsal our two actors playing Philo and Demetrius have been warned against 'ponging' their lines.

'You're signalling to the audience that it's the start of the play. You're trying to give it a lift. Don't!' says Glen. 'Say it quietly, as if you don't want to be overheard.'

And tonight they get it right. I give a final twitch to my costume and run on with Peggy. I had suggested this entrance to Glen. Cleopatra has a sort of giant daisy-chain, a long rope of water-lilies, and snares Antony with them on the line 'If it be love indeed, tell me how much.'

The entrance goes well. From the word go, from my first line, I sail through the performance without a single fluff or dry. Only to be trapped at the winning-post by an alliteration. As Antony breathes his last, buoyed up with confidence and a wondrous sense of relief, I decide to give him a really good send-off, and on the line 'A Roman, by a Roman valiantly vanquished,' I gave him literally an extra dying breath by pausing naturalistically, as if searching for the adjective. The prompter, who has sat all evening in his corner feeling thwarted after what happened at the dress rehearsal, seizes this briefest of pauses to ply his trade, and his voice rings out loud and strong.

'Never, *ever*, prompt me again,' I curse at him, poor fellow, after the curtain-call, with mingled exasperation and relief, 'even if you have to wait an eternity.'

Acting together, Peggy and I succeeded. Writing of her performance, Kenneth Tynan, who at this stage of his career had adopted the role of the theatre's chief iconoclast, used the opprobrious term 'Kensington', meaning, of course, that her accent was too 'refined'. And, true, if you wanted to listen for it, her vowel sounds would have given her away. But her acting was on a level which takes no account of vowel sounds. With no other actress since Edith Evans had I found such support and mutual help as I found with Peggy. Acting with her my chief emotion was the same as when acting with Edith : a feeling of great safety, and great freedom.

After *Antony and Cleopatra* had finished its season at Stratford and a six-week season in London, we did a short Continental tour. At The Hague the audiences were ecstatic. But on our first night in Paris, as Peggy and I came running on for our entrance, I was alarmed by the sound of a distinct chuckle. Was it our clothes ? 'Peggy must have some new costumes,' I had warned Glen, for though I had never played in Paris until that night, I knew how in the French theatre the actress would put in the programme : *Mlle Telle-et-telle, habillée sur la scène et en ville par Tel-et-tel*, and I feared lest French audiences should find us dowdy. The laughter subsided and we continued, slightly shaken.

(An untoward laugh can temporarily wreck an otherwise fine performance. I remember an unfortunate Macbeth who listened to Lennox's gory catalogue of disasters in Act Two, Scene Three, thinking, My God, this fellow's slow, and snapping impatiently at the poor actor, ''Twas a rough night.' He must have overlooked the obvious double meaning which the adjective *rough* might have for an American audience. There was no mistaking their reaction. It was in New York, and I was the unfortunate Macbeth.)

After the performance, at supper given in our honour by some of the actors from the Comédie Française, I found myself seated at table next to a celebrated poetess. I asked why the audience had laughed at that particular point. 'Ah that!' She smiled. 'It's very simple. In France, in tragedy, *on ne court jamais*. You *never* run !'

XIX

I HAD long wanted to play Hector, Jouvet's part, in Giraudoux's play *La Guerre de Troie n'aura pas lieu* (*Tiger at the Gates*, in Christopher Fry's translation). It was one of the plays Michel Saint-Denis had had in mind for our season at the Phoenix before the War, where I had played another of Jouvet's roles, Sir Andrew Aguecheek in *Twelfth Night*. Giraudoux himself came to London, reportedly to satisfy himself that I was mature enough to play Hector, but then came the Munich agreement, which seemed to put a temporary question mark over Giraudoux's parable on the inevitability of war. And soon after that our finances ran out, and all our plans for the company were shelved.

Since then there had been one or two vague offers from across the Atlantic, but they had not materialized. And now my eye caught a paragraph in one of our trade papers: the American impresario Roger Stevens, it said, was planning a production of Giraudoux's play in London and New York; Harold Clurman would be directing the play; Clurman was coming to England, hoping to persuade me to play Hector. Clurman ... the Group Theatre ... *The Fervent Years*! Admiration made me shy at the thought of meeting him. There was no need. Whatever I had expected, Clurman's warmth, humour, and knowledge of the theatre dispelled my shyness at once. Within an hour we were friends and colleagues. No one since Michel had made me so sure that this was where I wanted to be, this was what I wanted to do. There are directors in the theatre who say a lot and achieve little. And those, more rare, like Clurman, who seem by their presence to extract the very best their cast is capable of. What I got from Clurman is all-important: the feeling that he was getting something from me, and that it pleased him.

He agreed with me that the American translation, which had been going the rounds for years, was quite inadequate, and suggested that Christopher Fry do a new translation, to which I agreed at once. We also agreed, with scarcely a demur, on the casting. (At rehearsals I began to have some doubts about Diane Cilento's playing Helen of Troy. I wondered how an audience would react to her flat Australian vowels and her direct, high-voltage sex appeal – an English audience, that is, conditioned in their response to Helen by Christopher Marlowe's 'Was this the face that launched a thousand ships . . .' to expect abstract beauty rather than sex appeal. Harold said, 'I know what you mean, but wait until the first night in New York.' He was proved entirely right. From the moment she began to speak, the American audience was with her.)

Unknown to me, Vanessa and Corin had asked Clurman if they could watch rehearsals. He gave his permission, so long as they remained out of sight. And this they did, sitting each day discreetly at the back of the stalls in the darkened auditorium of the Apollo. It was the school holidays. I had expected they would soon find something else to do, but to my surprise they came each day of the four-week rehearsal period. Vanessa was eighteen now, and without question too tall for the ballet. At my insistence that she should learn another language, she had spent six months in Italy. She had come back, closeted herself in her room for another three months, and passed her A-level exam in Italian. Now she was in her first year at drama school. The most I could say at this stage was that I knew she would be an actress. I had seen one of her last school plays, something written by her, in which, because she was the tallest, she played a man's part. I was impressed by an immensely long pause she made, and held, and afterwards asked her was it art, or was it a dry?

'Art, of course.'

'I'm not sure that I believe you.'

She made an impromptu show of being hurt at my disbelief, and then laughed and confessed it was a dry. That impressed me even more.

In London, *Tiger at the Gates* was successful. That is to say, the applause was generous, in that English way which Irving, knowing that audiences need encouragement, would fill out by having his drummer in the pit sustain it and swell it with a sostenuto roll on the bass kettledrum. The notices were excellent – though of that English kind which makes an actor say, 'Yes, but is that all?' and which made Garrick and Irving buy their own periodicals in which to praise their own performances and answer their detractors. On the whole the English actor will not complain, for audiences in London repay him for any lack of warmth in their ovation by their loyalty and by their long memories.

In New York we were a 'hit'. I recall Leonard Bernstein's flinging his arms around me: 'Oh, Michael, you're a doll!' I recall Ruth Gordon's note to me on the first night. I rarely read wires or notes before the first performance. This one I read; it said, 'Remember, they are longing to like it!'

The same good wishes would have been more to the point before the first night of my next production, Terence Rattigan's *The Sleeping Prince*. By ill fortune we opened on Broadway in the autumn of 1956, when the twin crises of Eden's Suez adventure and the Hungarian revolution were in full flood. In the play's First Act the young King, who suspects his father, the Prince Regent, of plotting behind his back, bursts out, 'I will not have my country made the pawn of British imperialism and French greed.' At this, an audible *frisson* ran through the audience. The performance had not started well and proceeded from bad to worse. When the Prince Regent airily remarks that the music which is coming from beyond the door is 'probably some Hungarian violinist', our doom was sealed. I had suggested to Rattigan that these lines might, perhaps, given the circumstances, be cut. But Terry, convinced that art outlives contemporary events, was insistent that they be spoken. Not for the first time, contemporary events proved themselves the stronger.

And yet my contribution was perhaps principally to be blamed for our lack of success. *The Sleeping Prince*, subtitled *A Ruritanian Comedy*, is an impudently light-weight play whose characters, like insects on the water's surface, are borne aloft by nothing more than surface tension and the skill of the principal performers. How easy it is for an actor, tempted by the kind of success which only Broadway can offer, to choose such a vehicle for his next appearance. Especially when six uniforms, specially designed for him by Bermans in London, each one more gorgeous than the last, add their lustre to the possibilities of self-deception. We had opened in New Haven before a largely student audience from Yale which had roared with laughter. Yet even before the first performance in New York I was reminded that between the poles of success and failure in that city there is scarcely any middle ground. The management did something which I have never encountered before or since. Two days before the opening night I was met at the theatre by a representative from the management who suggested with no visible embarrass-

211

ment that another actor might be brought in to rehearse my part with me in the hope that it would help me get more laughs. Whom, I asked, politely, did they have in mind?

'Well,' they said, 'it would have to be a British actor. How about Cyril Ritchard?'

'But surely Cyril will not want to take on such a job at two days' notice. Besides, would he be free?'

'He's here, and free,' came the reply.

'And waiting in the lobby?'

'Exactly. He's in the lobby. Shall we ask him up?'

'It would be discourteous not to,' I said.

Cyril Ritchard, an old friend of mine, came into the room, embarrassment writ large across his usually cheerful face. I could not help thinking how good he would have been in the part. He stayed and chatted for a few awkward moments, in what was clearly an untenable situation, and made his departure, offering his apologies if he had wasted anybody's time.

The first night was a disaster. Yet at this distance of time I am inclined to shoulder at least half the blame. When one is half the management, the director, *and* the leading actor, one can but say, *La débâcle, c'est moi.*

The Sleeping Prince was due to end its run after ten weeks, and I was expecting to be home for Christmas, when I was offered a television 'spectacular': *Ruggles of Red Gap.*

I had never learned very much about television; I had had little opportunity to do so. My first acquaintance with TV cameras, in 1936, with Jean Forbes-Robertson in *Scenes from Romeo and Juliet* at Alexandra Palace, was something that, in later years, I found useful as a conversation-stopper whenever the 'old boys' at Television Centre began to reminisce, but of little practical value apart from that. Few people could have witnessed this spirited pioneering attempt to put Shakespeare on the box. To see it, Rachel had had to visit Selfridges in Oxford Street, where they had a demonstration TV set.

On another occasion, but with the same cultural urge, I attempted Chekhov's famous one-acter *The Bear* on television. It was 1948, and I was playing Macbeth on Broadway. Of *The Bear*, which is virtually a monologue, I recollect only that it suffered for lack of rehearsal. According to my great friend Norris Houghton it was a lesson, brilliant of its kind, in improvisation.

Ruggles was to be a musical, with a delightful score, specially commissioned from Jule Styne, and a starry cast. It sounded like a busman's holiday, and I agreed to do it. And then my agent phoned with the bad news. A film company was competing for my services, and it rather looked as though the television company would win. The film was Graham Greene's *The Quiet American*. They wanted me to play Fowler – 'Just about the best part this year,' my agent said. I have never taken kindly to any attempt to thwart me from something I wanted to do, and I very much wanted to play Fowler. No contracts had been signed, I pleaded. The answer came back that the verbal agreement I had given was, of course, sufficiently binding. Couldn't the film company wait a few days? I asked. Very difficult, came the answer. Locations were to be in Saigon, and Joseph Mankiewicz, the director, wanted to use scenes of the Indo-Chinese New Year, so the schedule was tight. By now I heartily wished I had never heard of *Ruggles*. Even if, by some unlikely good fortune, the film company could accommodate the dates, the last thing I could wish for, before a film as heavy as this, would be to be up to my ears in a TV spectacular – a 'live' spectacular, as all TV productions were then. In desperation, I hired a lawyer – 'the very best', I was told, for this kind of job, a real shark. Within twenty-four hours he rang me back. 'I've fixed it. You can do them both.'

4 February 1957

The morning run-through wasn't too bad. Then I sat at the local restaurant for fifty minutes and was given an almost uneatable steak. Lack of food and too much vodka made me sleepy and cross. The dress rehearsal seemed endless and dismal. After the morning run congratulations poured in effusively; after the afternoon – none. I haven't yet been through a performance without 'drying', and indeed cutting chunks of the almost unspeakable script.

Take a shower and shave and chew a few mouthfuls of dry chopped steak. Very nervous. I have the feeling that with my illnesses and absences and lack of precision I have turned all the cast against me, including sweet little Jane Powell, whose acting is, it is true, of the 'do-it-by-numbers' style.

But the performance goes – it goes. Imogene Coca does her damnedest and is pretty good. David Wayne also nervous but as always keeps a definite pattern and is reliable. Peter Lawford very nervous. The only people really relaxed and good are the dancers and singers. There was a party afterwards at which everyone *seemed* elated.

So by car to Idlewild, and at last off to Saigon. Our plane is a little late leaving and there is a nervous moment when we are told 'the field is closed.'

6 February

Not a very comfortable berth. Too short, and sleeping diagonally was uncomfortable. I sat up late with David Wayne, who told me of his experiences in the 8th Army, and his love of the British. We became close, though a bit alcoholic.

He gets out at Los Angeles, sunny and warm. I give two of my hand luggage pieces for someone to send along, not realizing that the plane is an hour late, and that I have only one hour to catch the plane on to 'Frisco. Get fussed and wonder why airports always assume you know what that Big Sister voice means.

On to 'Frisco sitting next to a vivacious pregnant woman who shows me photographs and talks (with enthusiasm!) about *Ruggles*.

At 'Frisco I have twenty-five minutes, and no baggage problems. The air is crisp and the sun warm. We fly on to Seattle, which is overcast and drizzly. Here I am given an executive suite which has everything but a bed.

After a good dinner back to the airport. A long wait before the plane leaves, an hour and a half late.

7 February

It appears we take a northerly route to Anchorage, Alaska, and Shemya before heading for Tokyo. I take two Doridon, and then another in the night in hot milk, and sleep – I have no idea for how long, as my watch says twelve and is still going, which looks as if I had at least ten hours. Is that possible?

The sun is up and we are still flying about the north. We touched down at Anchorage but not at Shemya, they say, not yet.

There were several wires on the first night – what am I talking about? – the first *and last* night of *Ruggles*, though Alexander Cohen [the New York impresario] *has* in fact inquired as to my interest in a Broadway version for the fall – including one with the strangest signature 'From Saigon'. Joe Mankiewicz? DEAREST MICHAEL AT A MOMENT LIKE THIS THERE IS SO LITTLE WE CAN SAY STOP CHIN UP BE BRAVE REMEMBER REMEMBER THAT THIS TOO SHALL PASS AWAY STOP COME TO US QUICKLY STOP NOT NECESSARY KNOW OUR LINES BUT FOR HEAVENS SAKE FORGET PRESENT ONES ALL LOVE THE QUIET AND DISQUIETED.

It looks sunny down below. 'Will passengers please fasten their seatbelts at this time in preparation for landing at Shemya, Alaska.'

Suddenly we are in dense cloud, and I think of *The Night My Number Came Up*. No wonder all these people who make a living out of flying seem so calm.

Why at this moment should I think of Paul Dehn? I must write to him this afternoon. I suppose it's because I have written this as I haven't for ages written anything, and remember my postcard to him from Eze about why Mme de Sévigné or whatever her married name was had no time to write to her mother. ...

Alex Cohen told me in a recent letter that Mankiewicz had told him 'in strict secrecy' about plans for filming *Twelfth Night* in Rome in November. I wonder how I shall greet this when it is properly broached to me. (Maybe it won't be, though, for I am by no means sure I'll be able to do Fowler to J. M.'s satisfaction or to mine.) Come to think of it, it's not the first time this project has been mooted. I put the idea to John Huston once. He was very excited. We talked of casting. Orson, Danny Kaye, self ... Next morning I met him: 'How did you sleep?' 'Great! Dreaming about *Twelfth Night*.' 'Yes?' 'Yes. Orson was Sir Toby, Kaye was Sir Andrew and you ... ' 'Yes?' 'Funny ... you weren't in it.' ...

Now we have Japanese stewardesses, and one has just given a lifebelt demonstration which seemed calculated to make one forget the practical side of the matter. We have been in the air for about twenty minutes. Tokyo by night from the air resembles the slums of Los Angeles. The whole personality of the aircraft, if such a thing has such a thing, seems changed.

I realize after several sips of gin and tonic that what is depressing me, apart from tiredness, is that the whole personality of the aircraft has *not* changed. It's only that before I had a large berth, and a Mr Eugen Johannsen, of Kristiansand, Norway, and I had this whole rear cabin to ourselves and now I am surrounded – surrounded? There are only six others, mainly Japanese, with me. But I'm feeling foolish and resentful because the company didn't book a berth for me for this part of the journey, and I didn't feel like parting with fifty-five dollars in travellers' cheques even if I could reclaim them. ...

At Manila Airport, after all my dread about baggage, money, health certificates, and Customs, I sailed through, thanks to a Filipino official who looked about 15½ and said, 'I've seen *all* your films.'

Audie Murphy, the most highly decorated soldier in the States, was to be my co-star in *The Quiet American*. I was eager to meet him. But the first news that greeted me as I stepped off the plane at Saigon was that Murphy had contracted some germ or other in Hong Kong, and was confined to hospital there. The numerous shots of penicillin he had received during the War made it unwise and, indeed, useless for him to receive any more.

So, leaving Audie to fend for himself, and with no thought of jet lag on my part (it had not yet been invented), we started shooting.

Vietnam, following the Geneva peace conference three years before, was a divided country. Saigon, with its pleasant tree-lined boulevards from the days of French colonial rule, was now like a shabby French provincial town. There seemed little trace of the war that had been fought or the war that was to come. Americans we met were mostly attached to the diplomatic service. They talked eagerly about the film, in the manner of those who seek distraction from the boredom of service in a routine provincial posting.

Only once did we see a sign of conflict. It was whilst we were shooting the scenes of the Indo-Chinese New Year. Placards borne aloft in a religious demonstration were suddenly turned around, revealing on their reverse side anti-Government slogans. When this was pointed out and interpreted for us, someone suggested we should have to cut those shots, or else reshoot them. 'Leave them in,' said Joe. An erudite, frequently witty man, he also cultivated a 'tough guy' image. 'What the hell? No one'll know what they mean.'

21 March

[We were in Rome now, at Cinecittà, for the interiors.] A miserable day for it seems to me I'll never adjust to the problem of acting with someone like Murphy, a 'natural' with a mass of experience but no technique. Joe seems unaware of the problem; perhaps for him it *isn't* a problem. I feel like telling him it's one thing to get a performance out of an amateur, another thing to give a performance with one.

I have a streaming cold. At the end of the day Joe annoys me with, 'Take care of that cold,' to which I reply, 'What do you *think* I'm going to do with it?'

27 March

Vexed from the word go. Joe meets me on the stairs and says in his peculiar 'tough' way, 'Well, how y'a feeling?' and I am so exhausted and stopped-up with cold that I feel a sort of baleful dislike of him and the whole set-up.

28 March

Everything seems much better today. My cold less heavy – irritation less. Only once in the morning do I feel ragingly impatient with Joe. After doing the 'Continental' scene with Audie for three hours, right on form, I think, we eventually get to my close-up. Audie's off-camera lines are not very stirringly delivered, to put it mildly; the need not to 'overlap' the lines in a close shot also slows the scene up, and Joe impatiently says, 'No, cut! Start again – it's getting spongey.' Spongey! For a moment I feel like telling him what I think of this, but decide to 'use' my irritation in the playing of the scene.

20 May

A letter from my agent, Cecil Tennant. I look at the date. It was dictated and sent on April 25th. That was mysterious enough. But the conclusion of the letter is hideously depressing, crowning my misery at Joan's [my secretary, Joan Hirst] information that the reason we have only £2,000 in the bank is that £8,000 of the *Quiet American* cheque went to the bloody tax people. But Cecil's letter is worse, for he advises, after this, two films, or at least one Hollywood film, and certainly not more than two plays at Stratford, and why not Stratford in '59 rather than '58?

This makes all my plans for Stratford next year, following a play in London, mere wishful thinking. And here I have been encouraging Glen [Glen Byam Shaw, Stratford's director] that there may be hope of three plays at Stratford, and writing to Peter Hall – though I could still not post the letter – that I might like to do John Whiting's *The Gates of Summer*, which he sent me, together with [Jean Anouilh's] *Ornifle*.

Oh, Lord, it is so disappointing to feel I'm back on the treadmill, or certainly will be if I don't follow Cecil's advice. Yet if I do follow it, it means not doing what I want to do.

All the same, it's all very well of Glennie to quote Irving saying to his financiers, 'Gentlemen, I was not sent on earth to make money.' I know that, even if I have not always the same belief in myself to phrase it so. The point is, Irving paid 6d – or was it a shilling in the pound? – income tax.

5 June

A happy day, because a cable came from Rachel this morning saying that Vanessa shares the Sybil Thorndike prize for best performance by a girl at Central School. I've been childishly happy ever since.

I'm still waiting to hear from Glen, though I've made my mind up, I think. I shall have to do Stratford. I can't let him down. And after all, it's what I wanted to do. The advantages Glen offers, £60 a week for me plus £40 for Rachel, plus the main house at Avoncliffe, plus *quelques choses* – well, all very well. But somehow, because of V's prize, I feel all the more inclined to do what, after all, I want to do.

Joe thinks, and Cecil thinks, that I shall be what is known as 'hot' after this movie, may get an Oscar, etc., and I know I'll probably never have such a chance again. But one's career teaches one that blind gropes in the dark are the ones which pay best in the end.

XX

I<small>T WAS</small> the autumn of 1957. I had not acted in London since *Tiger at the Gates*, two years before. I was looking for a play, and I was faced with a number of choices. And then a script arrived from Binkie Beaumont, a new play by N.C. Hunter. This puzzling work read as if Norman Hunter, tired of being called 'the English Chekhov', had decided to be the English Ibsen. It was concerned with money, and the effect which a sudden glimpse of wealth, in the shape of rich relations, has on a not-so-well-to-do schoolmaster's family. But so unremittingly was this theme driven home that it quickly became very boring, and the principal character, the schoolmaster, insufferably priggish.

I made these points in a letter to Binkie, who relayed its contents to Hunter. To my surprise Hunter sat down and rewrote the play in the shape of my suggestions. In its new form, *A Touch of the Sun* appealed to me. All the parts were good acting parts, which is never to be sniffed at – and there was a nice part for the schoolmaster's daughter. It crossed my mind that Norman might have written it for Vanessa. A short tour was planned, and then into the Saville, which someone said was an 'unlucky' theatre, but I said, rather arrogantly perhaps, 'No theatre is unlucky when it's filled to the brim.'

At Blackpool we went our separate ways – I to my hotel, Vanessa to her digs. From the start of rehearsals, though she was still living at home, we would as a rule travel separately to and from the theatre. Occasionally, and usually only when she asked for it, I would give her a note. She listened gravely and attentively. Vanessa is great on gravity. In Robert Beulah's portrait of her as a little girl, she looks severe, almost cross. Gravity can be mistaken for severity.

The first performance went well, astonishingly well. 'Vanessa a distinct hit with the audience (and with Binkie),' I noted in my diary.

At a supper party after the show, Ronnie Squire, who played the father, immaculately, told me he was bequeathing me Irving's powder box.

After the first night at the Saville, Binkie reminded me of Larry's curtain speech at the Vic on the night Vanessa was born: 'A great actress has been born.' 'Great?' I asked, thrilled but not fishing for compliments. 'Yes, great. A remarkable actress.'

We had known since she was a baby that she had an actress's gift. It flowered early, and beyond expectation. But great? About such matters one must be careful not to exaggerate. And not to underestimate. In Robert Bolt's *The Tiger and the Horse*, in which we played together in 1960, I recall being almost thrown by the force of her concentration. Hers was a part that required concentration, certainly, and it was there, bang, unmistakably there. That is one half of the gift of acting. The other half, no less important, though more rare, she had also: the ability to switch oneself off, to absent oneself from a scene that belongs to someone else. So many actors, finding that they have been given little to do in a certain scene, start inventing bits of business, nods and becks and wreathed smiles, when they should simply absent themselves awhile.

It is hard for the child of whom great things are expected, but harder by far for the one who is adorable and sweet, and of whom no one expects anything very much. Lynn, growing up in the shadows of her elder sister and brother, spent much of her time with Rosalinda, the pony which her godmother, Edith Hargraves, had given her. There was even talk of her joining Pat Smythe's stable and taking up horse-riding. One afternoon at Stratford, when she was sixteen, Lynn arranged a small hurdle for her pony to jump. She had won dozens of rosettes for jumping and gymkhanas, but now – probably because she was fraught with doubts and confusion – she fell and lay there winded. I was about twenty yards off and it took me some time to realize that she wasn't moving. Perhaps that fall tipped the balance between horse-riding and the theatre.

She had said nothing about the theatre. But, next year, staying with Vanessa at Stratford, she surprised us all by suddenly announcing that she was going to act. She bundled off to Central School, where Vanessa had been. I went with some apprehension to the Embassy Theatre to see her first public performance there. The image of this divided, decidedly plump young girl troubled me. Memory insists that it was a scene from a Shaw play, though I recall no telephone in Shaw and in this there was certainly a telephone. Lynn came on and, for a split second, looked exactly like Rachel. I had never been able to see the likeness till that occasion. I was astounded. This was a mature young woman, and the last thing I had expected of Lynn was that she was capable of suggesting maturity.

Such early images are haunting. Time has overlaid them with later images: the pride and thrill of seeing her on Broadway in *My Fat Friend*, when the audience applauded as she removed her coat in the final act and revealed a graceful woman. But, for a while, it was as though I could not quite synchronize with Lynn and her achievements. I went to see her at Southsea in *Billy Liar* when she was nineteen, and had to leave after the first act to get back to Chichester. There were about fifteen people in the house, and a very brash young actor was playing the lead. 'Very good,' I told her, 'but of course impossible to play with a young man like that,' only to find that the young man in question was standing beside me.

Something unfortunate happened also on the occasion I went to see her in her first West End play, *The Tulip Tree*, which, as it happened, was also by N. C. Hunter. She played a young girl who longs to be a dancer, and had a touching scene to herself where she brought on a gramophone and danced to it, and was then surprised in the act by another character. She played it very truthfully, moving the audience by the concentration with which she danced as well as she could, where another actress might have played for sympathy or laughs by exaggerating the young girl's awkwardness. But at the appointed moment the other actor failed to appear. Lynn danced on, improvising her steps as best she could. 'Very good,' I comforted her, 'the way you carried on dancing.' And so it was, though for her the scene was ruined.

Like myself, Corin, when he arrived at school, coming from a theatrical family, was expected to take the leading women's parts. When he played Portia, topped off with a bird's nest of a wig, there were moments when a promising actor shone through the insecurities inevitable in a school production. A little later I heard him at home, in a next-door room, practising some speech to a tape recorder. Fragments of Mark Antony reached me and caught my attention. That's good, I thought, very good, and wondered whether to go in and tell him, then thought better of it.

As Palaestrio in Plautus' *Miles Gloriosus* in his school's annual Latin play, he was impressive. True, a foreign language, especially Latin, might be said to smooth an actor's path, for the audience is bound to think, How clever, but there was no mistaking two attributes which proclaim an actor in the making: personality and authority.

At Cambridge, which was noted for the number of amateur actors straining to go on the boards, he did his share of acting and production. At the end of his third year George Devine offered him a job as an assistant artistic director at the Royal Court and for a moment it seemed that one of the children would do something other than act. But within a month or so he, too, was acting, with Lynn in *A Midsummer Night's Dream*.

Parents and children were now all on the stage. We had arrived at the intersection of our private and our public lives. There was pleasure and satisfaction in that, each supporting the other. As Vanessa once said, 'Ours is a family that rejoices in each other.' Some loss, too. No longer the Redgrave family, but the family Redgrave, a being in the public eye which interrupts the normal flow, the ups and downs of personal relationships.

It was in 1958, during my last season at Stratford, that Mother died. They called me in the morning and I held her hand whilst she was semi-conscious. It was a matinée day, but I went back between the shows – and she had died.

I thought of the last time we had been at Stratford together, the last and happiest time, clouded over since by the squabbles and scenes, hurtful and sometimes alarming, of her final illness. It had been during the history cycle in 1951. Mother was playing in *Man and Superman* under John Clements's management, and he was about to begin rehearsals of a new play. Most surprisingly he offered Mother a part in it, which would mean her coming off after Act One of the Shaw, taking a taxi to another theatre, and appearing there in Act Three of *And This Was Odd*. 'The most chic thing you can do,' I told her, 'is to appear in London in two plays at once.'

Mother had immense respect for Clements, and he had infinite tact and patience with her. Just as well, for she was inclined to interrupt him, as he was describing the new play to her, with, 'Now I'll tell you a play you ought to do, *much* more suitable than this.' She agreed, somewhat reluctantly, to John's proposal. She was dissatisfied with small parts, but found it increasingly difficult to learn new ones, and was beginning to lose her way on-stage.

Clements suggested she should take a week off from the Shaw, and I proposed that she should spend it with me at Stratford. I could hear her in the early mornings, reciting her new lines, and I would make her a cup of tea. Our talk was nearly all of the theatre. She had an astonishing memory for names, especially actors' names, and that week at Avoncliffe those names came flooding into our memories. Dorothy Green, an excellent Cleopatra; Edmund Willard, a fine Macbeth; Baliol Holloway, '*There* was an actor'; Vivienne Bennett, who could play boys' parts ... and further back in time to the old Savoy Theatre with H. B. Irving. That week at Stratford, thanks to Clements, made it possible to forget the unhappiness of the last years of her illness.

'What on earth are those kids of yours up to now?'

My questioner, an elderly member of the Garrick Club, clearly doesn't expect an answer. He presses on, outraged. Have I heard, did I know, that they're invading people's dressing-rooms, haranguing them by the hour?

I have grown accustomed to such stories. I shrug and raise my eyebrows. I rather like being buttonholed about my children. I do not understand their politics, but I like the revolutionary flavour.

Only once, I recall, did I try to influence their outlook. Their nanny was a staunch reader of the Tory *Daily Mail*. Under her influence, and the *Daily Mail*'s, they seemed to be growing up as little Conservatives, and I felt I should try to redress the balance. 'If you're going to read *that*,' I said, bursting into their nursery, 'you ought to read *this* as well,' and I handed them a copy of the liberal *News Chronicle*. They looked understandably baffled.

Since the days of Oliver Baldwin, I had considered myself a socialist – and still do. As a young schoolmaster at Cranleigh I had had modest success in encouraging the boys to talk about politics, rubbing it into them that the views of their parents need not necessarily be their own. As a young actor I made no attempt to disguise my left-wing opinions, when asked. It was during the Depression, and for an actor to be a socialist was not unpopular. When I signed the People's Convention, I was asked to stand for Parliament. 'You could be the most popular actor in England,' someone said. I toyed with the idea for all of twenty minutes before rejecting it, knowing perfectly well that I could never carry it through. But my political development stopped with the People's Convention. The fear that I had been used by people and a party I did not wholly trust, for a cause I did not fully understand, made me cautious, and in time my caution turned to conservatism, though with a small 'c'.

I had the same fear for Vanessa and Corin at first. On two or three ~ccasions I went to Hyde Park to hear Vanessa speak for her party, standing at a distance so as not to be seen by her. I remember thinking that, as yet, she was more persuasive as an actress than as a public speaker. But to those who seemed to think that her politics would diminish her acting, I would reply that, on the contrary, each strengthened the other and both were strengthened by her sense of purpose. As she grew up, her life became a study in purpose. How many parents could say of their children, I thought, that they had purpose?

Not long before the final season at Stratford, the tax collector and my own financial imprudence caught up with me. I was forced to do six films in succession to pay my arrears, and then to sell our house in Chiswick.

The human condition postulates some anchorage or other, and in this we were blessed beyond an actor's dreams. Rachel was given Wilks Water, an eighteenth-century farm labourer's cottage set among the fields and woods of what was once a Hampshire estate. For this gift three generations of Redgraves and Kempsons have now rejoiced for more than twenty-five years. Rachel poured her talent for making a family, and all that a family demands, into a haven which would be the envy of any theatrical country-lover.

Much as I love New York, California, and the lengthy tours which have taken up such a large part of my later life, I cannot now imagine an existence which did not contain something like Wilks Water, nor Wilks Water without Rachel running out of the front door to meet me.

As an actress matures, it often happens that she finds roles which deepen her gifts. Rachel left the Royal Academy of Dramatic Art in 1933 with an exciting vista of beautiful young parts ahead of her. In her first professional engagement at Stratford that year, she played everything from Juliet to a witch in Komisarjevsky's production of *Macbeth*.

The births of our children were joyous events, but they cannot be said to have enlarged her theatrical horizon. She made a modest, but definite, success as Charles Boyer's wife in the Hollywood film *A Woman's Vengeance* from Aldous Huxley's *The Gioconda Smile*, in Christopher Fry's *Venus Observed* with Olivier at the St James's in 1949, and in a variety of parts in George Devine's first season at the Royal Court. But the real showing of her talent has come later, as

Somerset Maugham's *Jane* on television, and only a year or two ago as the irascible elderly social worker *Kate, the Good Neighbour*.

When she is in a play in the West End, I selfishly hope it will not run too long, for that means she will stay at the cottage only from Saturday night till Monday afternoon. But often – too often – it does.

XXI

W HEN THE phone call came from Larry Olivier suggesting *Uncle Vanya* for the opening season at the Chichester Theatre Festival in 1961, I said yes at once.

Rehearsals began in a drill hall behind Sloane Square. 'I know you think there's no such thing as a definitive performance, but *this* . . . ' Larry murmured in my ear at the first reading as he closed the book on the last page. It was rumoured that he had insured the Festival against loss, and looking about one at the cast he had assembled for *Vanya*, I thought, What an insurance! Joan Plowright, Sybil Thorndike and Lewis Casson, Joan Greenwood, André Morell, Peter Woodthorpe; and Larry himself as Astrov.

The first two plays, *The Broken Heart* by Ford, and *The Chances* by Beaumont and Fletcher, gave little promise of what was to come. But there was no mistaking the triumph of *Vanya*. Even those who vowed that Chekhov could never work on Chichester's open stage were dumbfounded.

Larry and I had not worked together since *Hamlet* in 1937. During the War, while I was acting in *A Month in the Country* at the St James's, Alan Dent, the critic and theatre historian, had brought me a message from Olivier asking if I would like to play the Dauphin in his film of *Henry V*. At that time I was firmly of the opinion that any film of Shakespeare was doomed to failure, and I helpfully gave Dent the reasons for my prejudice, the gist of which was that, in the unequal fight between the image and the word, the image must always triumph at the expense of the word, and – 'Stop! Stop!' cried Dent. 'If I'm not careful you'll persuade me to think likewise.'

After the War, Rachel and I stayed several weekends with the Oliviers at Notley Abbey. Larry's energy was impressive. Quite early on a Sunday morning he would be pruning what he called a 'where'er you walk' of pleached hornbeams or beech. A big party would assemble in the afternoon, some twenty or more guests. It was the heyday of the game called 'the Game'.

One evening at Chichester, as we were going out to supper, Olivier said, 'I think we'll have to keep *Vanya* going next year.' It may have been that evening also that he told me, in the way he had of dropping such hints, that Chichester was to be the launching pad for the National Theatre, and that he and I would lead the company in the National's first season. I was overjoyed. I showed Larry a photograph of the model of what was to be, at some distant future date, the Yvonne Arnaud Theatre at Guildford; I had been asked to direct their opening festival. Laughingly I said, 'You've got your theatre, and I've got mine.'

'Would ya keer ta swap?' said Larry.

Those two seasons at Chichester rank amongst my happiest times in the theatre. I was proud of my work, proud of Larry's company. In the 1940s and 1950s I had been sometimes boosted in the press as Olivier's rival, and, it is said, by Sally Beauman in a recent history of the Royal Shakespeare Company, though on what authority I don't know, that Larry was conscious of this. At Chichester we worked together in complete harmony. I thought his Astrov faultless. I wished fervently that Mother could have lived to see our *Uncle Vanya*. No actor alive could meet her expectations, but of them all, Olivier came nearest to everything which she thought an actor should be, and which I should try harder to outstrip, though that was never my intention.

'The National Theatre at the Old Vic' was now the proud blazon across the façade of the dear old building in Waterloo Road. Denys Lasdun's building on the South Bank was, as yet, only a forest of girders, cement, and holes in the ground in the autumn of 1963, and for some time to come the Old Vic was to be our home. It was given a face-lift in honour of the occasion. Some noisy alterations were in progress, and a revolving stage was being installed, making our opening rehearsals very difficult.

At Chichester Olivier had opened the proceedings with two almost unknown Jacobean plays, as if to give his company a chance to stretch their limbs in unfamiliar surroundings. But for the National's first production we were to start at full throttle. *Hamlet* was to be the first production, with Peter O'Toole, directed by Larry himself. I was to play the King.

'We'll e'en fly at it like French falconers.' Good advice, if only one could take it. But somehow I couldn't. For my first entrance, with

Diana Wynyard as the Queen, I had to descend an immense flight of stairs, from the flies to the stage. Heights have always unnerved me, and I dearly wished for another, simpler entrance. But Diana didn't seem too nervous, so I thought I'd better persevere. By the time I reached the bottom step, all attack had deserted me.

Larry had indicated that the King and Queen should come to rest on two blocks – presumably thrones – at the foot of the staircase. Somehow my feet always seemed to carry me to the throne nearer stage centre. Time and again we made our entrance, and time and again I heard Larry's voice saying, 'The other throne, Michael. The *other* throne.' Poor Diana! After a while, when it must have looked as if I would never get the move right, she came storming into my dressing-room, saying, 'Michael, do you realize you've got that move wrong seventeen times?' 'Oh, sorry,' I said, privately thinking, Well, if an actor makes the wrong move so many times, it must be because the move itself is wrong. And then Larry said the same thing. Next day, giving notes, he said, 'When you came on as Macbeth, it was as if you were saying, "Fuck you, I *am* Macbeth." As Claudius you are *dim*.' These were portents.

We opened in November to indifferent notices all round. Performance after performance, I ploughed heavily through the part of the King and, as time went on, I thought I was neither so bad nor so ineffective as I had thought myself at the beginning. I no longer remember the details of my performance. I remember only a great feeling of tiredness. I frequently caught myself looking at some object, fixedly staring. I began to think that I was ill.

Our next play was *Hobson's Choice*. When Larry had asked me over the phone to play Hobson, my first reaction was 'What on earth makes you think I could play that?' 'You're a good character actor,' Larry said.

Harold Brighouse's play is a Lancashire comedy, as much of its time and place as the Neapolitan comedies of Eduardo da Filippo. Its humour lies, to a large extent, in its observation of status. Hobson is a Salford shopkeeper, but a tyrant in his own world. My chief difficulty was with the dialect. Usually I had no trouble with accents. But Hobson's demands a Lancashire accent, something with a strong bite to it, and when in rehearsal I tried to apply the 'bite', I thought I sounded slightly absurd. One of my fellow-actors gave up part of his Sundays to help me with it. Still it sounded off-key. Possibly not to everyone, but even the kindliest Lancastrian in the audience, I thought, would have awarded me no more than '2' for trying. Perhaps I could also plead that, but for the demands of repertory, I would never have been cast in the part of a North Country bully.

None of these excuses could be applied to Solness in *The Master Builder*, a part which might be said to be right up my street. Yet, once again, the lines would not stick. I had the feeling that the rest of the company were whispering about me. More and more I retreated into myself.

Diana was playing Mrs Solness. One afternoon after rehearsal a number of the cast were crowded into my dressing-room, making a slight hubbub, when in came Diana from her dressing-room next door, almost frantic with distress, saying, 'Oh, do be quiet, please, please be quiet.' She died the next day. She had become, after Edith, my closest woman friend. From the time we first worked together through the Blitz in *Kipps* I loved her for her beauty, her gaiety, and the sense of light-heartedness she unleashed in me.

Celia Johnson took over Diana's part. Rehearsals continued. I found myself at odds with everything, hating the production, hating the set. I could see the look of bewilderment on the faces of my fellow-actors when, in the final runs-through, I tried to apologize for not knowing my lines. I could hardly have blamed them if they thought that the serious memory gaps I began to suffer were due to the demon drink. I partly thought so myself.

On the first night I managed without a prompter, but my unease communicated itself to the audience, as it must have to the rest of the cast.

I kept telling myself when I woke up on Ibsen days that tonight I would get it right. Yet, as I taxied to the theatre, my confidence always slowly ebbed away, and as the taxi crossed Waterloo Bridge I would begin to tremble.

The season came to an end, and new contracts had to be drawn up. *Vanya* was to be withdrawn from the repertoire. It was assumed that I would go on playing my other three parts. But I stood firm on Solness. I would not take on that part again. Larry said that *The Master Builder* had been an expensive production and had to be revived, and that if I would not do Solness he would have to undertake it himself. I knew that he was loath to do this because of the heavy parts, including Othello, which he had coming up, but I was obstinate. So he took on the part. On his first night I sent him a wire quoting Solness's famous line 'It will be wonderful, wonderful, wonderful.' And so I was sure he would be, though I could never bring myself to see his performance.

For the opening festival of the Yvonne Arnaud Theatre at Guildford in 1965, I played safe by choosing parts which I had played before and therefore knew already. In the case of *Samson Agonistes*, which I had played at Cranleigh, this proved to be a mistake. It was one thing to ignore Milton's damnation of the theatre by rigging up an impromptu performance in the school library, but quite another to present it as a play to the citizens of Guildford. They came, audibly bracing themselves for the ordeal. But *A Month in the Country*, which I had played twice before and directed in New York, paid off very well. It was not the best-acted version I had been in, but the presence of Ingrid Bergman made it, whatever its shortcomings, a joyous occasion. We had acted together not long before in a television production of *Hedda Gabler*, and at the suggestion of a friend I had rung her, asking her to come to Guildford to play Natalya Petrovna. She agreed there and then, and the success of the season was assured.

It should be easy to describe Ingrid Bergman's art, and perhaps for that very reason it is difficult. In *A Month in the Country*, truth to say, she was not at the top of her form, but in most people's opinion and in mine it simply didn't matter. Her capacious good nature shone through everything she did. She was a lovely paradox: a very private person whose whole personality was on display.

It was a happy season, followed by a very successful six months' run of the Turgenev at the Cambridge Theatre in London. I had put the National Theatre behind me and out of mind. I was in good spirits and good health, or so it seemed. The only symptom that anything was amiss was an occasional spell of dizziness, and that could be put down to poor circulation.

I realize now that my loss of memory at the National, the shaking as I crossed Waterloo Bridge before *The Master Builder*, and the feeling I had that the company – 'they' – were against me, were all symptoms of the onset of Parkinson's disease. Yet the disease itself was not diagnosed for another nine years.

Parkinson's disease takes so many forms that no two cases are ever identical. It can strike so severely that its victim is completely incapacitated, or so lightly as to leave him in full possession of all his faculties, with nothing but the faintest tremor to indicate its presence. It is as old as recorded history. References to it are found in Galen, and in the Bible, where, in the Authorized Version, it is called 'the Palsy'. The physician James Parkinson, in honour of whose work the disease takes its name, called it the 'shaking palsy'. *Paralysis agitans*, its Latin title, expresses its nature and its essence better than any other, for the disease exhibits itself as a sharp and sometimes painful contradiction: it impels a person into bouts of restless movement, and yet paralyses him at that point where he *wants* to move.

The next period of my life remains, therefore, a grey expanse, with intermittent shafts of light. For much of this time my abiding feeling was simply of an absence of well-being. Weeks and sometimes months would pass pleasantly enough, but without my being able to summon the energy to accomplish anything very much. At such times it seemed as though my old enemy, procrastination, now ruled my life. Not an unprofitable drifting, at least not financially. Numerous films came along, some very good, like *The Go-Between*. Unconsciously, I sought to avoid situations where the symptoms I had felt at the National might recur. When I did return to the stage, in 1971, it was not, as I recall, from a conscious deliberation that I should do so. Simply that I liked the play, and thought, Why not?

I was happy enough rehearsing William Trevor's play *The Old Boys* with Sylvia Coleridge at the Mermaid Theatre in 1971. Happy enough to think that all was going well. Which it patently wasn't. At the dress rehearsal in the afternoon, I met Josephine Miles, the wife of the Mermaid's director, at the stage door. Or, rather, we bumped into each other. Till then she had appeared to be avoiding me. 'It's a very funny play, isn't it?' I said. 'Will your husband be out front?'

'Very funny,' she said. I noticed she was blowing her nose. I looked again, and saw that she was crying. 'Yes, a very funny play,' she repeated. I looked at her intently. The play wasn't as funny as all that. At that moment Bernard Miles appeared. 'I've sent for one of those contraptions,' he said. 'I think it might help you.'

When it arrived we spent some time practising how to use it. It seemed to be some sort of hearing-aid. Turn it up, and the prompter's voice bellowed and crackled in my ear; turn it down, and it murmured inaudibly. I ploughed through the dress rehearsal as best I could, with Sylvia doing her utmost to help me. I had not till that moment thought that anything was wrong. At the first performance I decided to brave it out. But unfortunately Sylvia and I, in a bit of rough-and-tumble, were more energetic than was strictly necessary, and the hearing-aid, making a few squawks, disintegrated and scattered in pieces around me. The loyal Sylvia started picking them up. 'I'm afraid it's broken, darling,' she muttered in a stage whisper.

At the Hospital for Nervous Diseases in Queen's Square, Professor Watkins diagnosed Parkinson's and prescribed L-dopa. I started taking it and was surprised at how cheerful I felt. I put this down to my cheerful nature; then I found it was an effect of the drug.

L-dopa by this time (1972) had been in use for some five years. At first it had been hailed as a miracle drug. Perfectly healthy people experimented with it in California in the belief that it was the elixir of life. Like all drugs, it is a stopgap, and until such time as the cause of the cell damage which is Parkinson's is understood and can be cured or prevented, L-dopa, or some derivative grandchild of L-dopa, will probably continue to be used. It is certainly useful, but it bestows its benefits in a capricious way. After the cheerfulness came sudden bouts of nausea. Later came hallucinations – voices from the next-door room, the corridor outside, or the pavement beyond my window, whispering about me or against me. The drug needed periodical fine-tuning of its dosage to overcome these unpleasant side-effects.

'I think that, after all, an operation won't be necessary,' said Dr Cooper. I felt relieved and rewarded. I had come to the Bronx at the suggestion of Lynn and her husband, John Clark, to be treated at St Barnabas Hospital, where Dr Irving Cooper had performed a number of operations on Parkinsonian patients, with some success. I had had numerous tests and observations. So impressed was I with the efficiency of this hospital and the wonders of modern medicine that I had gradually put myself in a frame of mind where I was ready for the operation on the morrow. To be told now that it wasn't necessary was like an unexpected reward for my bravery. 'Fine,' I said. But what next?

Illness played tricks with my memory. I found I could still retain large chunks of parts I had played before, but could not memorize new ones. I began to think I should be confined to radio broadcasts for the rest of my working life. Not an invigorating prospect, much as I enjoy broadcasting from time to time.

Suddenly, in July 1973, came an unexpected bonus. Would I care to accompany Peggy Ashcroft and others to Central City, Colorado, for a few performances at its festival of *The Hollow Crown*? This was an anthology devised by John Barton for the Royal Shakespeare Company about the kings and queens of England. Originally intended as a one-off divertissement in 1960, it had proved so successful and durable that it remained in the repertoire on and off for the next twelve years. It made an interesting, varied recital of pieces as diverse as Richard II's return from Ireland and the nine-year-old Jane Austen's potted history of England. They were divided among four actors, with good parts for all, and there was the added advantage of a production which allowed us to carry our scripts so as to read our parts when necessary.

We performed for two weeks in the neat little Opera House in the ruins of the city of the great Gold Rush. From there we moved to Washington, D.C., where we played another two weeks in the Opera House of the Kennedy Center. It was the beginning of the 'Save Michael' campaign, for the following year a new tour was mounted of *The Hollow Crown*, and the year after, another, and for the next three years there were tours of *Shakespeare's People*. One hundred and twenty-six theatres in one hundred and fifteen towns across four continents.

The date is 15 April 1974; Brooklyn; towards midnight. A dark and almost deserted place. We have just finished our first perfor-mance of *The Hollow Crown* in the Opera House of the Brooklyn Academy. Next week, Nazareth College, Rochester. Then Prince-ton. Then Harvard. (The emphasis seems to be on academic dates.) But then we travel west, to towns with charming names like Spokane, Tucson, Flagstaff . . .

The temperature rises, but, thank heavens, the bus is air-conditioned.

> Our driver's name is Mr OSCAR BRADFORD. The following rules have been found to be mutually beneficial, and we hope they will enable everyone to enjoy what is in effect our home for the next eleven weeks – 'THE BUS'.
>
> The bus will be divided into SMOKING and NON-SMOKING areas.
>
> Each member of the company will have a double seat to themselves, and that seat should be the same for the duration of the tour. When leaving the hotel in the morning it is customary that the first few hours of travel take place in silence, thus enabling the 'slow wakers' to do just that. Games that rattle or bang must be avoided.
>
> *Time Changes*: We will announce the fact when we go through a time change. After this announcement you will each be responsible for responding to calls on the new time.

1975. A marvellous homecoming. Our final performance of *The Hollow Crown*, newly-returned from the Antipodes, is at the

Redgrave Theatre in Farnham, Surrey. All that hectic fund-raising seems light-years away. The result is delightful, a tonic to the spirit of one who has never grown out of the childlike pleasure of seeing his own name in print.

The year is 1976. The programme of *Shakespeare's People* consists, for my part, entirely of pieces which I have known and played so often that I do not need a script. And who could resist a tour whose itinerary begins: 'September 20–24: Rehearse at Prince of Wales pub, Drury Lane. September 28: Depart Heathrow. September 29: Arrive Rio de Janeiro'?

The performance goes especially well in Rio. The Teatro João Caetano turns out to be a fine, sumptuously-appointed opera house of the 1860s, perfectly proportioned, with a row of boxes surrounding what was once the pit, each furnished with its little ante-room where ladies could retire or entertain.

No audience anywhere, at any time, is ever 'typical', but this one in Rio cannot be, for our brief stay – two nights – will attract only the English-speaking, the Shakespeare-lovers, those who want to see, and those who want to be seen. The applause is deafening, especially for *Macbeth*, Act One, Scene Three. Rosalind Shanks is a very attractive Lady Macbeth. There are five of us in *Shakespeare's People* – Ros and I, David Dodimead, Philip Bowen, and Rod Willmott and his lute – all on stage together throughout the evening. At the end of the performance the applause outdoes anything in any other continent. Cheers, stamping feet, flowers from the gallery . . .

It is 1977. Behind us are Indianapolis, Chattanooga, Knoxville. Ahead: London, Ontario, where I first played Macbeth before opening on Broadway twenty-nine years ago, and where once again we'll have to suffer Canada's liquor laws: 'The consumption of alcoholic beverages on public highways is illegal. Alcohol may be transported on the bus, but must not be consumed while we are in transit. No open bottles will be permitted when entering Canada, so you should plan accordingly.' After London: Kalamazoo; Bloomington; and Normal, Illinois. Tonight: Terre Haute, Indiana, in the Tilson Music Hall. If I close my eyes, as I frequently do on the bus, I can picture Terre Haute as a two-horse town with its dusty main street, John Wayne stepping out of the saloon bar, and gaily made-up ladies leaning against the piano of the Tilson Music Hall. But no, there will be a Howard Johnson's motel, and the Music Hall will be a large, well-equipped theatre. I *like* Howard Johnson's motels, for their sameness and efficiency. I like touring – love touring, in fact. No letters, no phone calls, no messages. Ideal – were it not for the loneliness.

I get to the theatre just before the 'half' and take a look at the stage. An actor with experience instinctively knows if it's a good auditorium to be seen and heard in: 'If in doubt, shout.' The university theatres have immense auditoriums, so large that only a small percentage of the audience can possibly see one's expression. But university audiences are amongst the best. The most fascinating theatre on this tour was Frank Lloyd Wright's building at Tempe, Arizona: round, pink, situated in a vast open space, and with a delightful impromptu air, despite the comfort and expense of all its fittings.

In my dressing-room I sing a little, to bring the voice forward. The 'five' is called. I put on my costume – a dark, full-sleeved Hamlet shirt, dark trousers.

The performance goes well. This is the third year of *Shakespeare's People* and my performance doesn't vary a great deal. On each tour I've tried to simplify it. 'The cardinal labour of composition is excision,' says Virginia Woolf, which in the language of acting means learning to do less.

There are a few visitors after the performance. It's nice to have visitors, of course, with their congratulations, but it's embarrassing somewhat, because unless they are professionals they find it very hard to leave. I've found it best to help them, and myself, by standing in the doorway of my dressing-room holding something over my arm, making as if I'm in a bit of a hurry. In the distance one can hear the stage staff packing the furniture, and over the public address system comes the stage-manager's voice announcing the time of departure for our next port of call, across the border and into Canada. The dramatic critic of Terre Haute's newspaper will be at work on his review, but we shan't be there to read it. Strange – notices are part of our addiction to receiving praise or blame, but when you're hurtling from one place to the next in a bus, it's amazing how well you manage without them.

'Would you prefer to cancel the performance tonight, Sir Michael? You may find it difficult to keep your feet.'

'Then we'll sit. No, we won't cancel it.'

The *QE2* is rolling heavily in rough weather. Half the passengers have kept to their bunks, and the other half have crowded into every corner of the main ballroom. An audience mainly middle-aged, middle-class, middle-brow, many of whom would not have come had the play been performed in their home town in England, but who come tonight because it's something different on board a ship, and find, to their surprise, that they enjoy every moment of it. 'I can't wait to get home and read it all again,' says one, with tears in her eyes. It's a comment I've heard before – typical, I think, of many of our audiences in the English-speaking countries. 'Did you find the audiences varied enormously?' I'm asked. True, we have played it across three continents. But no, the answer is no. Performances vary, and no audience is ever quite the same as the previous one. But essentially audiences, whatever the country, laugh when they're amused, and are amused in much the same way; sit silent when they're absorbed, and are restless when they're not; and are absorbed by what we, the actors, do, when it's done well and truthfully.

XXII

SCUDAMORES, REDGRAVES ... Dockyard workers, wain-
wrights ... Fortunatus Augustin Scudamore, his actor children
Dolly and Lionel ... A distinguished cleric, Roy's uncle, the
Reverend Henry Hymer Redgrave, who lived well into his nineties,
performed a christening service for Lynn, and in his extreme old age
was still working on a concordance to the Bible ... Grace, his
daughter, an acrobatic dancer ...

Nor should the offspring of Roy's first marriage be overlooked.
Judith Kyrle, Roy's first wife, gave up the stage and married a man
whose financial prospects were a great deal more stable than she
could have hoped for during her marriage to Roy. As a wedding
present, her new father-in-law gave her an oil well in Rumania.
Their son Robin, my half-brother, I met more than once, the air on
such occasions being filled with conjecture and surmise. The grand-
son, christened Roy, a General when I met him, on leave from
command of Her Majesty's forces in Hong Kong ...

Mabel, my actress aunt, who signed all her letters to me with the
drawing of a little imp. 'Impy' was a little ragged doll made out of
hairpins, with a goblin cap and a red bobble on it, and even now I
have only to say 'Impy with his knitty wire hand' to be back in the
days of my childhood and Mrs Gold.

I last saw Mabel when I was an undergraduate. A letter arrived
saying that she and her husband's company were playing at Saffron
Walden, and would I care to come over from Cambridge to see a
performance. I had not seen Mabel since the days when, with the
help of her dressmaker, Mother had fitted her up with the costumes
for *A Royal Divorce*, in which she played the Empress Josephine with
her husband as Napoleon. But those were the palmy days.

The Woman Always Pays, said the poster outside the village hall.

236

No mention was made of the author. Inside I found Mabel in the box office selling tickets. She greeted me with a cheerful smile and hurried backstage.

The play – seeming strangely familiar – was performed at a brisk pace. Henry Beckett, Mabel's second husband, was a fine actor who had played many seasons at Bridport.

'Did you like it?' asked Mabel.

'Yes, very much.'

'We had to change the title, of course. Good, don't you think? Good for the box office.'

'But what is the real title?' I asked.

'*Hindle Wakes*. Didn't you recognize it? Good little play, but of course we couldn't afford the royalties.'

'We live and learn,' said Mabel.

Mother said, 'What do you mean?'

Mabel fell silent. But not for long. 'At least,' she said, 'we learn who are our friends and who are not.'

'Nonsense.' Mother had a real sweetness of her own, but in her old age she could not stand nonsense.

Mabel continued. 'Who was it who said it would be better if we were born old and grew young?'

'I can't imagine.'

'Who said that? That dreadful man who thought you could find the truth by turning everything upside-down – you know, you hate me quoting him ... ?'

'*What* about it?'

'Well, try another favourite of yours, Goethe's *Poetry and Truth*: "What a man wants in his youth he gets in plenty in his old age." What about that?'

'It's all relative,' said Mother. 'Relatively there is progress, absolutely there is no such thing.'

'What do you think, Michael?' I had been listening.

'"The sixth age shifts into the lean and slippered pantaloon ... "' I began.

'That's enough, Michael. We don't want to know what the old idiot does or doesn't. That's enough.'

LIST OF PERFORMANCES AND PRODUCTIONS

Films are listed by their general release date.
Plays produced/directed by Michael Redgrave are asterisked.

AMATEUR AND SEMI-AMATEUR

Date		Character	Play or Film and Author, etc.	Theatre
1921	July	Walked on	Henry IV, Part 2 (Shakespeare)	Memorial Theatre, Stratford-on-Avon
1922	June	Second Niece	The Critic (Sheridan)	Clifton College
	December	She	A Pair of Lunatics	
		Barbara	The Private Detective (J. A. O. Muirhead)	
1923	June	Lady Mary	The Admirable Crichton (Barrie)	
	December	Cosmo Lennox	The Refugee (J. A. O. Muirhead)	
1924	June	Mrs Hardcastle	She Stoops to Conquer (Goldsmith)	
	December	Clarence	Richard III (Shakespeare)	
1925	June	Lady Macbeth	Macbeth (Shakespeare)	
	December	Reginald	Pigs in Straw (M. Redgrave)	
1926	June	The Young Man	The Bathroom Door (Gertrude Jennings)	Orthopaedic Hospital
		The Old Man	The Maker of Dreams (Harold Chapin)	
		Captain Absolute	The Rivals (Sheridan)	Clifton College
	August	The Young Man	The Bathroom Door (Gertrude Jennings)	Duke of York's Camp
	October	The Cook	The Taming of the Shrew (Shakespeare)	Apollo
1928	June	Florindo	The Servant of Two Masters (Goldoni)	A.D.C., Cambridge
	November	The Soldier	The Soldier's Tale (Ramuz-Stravinsky)	
		The Lover	A Lover's Complaint (Shakespeare)	

Date	Character	Play or Film and Author, etc.	Theatre
1929			
March	Edgar	King Lear (Shakespeare)	King's College, Cambridge, and 46 Gordon Sq., London
November	Mr Voysey	The Voysey Inheritance (Harley Granville–Barker)	
December	Second Brother	Comus (Milton)	
1930			
February	Rumour and Prince Hal	Henry IV, Part 2 (Shakespeare)	A.D.C., Cambridge
March	Mr Pepys	The Battle of the Book (Redgrave–Turner)★	Arts, London
December	The Lover	A Lover's Complaint (Shakespeare)	A.D.C., Cambridge
	Second Brother	Comus (Milton)	Cranleigh School
1931			
June	Captain Brassbound	Captain Brassbound's Conversion (Shaw)	Guildford Rep. Co.
1932			
June	Hymen	As You Like It (Shakespeare)★	
November	Ralph Rackstraw	H.M.S. Pinafore (Gilbert–Sullivan)★	Cranleigh School
1933			
March	Samson	Samson Agonistes (Milton)★	
June	Hamlet	Hamlet (Shakespeare)★	Guildford Rep. Co.
October	John Worthing	The Importance of Being Earnest (Oscar Wilde)	
November	Menelaus	The Trojan Women (Euripides)	
1934			
February	Prospero	The Tempest (Shakespeare)★	Cranleigh School
	Clive Champion Cheney	The Circle (W. S. Maugham)	
March	Young Marlow	She Stoops to Conquer (Goldsmith)	Guildford Rep. Co.
June	Lear	King Lear (Shakespeare)★	
July	Mr Browning	The Barretts of Wimpole Street (Rudolph Besier)	

PROFESSIONAL

Date	Character	Play or Film and Author, etc.	Theatre
August	Roy Darwin	Counsellor at Law (Elmer Rice)	Liverpool Playhouse
September	Charles Hubbard	The Distaff Side (John van Druten)	
October	Dr Purley	A Sleeping Clergyman (James Bridie)	
	The Man	The Perfect Plot (Aubrey Ensor)	
November	Mr Bolton	Sheppey (W. S. Maugham)	Liverpool Playhouse
December	Ernest Hubbard	Heaven on Earth (Philip Johnson)	

Date		Character	Play or Film and Author, etc.	Theatre
1935	January	Melchior Feydak	Biography (S. N. Behrman)	
	February	Gaston	Villa for Sale (Sacha Guitry)	
	March	Sir Mark Loddon	Libel (Edward Wooll)	
		Richard Newton Clare	Flowers of the Forest (John van Druten)	
	April	Horatio	Hamlet (Shakespeare)	Winter Gardens, New Brighton
	May	Bill Clarke	Too Young to Marry (Martin Flavin)	
		Oliver Maitland	The Matriarch (G. B. Stern)	
	June	Sir Mark Loddon	Libel (Edward Wooll)	
	July	Charles McFadden	Counsellor at Law (Elmer Rice)	Liverpool Playhouse
	August	Bill Clarke	Too Young to Marry (Martin Flavin)	
	September	Randolph Warrender	Youth at the Helm (Hubert Griffith)	
	October	Richard Barnet	Barnet's Folly (Jan Stewer)	
		Robert Murrison	Cornelius (J.B.Priestley)	
		Richard Brinsley Sheridan	Miss Linley of Bath (Mary D. Sheridan)	
	November	Max	The Copy (Helge Krog)	
		Trino	A Hundred Years Old (Quintero Brothers)	
	December	Gilbert Raymond	The Wind and the Rain (Merton Hodge)	
		BBC Official	Circus Boy (Michael Redgrave)	
1936	February	Rev Ernest Dunwoody	Boyd's Shop (St John Ervine)	
	March	A Radio Announcer	And So To War (Joe Corrie)	
	April	Richard II	Richard of Bordeaux (Gordon Daviot)	
		Richard Burdon	Storm in a Teacup (James Bridie)	
	May	Tom Lambert	Painted Sparrows (Guy Paxton and Edward V. Hoile)	
	June	Malvolio	Twelfth Night (Shakespeare)	
	September	Ferdinand, King of Navarre	Love's Labour's Lost (Shakespeare)	Old Vic
	October	Mr Horner	The Country Wife (Wycherley)	
	November	Orlando	As You Like It (Shakespeare)	
	December	Warbeck	The Witch of Edmonton (Dekker)	
1937	January	Laertes	Hamlet (Shakespeare)	

240

Date	Character	Play or Film and Author, etc.	Theatre
February	Orlando	As You Like It (Shakespeare)	New
March	Anderson	The Bat (Mary Roberts Rinehart and Avery Hopwood)	Embassy
April	Iachimo	Scene from Cymbeline (Shakespeare)	Old Vic
	Chorus	Henry V (Shakespeare)	
May	Christopher Drew	A Ship Comes Home (Daisy Fisher)	St Martin's
June	Larry Starr	Three Set Out (Philip Leaver)	Embassy
September	Bolingbroke	Richard II (Shakespeare)	Queen's
November	Charles Surface	The School for Scandal (Sheridan)	Queen's
1938 January	Baron Tusenbach	The Three Sisters (Chekhov)	
April	Chorus	Henry V (Shakespeare)	Old Vic
July	Orlando	Scenes from As You Like It (Shakespeare)	The Barn, Smallhythe
October	Alexei Turbin	The White Guard (Michael Bulgakov, adapted by Rodney Ackland)	Phoenix
December	Sir Andrew Aguecheek	Twelfth Night (Shakespeare)	Phoenix
1939 January	Gilbert	The Lady Vanishes (dir. Alfred Hitchcock)	Film
March	Lord Harry Monchensey	The Family Reunion (T. S. Eliot)	Westminster
April	Alan Mackenzie	Stolen Life (dir. Paul Czinner)	Film
May	Nicholas Brooke	Climbing High (dir. Carol Reed)	Film
October	Henry Dewlip	Springtime for Henry (Benn W. Levy)	Provincial tour
1940 February	David Fenwick	The Stars Look Down (dir. Carol Reed)	Film
March	Captain Macheath	The Beggar's Opera (John Gay)	Haymarket
	Romeo	Scene from Romeo and Juliet (Shakespeare)	Palace
June	Peter	A Window in London (dir. Herbert Mason)	Film
	Charleston	Thunder Rock (Robert Ardrey)	Neighbourhood
July	Charleston	Thunder Rock (Robert Ardrey)	Globe
1941 June	Kipps	Kipps (dir. Carol Reed)	Film
July	Entered Royal Navy		
	Charles MacIver	Atlantic Ferry (dir. Walter Forde)	Film
September	Stanley Smith	Jeannie (dir. Harold French)	Film

Date		Character	Play or Film and Author, etc.	Theatre
1942	March	The Russian	The Big Blockade (dir. Charles Frend)	Film
	July		Lifeline (Norman Armstrong)★	Duchess
	October	Gribaud	The Duke in Darkness (Patrick Hamilton)	St James's
1943	February	Charleston	Thunder Rock (dir. Roy Boulting)	Film
		Rakitin	A Month in the Country (Turgenev)	St James's
	June	Lafont	Parisienne (Henry Becque, adapted by Ashley Dukes)	St James's
	August		Blow Your Own Trumpet (Peter Ustinov)★	Playhouse
	September		The Wingless Victory (Maxwell Anderson)★	Phoenix
1944	March	Harry	Uncle Harry (Thomas Job)★	Garrick
1945	June	The Colonel	Jacobowsky and the Colonel (Franz Werfel and S. N. Behrman)★	Piccadilly
	July	Flight Lieut. Archdale	The Way to the Stars (dir. Anthony Asquith)	Film
	October	Maxwell Frere	Dead of Night (Sequence dir. Alberto Cavalcanti)	Film
1946	April	Karel Hasek	The Captive Heart (dir. Basil Dearden)	Film
	July	Michael Wentworth	The Years Between (dir. Compton Bennett)	Film
1947	May	Carlyon	The Man Within (dir. Bernard Knowles)	Film
	November	Hamer Radshaw	Fame is the Spur (dir. Roy Boulting)	Film
	December	Macbeth	Macbeth (Shakespeare)	Aldwych
1948	March	Macbeth	Macbeth (Shakespeare)	National, New York
	November	The Captain	The Father (Strindberg)	Embassy
	December	Mark Lamphere	Secret Beyond the Door (dir. Fritz Lang)	Film
1949	January	The Captain	The Father (Strindberg)	Duchess
	April	Etienne	A Woman in Love (M. Redgrave and Diana Gould, from G. de Porto-Riche)★	Embassy
	October	Berowne	Love's Labour's Lost (Shakespeare)	New
	November	Young Marlow	She Stoops to Conquer (Shakespeare)	New
1950	November	Rakitin	A Month in the Country (Turgenev)	New
	February	Hamlet	Hamlet (Shakespeare)	New
	June	Hamlet	Hamlet (Shakespeare)	Kronborg Castle
	November	Filmer Jesson	Scene from His House in Order (Pinero)	Drury Lane

Date	*Character*	*Play or Film and Author, etc.*	*Theatre*
December	Solo performances of Shakespeare		Holland
1951 March	Richard II	*Richard II* (Shakespeare)	Stratford-on-Avon
April	Hotspur	*Henry IV, Part 1* (Shakespeare)	Stratford-on-Avon
May	Andrew Crocker-Harris	*The Browning Version* (dir. Anthony Asquith)	*Film*
June		*Henry IV, Part 2* (Shakespeare)*	Stratford-on-Avon
July	Prospero	*The Tempest* (Shakespeare)	
July	Solo performances of Shakespeare		Holland Festival
	Chorus	*Henry V* (Shakespeare)	Stratford-on-Avon
	Mr Lege	*The Magic Box* (dir. John Boulting)	
1952 April	Frank Elgin	*Winter Journey* (Clifford Odets)	St James's
July	John Worthing	*The Importance of Being Earnest* (dir. Anthony Asquith)	*Film*
July	Orin Mannon	*Mourning Becomes Electra* (dir. Dudley Nichols; released New York 1947)	*Film*
1953 March	Shylock	*The Merchant of Venice* (Shakespeare)	Stratford-on-Avon
April	Antony	*Antony and Cleopatra* (Shakespeare)	
July	Lear	*King Lear* (Shakespeare)	
November	Antony	*Antony and Cleopatra* (Shakespeare)	Princes
1954 January	Antony	*Antony and Cleopatra* (Shakespeare)	The Hague, Amsterdam, Antwerp, Brussels and Paris
September	Maître Déliot	*The Green Scarf* (dir. George More O'Ferrall)	*Film*
1955 January	Air Commodore Waltby	*The Sea Shall Not Have Them* (dir. Lewis Gilbert)	*Film*
	Colonel Eisenstein	*Oh, Rosalinda!* (dir. Michael Powell and Emeric Pressburger)	*Film*
April	The Air Marshal	*The Night My Number Came Up* (dir. Leslie Norman)	*Film*
June	Barnes Wallis	*The Dam Busters* (dir. Michael Anderson)	*Film*

Date	Character	Play or Film and Author, etc.	Theatre
	Hector	Tiger at the Gates (Jean Giraudoux, trans. Christopher Fry)	Apollo
October	Hector	Tiger at the Gates	Plymouth, New York
1956 November	Trebitsch	Confidential Report (dir. Orson Welles)	Film
December	Shylock	Tubal scene in The Merchant of Venice (Shakespeare)	Waldorf-Astoria
March	O'Connor	1984 (dir. Michael Anderson)	Film
April	The Regent	A Month in the Country (Turgenev)*	Phoenix, New York
November	Ruggles	The Sleeping Prince (Terence Rattigan)	Coronet, New York
1957 January	David Graham	Ruggles of Red Gap	NBC TV
March	General Medworth	Time Without Pity (dir. Joseph Losey)	Film
June	Narrator	The Happy Road (dir. Gene Kelly)	Film
September	Philip Lester	Vanishing Cornwall (Christian Browning)	Film
1958 January	Fowler	A Touch of the Sun (N. C. Hunter)	Saville
		The Quiet American (dir. Joseph L. Mankiewicz)	Film
March	Hamlet	Hamlet (Shakespeare (Director) Glen Byam Shaw)	Stratford-on-Avon
June	Percy	Law and Disorder (dir. Charles Crichton)	Film
August	Benedick	Much Ado About Nothing (Shakespeare)	Stratford-on-Avon
October	Narrator	The Immortal Land (dir. Basil Wright)	Film
November	Hamlet	Hamlet	Palace of Culture, Leningrad and Moscow Art Theatre, Moscow
1959 August	Sir Arthur Benson Gray	Behind the Mask (dir. Brian Desmond Hurst)	Film
May	H.J.	The Aspern Papers (Henry James: adapted by MR)*	Queens
December	Michael Collins	Shake Hands with the Devil (dir. Michael Anderson)	Film
	Mr Nyland	The Wreck of the Mary Deare (dir. Michael Anderson)	Film
1960 April	Solo performances of Shakespeare		Ordry, Budapest
August	Jack Dean	The Tiger and the Horse (Robert Bolt)	Queen's

Date	Character	Play or Film and Author, etc.	Theatre
1966 June	Narrator	Werther (Massenet)★	Glyndebourne Opera
October		The Lost Peace (John Terraine)	BBC TV
December	The Blue Caterpillar	Alice in Wonderland (Lewis Carroll)	BBC TV
1967 June		La Bohème (Puccini)★	Glyndebourne Opera
November	Commentary	October Revolution (Fred Nossif)	BBC Radio
December	Charles Dickens	Mr Dickens of London (Barry Morse)	ABC TV
1968 January	Monsieur Barnett	Monsieur Barnett (Jean Anouilh)	BBC TV
	Harris	Assignment K (dir. Val Guest)	Film
May	Reading from the Huntingdonshire Cabmen	World of Beachcomber	BBC TV
November	Prospero	The Tempest (Shakespeare)	BBC TV
	The Ghost	The Canterville Ghost	ABC TV
	Grandfather	Heidi	NBC TV
1969 April	General Wilson	Oh, What A Lovely War (dir. Richard Attenborough)	Film
September	Air Vice Marshal Evill	Battle of Britain (dir. Guy Hamilton)	Film
November	The Headmaster	Goodbye, Mr Chips (dir. Herbert Ross)	Film
1970 March	Mr Peggotty	David Copperfield (dir. Delbert Mann)	Film
August	The MP	Goodbye Gemini (dir. Alan Gibson)	Film
1971 April	The Commander	Hell scene from Man and Superman (G. B. Shaw)	BBC TV
April	Polonius	Hamlet (Shakespeare)	TV, USA; BBC TV, UK
May	James Wallraven	Connecting Rooms (dir. Franklin Gollings)	Film
July	Mr Jaraby	The Old Boys (William Trevor)	Mermaid Theatre London
August	Father	A Voyage Round My Father (John Mortimer)	Haymarket
September	Leo when older	The Go-Between (dir. Joseph Losey)	Film
1972 April	Grand Duke	Nicholas and Alexandra (dir. Franklin Shaffner)	Film
September		A Voyage Round My Father (John Mortimer)	Tour of Canada and Australia
December	John	The Pump (James Cameron)	BBC Radio
	Erik Fritsch	The Last Target (dir. George Spenton-Foster)	Film

Date	Character	Play or Film and Author, etc.	Theatre
1973 August		Reading of *Child's Christmas in Wales* for the National Theatre of the Deaf	CBS
		Reading *The Hollow Crown* (Shakespeare)	Central City, Denver and Opera House, Washington
1974			USA Tour
		Reading *The Hollow Crown* (Shakespeare) and *Pleasure and Repentance* (programme of poetry, prose and songs)	
1975 January		Reading *The Hollow Crown* (Shakespeare) and *Pleasure and Repentance* (poetry, prose and songs)	World Tour
1976 August		Reading *Shakespeare's People* (Shakespeare)	South Africa
October		Reading *Shakespeare's People* (Shakespeare)	Tour of South America and Canada
November	Reading	*The Wheel of Fire* (Shakespeare)	Theatre Royal, Windsor, and English Tour
1977 March		Reading *Shakespeare's People* (Shakespeare)	Tour of Denmark, Canada, New Zealand and USA
1978 January		Reading *Shakespeare's People* (Shakespeare)	Bermuda Festival
April		Reading from Hans Andersen	Palaeets Lesser Hall, Copenhagen
September		Reading *Shakespeare's People* (Shakespeare)	Arts Theatre, Cambridge
1979 May	Jasper	*Close of Play* (Simon Gray) Directed by Harold Pinter	National Theatre, London
October		*Close of Play* (Simon Gray)	Royal, Bath
		Close of Play (Simon Gray)	Olympia, Dublin
1982		Scene from *King Lear* (Shakespeare)	Roundhouse

INDEX

MR stands for Michael Redgrave